CHRISTIANITY AND SECULAR REASON

THRESHOLDS IN PHILOSOPHY AND THEOLOGY

Jeffrey Bloechl and Kevin Hart, series editors

Philosophy is provoked and enriched by the claims of faith
in a revealed God. Theology is stimulated by its contact with
the philosophy that proposes to investigate the full range
of human experience. At the threshold where they meet,
there inevitably arises a discipline of reciprocal interrogation
and the promise of mutual enhancement. The works in this series
contribute to that discipline and that promise.

CHRISTIANITY ᴬɴᴅ SECULAR REASON

Classical Themes & Modern Developments

edited by

JEFFREY BLOECHL

University of Notre Dame Press

Notre Dame, Indiana

Manufactured in the United States of America

Library of Congress Cataloging-in-Publication Data

Christianity secular reason : classical themes & modern developments /
edited by Jeffrey Bloechl.
    p.   cm. — (Thresholds in philosophy and theology)
   Includes index.
   ISBN 978-0-268-02228-0 (pbk. : alk. paper) —
   ISBN 0-268-02228-3 (pbk. : alk. paper)
   E-ISBN: 978-0-268-07587-3
   1. Philosophical theology.   2. Theology.   3. Secularism.   4. Reason.
I. Bloechl, Jeffrey, 1966–
   BT40.C488   2012
   261.2—dc23
                                       2012008949

Contents

Acknowledgments

Early outlines for several of these papers were presented in a seminar organized by the Center for Religion, Ethics and Culture at the College of the Holy Cross. The seminar, and thus much of this research, was made possible by funding from The May and Stanley Smith Charitable Trust. I offer the stewards of that trust my heartfelt thanks.

I am also grateful to William M. Shea, Director of the Center for Religion, Ethics and Culture, for providing a quiet and comfortable environment for serious reflection on important things, and to many friends at the College of the Holy Cross for indispensable moral and intellectual support during the planning and occurrence of the seminar. I also wish to thank my colleague Frederick Lawrence for responding, and in abundance, to my late call for an expression of the Lonerganian perspective that this volume would otherwise have all too evidently lacked. Finally, though surely not least, I am of course grateful to the University of Notre Dame Press, especially Charles Van Hof, who welcomed this volume for publication.

Introduction

JEFFREY BLOECHL

I

What is it that we are witnessing in the recent appearance, and indeed the proliferation, of rational principles, social structures, and a moral order no longer determined by a positive relation to religion, if not simply the continued unfolding of our secularity? This much can be conceded without implying any judgment on the rise and alleged fall of the secularization theory of modern society: we today have frequent occasion and perhaps greater cause than ever before to reflect carefully on a dimension of our humanity that seems not to derive its meaning from either a revelation or an inspiration that must be called "religious." And so one wants to know: Is that secular dimension of our humanity still contained within a religious constellation that it is now our task to redefine or perhaps simply reassert? Or must we recognize in it the arrival of a genuinely godless thinking for which religion is no longer the truth? Is it still possible to propose that every power of our reasoning and the full scope of the freedom our reasoning claims for itself on the basis of that power testify in the final account to a profound solidarity with God? Or is it time to recognize that our freedom and our capacities are more fully realized when that thesis of profound solidarity is set aside?

Like all important questions, these have attracted considerable reflection from a variety of disciplines and approaches. The authors contributing to this volume work at the undefined, or perhaps contested, boundary between philosophy of religion, Christian philosophy, and philosophical theology. Where this volume uses the word *theology,* what is meant is essentially the intelligence of a faith defined by openness to revelation. But in each instance here, that revelation is distinctly Christian, which means the theological work one encounters must not only draw on the considerable resources of that particular tradition but also meditate on any number of problems that may not trouble other traditions in quite the same way. Where there is philosophy, the approach is generally what some have called "continental," but what here might better be addressed as broadly hermeneutical. This is certainly not to discredit the considerable advances made by "analytic" philosophers, including advances on some of the themes taken up in this volume, but instead to explore the deep disturbances that both join and disjoin Christian theology and hermeneutical philosophy—whereupon the latter may become sufficiently self-reflective for the sustained engagement with analytic philosophy that must surely lie ahead.

Remaining within the field that the foregoing distinctions open up, we have at least two fruitful ways of pursuing the question of Christianity and secular reason. One prominent line—put back into the spotlight a few years ago by the public discussion between Joseph Ratzinger and Jürgen Habermas[1]—focuses on the relationship between culture, politics, and religion. Without separating itself from this concern, another line focuses more sharply on the relationship of selfhood, humanity, and world. Let us follow this latter line briefly, touching on what appears to be its ancient root and searching for a possible inclination toward its cultural and political counterpart. As Rémi Brague has shown in a suggestive investigation of the pertinent matters, Aristotle defines the relation of self to world by a fundamental openness and total concern such that, in an important sense, literally everything is the self's affair.[2] Without venturing far into everything that this involves, we may note two interesting implications: the very possibility of a relation to the world requires a distinction between me, as openness to that world, and myself as person available to be seen and described within that world; and this distinction is also the difference between me as myself and me as one instance of humanity. My stance in the world is thus oddly doubled: I look out on the world while also inhabiting it, and it is only accordingly that I am able to recognize an order and know a meaning that includes me no less than anything else belonging there. With this in view, there is no mistaking the robust primacy that Aristotle recognizes for what we, according to an undeniable anachronism, might wish to call natural reason in the disclosure of our world and everything in it: natural reason alone, and ceaselessly, makes present whatever it encounters. And this is to say that it is in a certain sense unlimited. Reason never ceases knowing the inexhaustible riches of a world that always gives itself to be seen.

To this we may add that although Aristotle's conception seems not to thematize a distinction between world and nature, such a distinction is nonetheless close to emerging from his implicit distinction between the self and the humanity in which one recognizes one's essential definition. The self that is capable of identifying its own humanity is a self that is marked by historicity, as must be its world. But this is a notion that does not emerge fully until the medieval introduction of a transcendent God. True, the believing Christian will with good grounds insist that God does appear in the world, and the philosopher will in turn argue capably that such a God is knowable by analogy; yet precisely the latter is meant to insure against the idea that God is wholly accessible by natural reason alone. This has the effect of submitting natural reason, as the proximate and discriminating norm in our worldly affairs, to an ultimate and divine norm that is most knowable in supernatural revelation. In the thought of a God who enters the world from beyond any measure contained there, there is also already the thought of a historicized world. Where previously there was the timeless order of natural and celestial movements, henceforth there is the linear history of worldly events. This world, as Karl Löwith famously observed (reminding us of the latter portions of Augustine's *City of God*), is properly called "secular" (from *saeculum*), that is, taking place in immanent time. And so likewise is reason, at least insofar as it functions as only the proximate norm in the life that seeks salvation.

It should be evident that this secularity that results inevitably from biblical religion has nothing at all to do with the considerably more debatable secularization envisioned by modern sociology from Max Weber to Peter Berger, if for no other reason than that the former represents an essential feature of the biblical religious worldview whereas the latter defines a departure from that worldview. Yet to the degree that one accepts the proposal that in our own time religious life and thinking truly are under pressure—even as the religions themselves, as moral and cultural communities, sometimes appear to reassert themselves—one must ask about the relationship between the secularity that is internal to religion and the secularization that seems to depart from it. Or, if one prefers, one may ask about the relationship between secular reason in the form that is still agreeable to religious reason and the secularized reason that appears to move decidedly away from it (and in fact this has been a latent concern of the present volume). For Marcel Gauchet, a crucial factor in the passage from secular reason to secularized reason is found in the process of disenchantment underway already in the late Middle Ages, as religious reformers began to center spiritual practice on an inner discipline in which the direct aim is individual godliness rather than the flourishing proper to well-ordered human nature.[3] Gauchet's argument is notoriously sweeping, but there is something persuasive about this feature of it, for the close association of individual godliness and a diminished concern for nature and world as an ordered expression of the divine will does become prominent in the more anthropological orientation adopted by Kant: in the first *Critique,* one is called to the world specifically by reason, which demands a unity, or ordered totality, that is impossible even if it is also indispensable. From Aristotle to Kant we have thus moved from a conception of the self in an ordered world to a conception of the self directed by the regulative ideal of world as ordered totality—and thus to an unmistakable sense of the difficulty of proving that the world is indeed so. For Kant, the world gives itself without the order that reason requires for its essential movement, and reason for its part deploys the ideal of such an order. Our relation to the world is dialectical; it bears the mark of a finitude with which modern thought has not yet fully reconciled us.

On the usual account, modernity's firstborn child is the self-legislating subject announced with most influence by Rousseau and Kant. The modern subject does not govern its action with reference to some external norm, be it natural or supernatural. As moderns, we can no longer say our private discernment is clearly the proximate norm of a life seeking salvation, but must affirm that discernment as something closer to the ultimate norm of such a life. To be sure, Rousseau recognized a calculus of freedom and the ceding of freedom built into social compact, and Kant's practical reason requires regulation by ideals that cannot be recuperated into reason itself, but with few exceptions the modern enterprise was for centuries oriented to, if not convinced of the possibility of, achieving a society, politics, and sometimes even a religion fully in accord with the exercise of a rationally determined freedom. The tendency, if not quite the confidence, is not without contemporary adherents. Husserl persisted in the quest for a transcendental logic capable of grounding the sciences even as his own successes exposed the need for genetic adjustments. The ideals of transparency and universality are also present in the earlier Habermas's attempt, in his pragmatics of communication, to identify universal conditions for the possibility of mutual understanding by demonstrating that our very comprehension of linguistic expressions already supposes an orientation to claims of validity, which in turn suggests that a rational telos is present already in the linguistic procedures by which any understanding is achieved.

Yet none of this can be argued without recognizing an only slightly more recent return of much of what those modern positions had relegated to the margins. One thinks, for instance, of the "material phenomenology" of Michel Henry, which exploits certain reserves in Husserl—as well as in Heidegger and Hegel—to resurrect the decidedly non-Enlightenment interest that Pascal or, much more decisively for Henry, Maine de Biran had in a pathos that is irreducible to *phainomenos*. Henry's later works move from a critique of the repression of affectivity, or "life," to an apologetic for the Johannine Christian thinking that on his understanding best attends to affectivity.[4] There is also the unexpected turn to religion by Habermas himself, who has defended a Christian identity for Europe, though without pretending that a Christian Europe would necessarily be a faithful Europe. One also thinks also of René Girard's generative anthropology, the fragile alliances sometimes forged between psychoanalysis and theology, the interest a post-Marxist like Alain Badiou has taken in St. Paul, and persistent suggestions that deconstruction has somehow been religious from the beginning—all of which one thinks of without forgetting the distant concerns of those for whom no thinking that does not confess a love of the Transcendent could ever truly be joined with the thinking that certainly does.

By what strange and differing paths will secular thinking have been led to rediscover its kinship with religion? And which kinship, if any, will one day prove authentic? It is the general hypothesis of the present collection of essays that a helpful start toward answering these questions may be found in reflection on the development of the thinking that had long refused to countenance them. If perhaps it is not yet clear that secular reason is fully secularized, and thus not yet clear what will define its essential relation to the religious, then perhaps we can suppose only that it continues to emerge from its break with what in comparison appears as a more strictly natural reason such as we find operative in the ancient world—a break which is announced in the revelation of a one true God.

II

This volume brings together a plurality of approaches to a loosely related set of questions, themes, and phenomena. Many of them are introduced, and indeed already developed, with some care by Adriaan Peperzak, in "How Rational Is the Heart? How Natural Is Reason? How Universal Is Faith?" This is not to say that the essay is without theses of its own, and a perspective that unifies them. For Peperzak, the time is ripe to seriously reconsider the premises and direction of a modern reason that is "deficient" if also remarkable in its extension. The critique that he sketches opens necessarily to new appreciation of some elements of a tradition, a worldview, and a conception of our humanity that modernity had supposed itself to render obsolete: no longer only reason but once again also heart, no longer the ideal of mastery but instead a positive sense of discipleship, no longer an insistence on egology but a renewal of openness to communication—listening and responding—and thus no longer a tendency to enforce self-assertion and the pretense of autonomy but a return to affection, rootedness, and faith.

This is first of all the world of Plato, Augustine, and Bonaventura, as Peperzak well knows. Their ambiance is also present in the medieval Christian thought taken up by Peter Casarella, in "*Naturae Desiderium*: The Desire of Nature between History and Theology." Casarella's focus is the conceptions of nature and soul in the twelfth and thirteenth centuries of Christian thought, and his stimulus is some recent work by John Milbank. The stimulus in question is in the first instance methodological: how does one properly read Thomas on this matter of understanding religious, natural, and eventually secular reason? According to Casarella, a good appreciation of what the *twelfth* century has understood about soul and nature is the necessary key to grasping what has in fact been argued in the *thirteenth* century. Now if one only recalls that Milbank's long and deepening critique of modern secular reason claims Thomism as its ground and bulwark, one immediately anticipates that a supplement, if not a corrective, to Milbank's reading of the Thomistic conception of nature will yield a somewhat different approach to the questions at hand in this volume. Inevitably, perhaps, the discussion concludes with new emphasis on the importance of thinking nature together with grace.

In "Athens, Jerusalem, and . . . : Overcoming the Exclusivist Paradigms of the Past," Kevin Corrigan identifies a split between the classical world of drama, poetry, and philosophy and the biblical world of witness, prophecy, and faith; in so doing he intends to haunt our modern world most poignantly with the pedagogy that is to convey what either world might offer us. In short, one contents oneself with quiet study of the fractures conceded in modernity and the fragments celebrated in postmodernity only at the risk of forgetting their effects on souls whose most natural desire is for unity and a sense of the whole. Sifting through both sides of the Athens-Jerusalem pairing, Corrigan finds each, in its contemporary state, to be racked by strife and division, but also, each of them, calling for repair. If in the classroom or the lecture hall there is dire need of new synthesis, at the desk or in the library it may appear possible for research and reflection to approach it.

Something very much like the latter is proposed, and at the very heart of modernity, in Cyril O'Regan's "Kant: Boundaries, Blind Spots, and Supplements." What truly is the legacy of Kant's turn successively from pure reason to practical reason, and then from there to judgment, and on, let us not forget, to *Christianity?* Is it certain, as we are sometimes told, that the project was first and foremost an attempt to admit the validity and use of modern science, and scientific reason, while also protecting religion from its march? O'Regan would have us attend to the incapacity of reason to provide itself with every necessary assurance, and in that sense to become sufficient unto itself. The problem, O'Regan suggests, haunts the Kantian project, driving it from one domain to the next until it now, with all the assurance that comes from scrupulous preparation, accepts Christian faith as its essential supplement. There is no summarizing O'Regan's tour through the Kantian enterprise, but there is also no mistaking the provocative suggestion: read carefully, Kant—or this new Kant read against the standard Kant—becomes a resource for resisting the Promethean ambitions of modern reason whose most forceful representative is the same Hegel who thought to transcend and complete the critical philosophy.

But perhaps Christianity is not the supplement of reason so much as its surplus. In "On Knowing God through Loving Him: Beyond 'Faith and Reason,'" Jean-Yves Lacoste approaches God as proposed to thought while also given to faith. The thesis is essentially Christological, according to an argument found in Kierkegaard's *Philosophical Fragments*: God appears precisely in Jesus Christ, as proposal to be grasped and integrated rather than merely recognized and described. Since, as the Gospels easily confirm, such a God must be thought of as love, the question of knowing God becomes a matter of responding to love. *Secularity,* as naming a dimension of human existence, is a name for the fact that this love can be missed, and secular reason presents itself as the self-interpretation of the life that thus unfolds. Faith, in contrast, embraces the proposal of God in Jesus Christ as promise of salvation, and this calls for rational articulation. Theology, Lacoste reminds us, takes shape in the hope that is grounded in that promise. Philosophy, for its part, attends to the thing itself, as given. This seems to invite a richer, more vital relation between philosophy and theology. If, as Clement of Alexandria already observed, philosophy can attend to the phenomenality of freedom, to faith in the divine proposal, and to the dawn of hope, then it can complement theology. Nothing prevents us from seeking this role for philosophy in the judicious use of phenomenology.

Of course, phenomenology has pondered its own relation with theology almost, as it were, from the beginning. Certainly for Heidegger and Scheler this relation was a recurrent question, but it should not be forgotten that Husserl, too, expresses occasional though also profound interest in the question.[5] For the founders of the movement, theology is always a question or difficulty, if not a problem. Later generations, from Lévinas to Marion, have been engaged in an effort of overcoming. For Lévinas, phenomenology is to be redefined in the wake of religious revelation; Marion claims to open phenomenology from within, and thus to satisfy its original impulse. This would be one of, in fact, many points at which to appreciate the unique provocation—and, it will surely be granted, idiosyncrasy—of the position taken in the late work of Michel Henry. As we find in Kevin Hart's "Phenomenality and Christianity," Henry takes Christianity itself as phenomenology par excellence. For Henry, appealing especially to the Gospel of John, God is Life, and Life appears—phenomenalizes itself—in the life we recognize and indeed share in ourselves. If we reverse this proposition, starting where in fact Henry himself starts in works dating from the 1950s and 1960s, we are led to think that an exhaustive phenomenology of being human grasps life anterior to the appearing of life, including in affective dispositions, but then finds the primordial condition of life in what Christianity alone calls Life. Needless to say, and as Hart does not fail to observe, the theological difficulties that this incurs are numerous and immense. But it also leaves us with an extraordinary proposal for how to understand the topic at the center of this volume: a strictly secular mind-set confines the meaning and truth of our condition to the play of an immanence (itself assimilated with appearance) that forgets or perhaps refuses its primordial horizon in life/Life. Whereas in the more recognizable phenomenological approaches taken by Lévinas and Marion, secular reason is in some sense inauthentic (in this they agree with Heidegger that this word ought not be invested with a strictly negative connotation), for Henry it must be something more like the figure of repression.

Michel Henry is also present in Anthony Kelly's "Making the Resurrection Reasonable—or Reason 'Resurrectional?,'" a courageous effort to recognize and address what many will agree is a matter of some difficulty for contemporary Christian theology. Irreplaceable within the life of the believer and ever-present at the root of Christian speech and history, yet incomprehensible by logical reason and unintelligible as an empirical event, the resurrection of Jesus Christ—what Kelly calls "the Resurrection event"—either renders faith unintelligible or marks it with an intelligibility all its own. Perhaps the difficulty predates the rise of secular reason, but then secular reason certainly exacerbates it, driving theology into a more acutely apologetic stance. Under various pressures, in recent times Christological reflection has been tempted to emphasize only certain aspects of the Resurrection's traditional meaning, evidently marginalizing others, and often those that are bound most tightly to the Resurrection: Incarnation itself, as distinct from the historical event confirming it; history of the Spirit, as depending on an insistence that the Resurrection was more than mythological; and so forth. Hence are we called by the tradition itself to a renewed, phenomenological attentiveness to the event itself, in its rich complexity. And this, in turn, requires us to admit and unpack what can only appear as a disruption of ordinary reason, and indeed a moment of "turbulence" (Voegelin) in its history. At such a juncture, theology is well served by phenomenology, and specifically that of recent figures including Lévinas, Marion, and Henry. Moreover, Christian theology itself has already moved on its own initiative toward such an approach in, for instance, the theological aesthetics of Hans Urs von Balthasar and, more recently, David Bentley Hart.

Each of the final two essays in this volume engages the Ratzinger-Habermas discussion that has done so much to put the question of religious secular reason fully on our intellectual agenda. In "Habermas, Religion, and a Postsecular Society," James Swindal reviews Habermas's earlier, highly theoretical understanding of secularization on his way to an account of Habermas's more recent view that we find ourselves in a situation properly termed "postsecular." Prompted in part by the events of September 11, 2001, which he received as fresh evidence against the secularization theory of culture, Habermas has made significant, at one time quite unexpected, concessions to the notion that certain spiritual factors remain present, perhaps indefinitely, in the public sphere even of northern Europe. Without abandoning his long-standing concern precisely with the public sphere, thus without ceasing to remain a philosopher of state rather than of religion, he has thus become genuinely agreeable to the theology of culture promoted by Joseph Ratzinger/Pope Benedict XVI. Both, in short, have an interest in recognizing the distinctly Christian features of European culture. Yet their differences are of course quite marked. For Benedict XVI, Hellenized Christianity represents the highest achievement of a unified rationality and indeed the sole avenue to truth itself. For Habermas, it is enough to say, and perhaps all that can be said, that European discourse and its root identity are profoundly Christian, at least at this historical moment. Would the Habermasian program truly contribute to the project of a Christian Europe, or would it in fact convince many that it is politically unnecessary? If the latter proves to be the case, then Habermas's particular version of postsecular reason may initially appear to support Benedict XVI's rather traditionalist theology, but without becoming the handmaiden of that theology any more than did its robustly secular predecessor. Wary of this, Swindal proposes that religious thinking preserve its own impulses for action in the public sphere, while also recognizing the need to sharpen its self-understanding through an open dialogue with the intellectual resources made available by a philosopher who is, at any rate, far from hostile to its presence.

In Frederick Lawrence's masterful essay "Transcendence from Within," Pope Benedict's predilection for Hellenized Christianity is examined at length, and submitted to some scrutiny according to impulses found in the work of Bernard Lonergan. The original context for "Hellenization" is the Athanasian shift from a God who is first-for-us to a God who is first-in-principle, with the latter necessarily implying a move away from symbols and metaphors to concepts, with the greater intelligibility the latter afford. Benedict's "Hellenization," like so much other good theology between Nicea and the early twentieth century, is substantially in keeping with this move. Yet it is also marked by a need to resist an extraordinary range of developments ranging from Catholic Modernism through the demythologizing hermeneutics of Rudolf Bultmann, all of which threatened to destabilize the philosophically informed but still biblically grounded theology found in the best of the tradition—especially, for Benedict, in its Augustinian current. Between Augustine or Bonaventura and us looms the influence of Spinoza, and indeed the modern scientific rationality that Spinoza welcomed. Benedict's love of the Augustinian tradition is alloyed with a tendency to withdraw from this major feature of secular modernity.

This was not the perspective or the approach adopted by Bernard Lonergan, though he did concern himself with Catholic Modernism as a critical expression of the impending need for theology to dialogue with modern science. Lawrence's interest in Lonergan is thus first of all an interest in comparing and weighing between distinct theological responses to some of the same social, cultural, and intellectual phenomena. Would Lonergan's less culturally pessimistic approach preserve theological identity and perhaps even enrich it with the findings of modern science? Could the engagement with scientific rationality yield new resources for an expression of faith in the God who is first-in-principle? Such an achievement would immediately extend the range of theological intervention in the public sphere. The missed exchange between Lonergan and Benedict would thus interrupt and, one may hope, enrich the recent and very real exchange between Benedict and Habermas. What could be expected of a discussion between Lonergan and Benedict, on the one hand, speaking from a genuinely pluralized theology, and Habermas, on the other, inevitably speaking for a secular thinking positively disposed to religious factors in contemporary society? At the very least, a joining of forces urging a reconsideration of the modern habit of associating our human condition too closely with its cognitive capacities, whereupon human progress and even human dignity are thought to lie with what human beings can do *for themselves*—yet this much without therefore rejecting out of hand the successes of a distinctly modern cultivation of human cognition, human freedom, and indeed human striving. The modern achievement, Benedict and Lonergan would surely agree, is of limited reach. What theology has to offer, Lawrence has them conclude, is the enlivened sense of personal goods that can come only in light of a commitment to the higher good of the universe itself. It seems unlikely that that secular reason and a secular politics could ever provide us with such an elevated sensibility.

III

I have observed that at the most apparent level this volume attends to the relation between Christianity and secular reason at points where each seems to contest the self-assurance of the other. I have also observed that at another level this volume is attuned to the fact that secular reason, whatever else may result from it, is deeply troubling to both Christian thought and the philosophy often called "continental." There are several strategies for finding one's way in this thicket of reciprocal interrogations. One may well begin with Adriaan Peperzak's topical approach to much of the discussion broached in this volume, and then follow the sequence of essays as they proceed through the approximate historical order of their central subject matter. One might equally begin with Peperzak's essay and then move from essay to essay as directed simply by one's interest and competence—thus, for example, from Peperzak's emphasis on "affection" into Kevin Hart's exploration of Michel Henry's attempt to develop a philosophical Christology from his understanding of that same theme; and then on, evidently enough, to Anthony Kelly's reflections on the promises and pitfalls that Henry's philosophy presents to theology. For those with more immediately pedagogical concerns, whether they are a matter of what Jesuit institutions have championed as the *cura personalis* or simply of the liberal arts curriculum, Kevin Corrigan's impassioned plea for a recovery of the spiritual must be the evident place to begin. Philosophers intent on grappling with the broader issue of "modernity" might concentrate especially on the essays by O'Regan, Swindal, and Lawrence. Theologians, however, are likely to respond more readily to Kelly, Casarella, or Lacoste.

Yet these very distinctions—this way of dividing the intellectual terrain—put us at risk of reifying disciplinary boundaries which, while quite real, have never inhibited the truly intellectual discussion that places its trust in the general lucidity of concepts and lines of reasoning. And in the final account, it is this sort of discussion, rather more than any particular set of conclusions, that binds together the essays in this volume. Indeed, any number of the essays will be found in plain disagreement on important points. Let it suffice to only touch on a few. What, for example, do we make of Jean-Yves Lacoste's call for some updating of the classical couplets of faith/reason and natural/supernatural, when exposed to the somewhat different argument, most clearly from Peperzak but also strongly implied by Casarella, that we reconsider the received understanding of just what those distinctions originally meant? Or, prescinding from the lengthy exercise in historical theology that this calls for, will it be enough to get on solid footing toward a proper understanding of faith if we withdraw it from a pairing with reason? There is evident agreement among the three authors, and very likely the other six contributing to this volume, that faith has its own intelligibility. But there is something less than unanimity over the degree or sense in which it would be truly prior to the intelligibility of secular reason, opposed to it, or simply distinct from it.

Another point of fruitful disharmony can be found in comparing the different attempts to handle the claims of modern reason to supply us with a productive hermeneutic of religion. O'Regan, for example, illumines the manner in which this works in the philosophy of Kant: reason exploits what I have just called "the intelligibility of faith" by taking it as a sort of foothold by which to extend reason's own reach toward unity and order. Lacoste would appear to have adopted an alternative tack, clearly inspired by Kierkegaard: reason is stung by the paradoxes of faith, which thus appears rational in precisely its own way. Of course, this sort of debate can be had without reducing it to a matter solely of competing rationalities. In one of its most sophisticated forms, Husserlian phenomenology, secular reason claims to have discovered the conditions for all intentional relations—conditions which by definition the things and life of faith cannot meet. Against this, Michel Henry would have us associate the Life that cannot appear without becoming captured and falsified *intendum* with the absolute God who is always infinitely greater than any image or idea we may form. Hart's development of this position might then be set in balance with the large portions of Kelly's study that treat the position taken most notably by Jean-

Luc Marion: our appreciation of the transcendence of God is enhanced, both in depth and in sophistication, by the success phenomenology has had in exploring the various dimensions and strata of human existence that, as the theologians tell us, comb and card the play of immanence.

Of course, none of this is quite the perspective nourished on the transcendental Thomism of Bernard Lonergan. There is no doubt an entire range of topics that one might debate within the difference between Swindal's approach to the Ratzinger-Habermas encounter and the approach taken by Lawrence. Evidently enough, a significant factor must be the forceful commitment Lawrence makes to the intervention Lonergan might endorse. In fact, a careful reading of Lawrence's essay, which does come last in this volume, might provoke a new engagement with many of those coming before it. As is well known, Lonergan's reading of Thomas Aquinas is greatly shaped by his sympathy for a quasi-Kantian interest in universal reason, a sympathy which nonetheless stops well short of endorsing the self-promotion of reason traced by O'Regan. One might go from here in either of two directions: on one hand, Lonergan's sense of "reason" must be considered to resemble that of Habermas at least in its primitive spirit, while necessarily resisting any reduction of Christian doctrine to mere cultural form; on the other hand, the very suggestion that a development as distinctly modern as is the Kantian critical philosophy might furnish some of the conditions under which Christian thinking might prove rational signals the presence of another voice in the discussion with Lacoste, Peperzak, and perhaps indeed all contributors to this volume over the essential limits of the intelligibility of faith.

Notes

1. See J. Ratzinger and J. Habermas, *The Dialectics of Secularization: On Reason and Religion* (San Francisco: Ignatius Press, 2007). In their contributions to the present volume, Frederick Lawrence and James Swindal each take up this discussion.

2. See R. Brague, *Aristote et la question du monde* (Paris: Presses Universitaires de France, 1988). This claim appears consistent with the classical conception of knowledge as presence in the mind of immaterial form. The medievals were captivated by the implications of a soul that is not limited by the

sensible contours of its objects. Inasmuch as the soul thus can know all things, it is also fitting to say that it is all things (*anima est quodammodo omnia*). On this notion, and the Thomistic manner of completing it in a theology of grace, see the final paragraphs of Peter Casarella's contribution to this volume.

3. M. Gauchet, *The Disenchantment of the World* (Princeton: Princeton University Press, 1997), 151 ff.

4. The Johannine orientation of Henry's thinking becomes evident in ch. 4 of *C'est Moi la Vérité* (Paris: Seuil, 1996), in which an early concern to think about what is variously called "affection" and "life" is brought into (surprisingly easy) contact with a Christian discourse dominated by the fourth gospel. Extended treatment of Henry's theology (which might best be termed a *proto*logy) can be found in Kevin Hart's contribution to this volume.

5. For an extraordinary reinstatement of Husserl's significance for religious thought, see J. G. Hart, *Who One Is,* 2 vols., Phaenomenologica 189 and 190 (Dordrecht: Springer, 2009).

1 How Rational Is the Heart? How Natural Is Reason? How Universal Is Faith?

ADRIAAN T. PEPERZAK

Instead of being a fable, truth bothers us as the most desired condition of an authentic life. It must be sought, however. Consequently, human existence has been experienced, represented, imagined, told, and dramatized as a journey, an exodus, a quest, a pilgrimage, an expedition, a ladder, a climb, an ascent.

To discover the truth that really, ultimately, and primarily matters, Bonaventura sketches a travel guide in six stages, for each of which we are equipped with an appropriate mode of climbing: the senses, imagination, reason, intellect, intelligence, and, finally, the very tip of the mind (*apex mentis*).[1] Together, in a cooperation of all, these modes of awareness and experience are driven by desire—a burning desire that inflames the human heart because the truth can be approached but not caught—a desire for "the Sought" that, all along the journey, remains more sought than found. To be successful in this "cordial ascent," as Bonaventura calls it, one must be full of a desire that is fueled by "outcries of the heart" and refulgent speculation. Only thus will a human mind be turned directly and intensely toward the light of truth.[2]

Bonaventura's methodical desire is not less intense than Plato's *eros,* Nietzsche's *pathos,* or the radical urge of St. John of the Cross. But what a contrast with the standard methods and methodologies of modern reason and experience! However, even the greatest thinkers of modernity were driven by a radical faith that can be compared to that of Nietzsche, John of the Cross, Bonaventura, and Plato.

Once we are conquered by the conviction that the framework and the procedures of modern philosophy have lost their power, it would be ideal to invent an alternative method as rich and diversified as, for example, Bonaventura's,[3] but we know that no realistic methodology can be written before much experimentation has been accomplished in the half-dark, half-luminous trial and error of postmodern (i.e., post-Hegelian) history.

In this essay, I will neither try to prematurely sketch an updated travel guide for philosophy, nor stage the birth of a brand-new kind of thinking. I prefer to remind you and myself of some lost or forgotten possibilities of Western thought that risk being destroyed altogether if we deem ourselves capable of beginning anew without relying on any memory. I will (1) briefly summarize a critique of the framework within which a modern philosopher is supposed to think, (2) ask the question of how we can remedy some of this framework's most blatant deficiencies, and (3) indicate a few desiderata with regard to a renaissance of thinking in a more radical and less restricted style than the one that during the last five centuries has been unfolded in remarkable but deficient ways.

While proposing my remarks to your critical attention, I am not overly concerned about neat distinctions between philosophy and theology. Moreover, I beg your pardon for the oversimplified, perhaps even caricatured, aspects of some sweeping statements, which I cannot avoid altogether.[4]

THE MODERN UNIVERSE

Since nothing new comes to life unless it is born from a pregnant past, while breaking away from that past's exhausted possibilities, modern philosophy was not quite as different from premodern epochs of thought as it wanted and thought itself to be. Gilson, Courtine, Marion, and others have sufficiently demonstrated how much, for example, Descartes owes to the scholastic tradition, and the same is even easier to prove for Spinoza, Leibniz, Kant, and Hegel. Even the very attempt to "begin anew" is a well-known feature of the various rebirths that punctuate Western thinking since Parmenides.

Descartes however, followed by many modern and postmodern philosophers, did not explicitly return to Greece or Rome, as most renaissances before and a few after him have done. He was too much impressed by the new possibilities revealed by modern mathematics and the mechanisms of early modern physics, and his philosophical successors remained fascinated by the transparent simplicity of the natural sciences. Past philosophy could be ignored. With regard to the scholastic past, a new foundation had to be laid, one that allowed for systematic constructions according to new principles of attention, perception, selection, observation, experimentation, measuring and calculation, logic, and argumentation. Let me quickly mention a few characteristics of the new project and its way to wisdom:[5]

1. Philosophy is a work of human reason in cooperation with empirical evidence.

2. This work must be accomplished autonomously: ignoring all authorities and traditions, reason should rely exclusively on its own principles and the data of universally available experiences in order to reconstruct the real world—preferably *ordine* or *more geometrico*—without bothering about beliefs or speculations inherited from the past.

3. Philosophers should be interested exclusively in clear, objective, universally valid, and certain—that is, empirically and rationally warranted—truths.

4. The subject of philosophical thought is any thinking ego (*ego cogito*), insofar as this ego can make abstraction from its own singular and particular properties, in order to think and speak in the name of *all* human individuals, that is, of humanity as a whole. The proper subject of philosophy is not any existent individual, but rather a transcendental ego. However, this transcendental subject always happens to be united with an—every time different—"empirical ego" who, in the mean time, is living a real (male or female, French or Persian, holy, mediocre or criminal) life, more or less in agreement with the culturally determined rules of a "*morale provisoire.*"[6]

5. The generalization of the scientific approach clearly shows in the framework of modern philosophy: the philosophical stage director displays the universe as a *theatrum mundi* before his observant and studious eyes. Very often, this director forgets that he is part of the universal theater. When he is aware of it, however, he abandons his empirical existence to the laws of the universe, while seeking a place outside himself and the world for the transcendental ego that rules all human thinkers, including himself. However, he cannot stop talking in a particular language and a unique style, while at the same time attempting to be a faithful messenger of the transcendental ego that cannot speak, because there is no transcendental language. To achieve this task, the speaking or writing ego must be a perfect translator—not of any language but instead of a prelingual, conceptually accurate but ineffable thought.

CRITIQUE

A serious critique of the modern idea of philosophy should, of course, try to discover the coherence and radical unity of all its features, some of which I have mentioned. Although all historical syntheses are even more simplistic than a quick selection of properties, the following indications might point in the direction of a kind of core that has unfolded in modern philosophy. We need such indications if we want to argue that the history of modern philosophy is dominated by a characteristic attitude or mentality.

With regard to this mentality (or position or "stance"), I want here neither to pronounce a global condemnation nor to repeat the many forms of praise that have saturated four centuries of our intellectual history, but instead to introduce a discussion about the reasons why the modern framework of thought (including its attitudinal and methodological presuppositions) should be replaced with another framework, in which the modern stance and procedures are still operative, though differently.

The constellation evoked by the five properties mentioned above can be interpreted as a specific form of egology and radicalized as expression of an egocentric will to intellectual mastery. A singular and solitary ego conceptually dominates the universe in the name of humanity by de- and re-constructing the universe as an all-encompassing but finite composition of objectified parts and relations. The thinker has become a universal engineer. Autonomy does not exclude an *initial* dependence on experience, but—as Spinoza and Hegel have argued— the completion of a philosophical system includes a demonstration of the thesis that the partly empirical, partly a priori point of departure contains in principle the full truth that progressively has unfolded that beginning. The secret weapon of the all-embracing thought that, in the end, displays the well-articulated totality of the all is *Reason*. If there is a God, his name is Reason, but one of the decisive questions that weigh upon the modern enterprise is whether there is a place at all for God within the confines of the universe.

If the Hegelian claim of an all-encompassing, self-enclosed, and completely demonstrated thought can be shown not only to have failed, but to be utterly impossible, the modern project is an illusion and we must ask which of its features are responsible for its failure. Is its use of reason founded in an overly optimistic trust? Was its appeal to experience too biased, too unfaithful, too much of a distortion of the evidence?

A few facts can be proven without great difficulties:

1. None of the systems that have been produced in the last five centuries has been loyal to the program of an autonomous thought that could do without all appeal to authorities.

2. None of the modern philosophers has demonstrated that reason is sufficient to think well. The claim that reason was the leading function for the human search of truth did not rest on a rational proof, but, as Hegel publicly declared, on *faith* in reason.[7]

3. The experience that was accepted by the classics of modern thought as a safe soil on which to build a system was restricted to an extremely poor and badly described form of givenness that from the outset was adjusted to an objectifying, quasiscientific, un- or even anti- existential conceptuality, which found its most admired paradigm in the most "ob-jective" of natural sciences.

Modern reason was different from ancient and medieval reason: much less open to the full range of human experientiality than the Greek *logos, nous, dianoia,* or *phronesis* and the medieval *ratio, intellectus,* or *extasis.* It looked down on all epistemic and gnostic possibilities that it could not test or control by its own means. Taste, receptive dispositions, and the purification of the mind's eye were deemed irrelevant: everybody was inhabited and led by reason, and this was the supreme criterion. If some training still was deemed necessary, it was in the discipline of logic and formal methodology. Descartes's weeklong *exercitia,* composed of metaphysical meditations, for example, appealed to the most common and easy kind of experiences and reason only. The more reason discovered its own a priori principles and laws, the more it withdrew into the boundary of formal structures.

The same was true of language. It was an indispensable presupposition of the modern project that the thought of the transcendental ego could be communicated by and to all human individuals in order to be checked, repeated, or amended. But which is the language of that universal ego? If it is not Greek, Latin, French, German, or any other language, we must hope that it can be translated without fail in one of them or that it can be reduced to notations so formal and abstract that they do not constitute any language at all, but only a conceptual system that extracts a core of bleak truth from the six thousand particular languages that exist. Those who spoke or wrote only Latin, French, German, or English might then imagine that their language was the most faithful to that system or instead concede that all languages had become superfluous for the search, like adornments or variations on one universally valid conceptuality that really counted.

The poorest and most abstract element of modern philosophy is the experience to which it appeals, albeit for its takeoff only. Reason must reduce all the human varieties of existing to experiences that are neither particular, individual, or unique, nor subjective, exceptional, or profound, but instead average and universally human: experiences that everyone everywhere can have and deem obvious—such as seeing a glass on the table or a cat on the mat.[8] Fond of experimentation within the geometric and physicalist horizons of a sharply defined and limited universe, modern thought hates the eccentricities of poetic, dramatic, spiritual, and mystical experiments in which entire lives are probed, purified, refined, enriched, and transfigured. No *katharsis* or mental growth is necessary for discovering what is real; experience is considered to be the easiest—yes, the most average, mediocre, uninteresting, and almost meaningless—part of modern philosophy. No wonder that a postmodern phenomenology had to emerge from the flattened scene into which philosophy had maneuvered itself through English empiricism, German idealism, and other forms of modern rationalism.

Phenomenology is indeed a liberating program for the philosophical rehabilitation of the whole range of human experiences that have taken refuge in modern art and literature since modern scientificity banished them from the anatomic theater of a "rigorous" thought, whose rigor lacked all the accuracy and refinement of ancient and medieval perspicacity and good taste. This premodern tradition found new expressions in the fragments of Pascal, Haman, Baader, and Jacobi, but a more radical renewal of philosophy did not erupt before the post-Hegelian attempts of Kierkegaard, Marx, Nietzsche, Husserl, Freud, Bergson, and Heidegger, followed by our French friends from Levinas and Ricoeur to Marion, Chrétien, and Lacoste. If, however, we wish to participate in the movement that today achieves a renaissance of philosophy as radically as is possible for us, we cannot avoid being at the same time philosophical historians of philosophy, because we cannot think without memory (and thus, without writing and rewriting genealogies of our own). But our looking forward can be focused by concentrating on a few key words of the tradition that most moderns despised. Sustained reflection about the questions indicated by these words might issue in a new style of thought that shows more affinity with premodern contemplation than with modern combinations of destruction and construction. Allow me, please, to briefly focus on four such words: *heart, communication, affection,* and *faith.*

The Heart

While modern reason is good at conceptual analysis and argumentation, it is weak in sensibility, feeling, desire, pathos, love, and other forms of intimacy. Reason dissects and reconnects, it legislates, critiques, and judges; but it neither desires nor decides. Kant's reason, for instance, tells us which kind of legislation issues from human conscience, but it is not able to bind us in obedience, awe, veneration, or love to the duties that are contained in its brand of rationality. The moral fact to which Kant appeals as foundation of his practical philosophy is an experience that precedes all operations of theoretical and practical reason; it is a spontaneous respect for the absolute "dignity" (*Würde*) that distinguishes humanness (*Menschheit*) from animality and all forms of exchangeable value and utility. That Kant recognizes this fact as irreducible to any other fact testifies to a moment of phenomenological sensitivity in his philosophy. That he interprets it as a fact of reason, however, and that he explains it as a humiliation (*Demütigung*) of sensible "self-love"[9] results from his absolutist veneration of reason. Reason cannot prove that it is the most radical core of being, desiring, acting, and enjoying humanly, since the necessity of faith in reason cannot be demonstrated by reason itself. Fundamental affections, and especially faith, issue from the heart, taken in its biblical sense as the living core of human existence.

All that is interesting comes from the heart. It is the heart, and not reason, that desires, trusts, evaluates, respects, and decides; for only the heart is in touch with a person's destiny. Only it "knows" whether one's stance and movement are well oriented and well adjusted, loyal, friendly, responsive, and faithful to what a human individual—in the end and from the outset—is meant to be. Only the heart is able to respect and to venerate, even if it needs imagination and reason to clarify its naïve but radical experiences of the other's face, its own self-evaluations, and the ultimate Sought of its endless longing.

The humanness (*Menschheit*) that demands awe and veneration coincides with each one's singular destiny as an absolute that is more important than life and immortality. It demands devotion to the unique and irreplaceable meanings of lives that perform what they are meant to be. That such meanings cannot be reduced to rationality or reasonability is obvious—even for philosophers. If their heart puts all its trust in reason, this addiction contradicts the deeper pathos that rules the reason provoked by it.

That *heart* is a name for the central and decisive core of each singular human existence does not imply that we should understand philosophy as an individualistic rivalry of isolated geniuses who live in ivory towers, for nobody can even begin to think without being initiated by others into an already existing history of thinking. And no thinker is able to think without listening and speaking to other thinkers.

Communication

The heart is a singularizing organ, but it does not isolate. On the contrary, it is always affected by and responding to challenges that come from the outside. It is constantly both addressed and addressing. In the dimension of thought, this means that thinking is always involved in communication.

All speaking is preceded by an earlier speaking, to which the speaker has listened. Speaking thus always emerges as a response, but, as a new (and to a certain extent original) speech, every response provokes a subsequent answering. Initiation, education, dialogue, and conversation unfold the nucleus of an initial provocation, which presupposes someone who turns to some other, who thereby is summoned to address the former. The response to a provocation should be appropriate, and this is possible, because each summoning address contains suggestions for such "appropriation."[10] Receptivity and listening, as forms of basic dependence, combined with a moment of originality, are constitutive of the pattern according to which all speaking and writing are practiced; and philosophy—even the one that is obsessed by the beginning of all beginnings—does not escape this pattern. The subject of philosophical thought is thus never a single ego, but always someone who, while speaking or writing, participates in a communicative *we*. If a transcendental ego exists—as an element of our own thoughts—it is shared by those individuals who compose the community of a *We*, even if the structure of such a *We* has not yet been recognized by those who try to impose a choice between contractualism and commonalism. The partial coincidence of unique but firmly linked destinies with the common destiny of a thoughtful republic generates philosophy as a living history. The search for the truth, therefore, is not a solitary adventure, but rather the orientation of a community that embraces a variety of traditions, schools, styles and fashions, heroes, educators and scribes, editors and salespersons, liturgies, memorials, fora, authorities, pressure groups, sophists, mafias, and impostors. Neither I alone nor "the tradition," neither "*die Sprache*" nor the Muses can replace the originating subject of modern egology, if a postmodern metaphilosophy is ipso facto a social and political—and then also an ethical—(re)consideration of philosophy as such.

Where does such a metaphilosophy find a standpoint if this can no longer be found in an all-overseeing ego? Only in an existent, unique, and singular but loyal and "solidary" (not solitary) thinker who receives, learns, practices, and—with some luck and originality—ameliorates a historical tradition of thinking in conversation with some of the others who are involved in the same history. Where, however, does the truth manifest itself in this history? Not in any majority or unanimity. Not even in a privileged or fortunate minority. Perhaps in a hidden convergence of "the best"? That is what we may hope for. But who is wise enough to recognize the best?

Doesn't this question again express our desire to sit on a top from where we can wrap up, synthesize, evaluate, judge, and conclude all the views and voices that can be heard? Thinking-as-ongoing-conversation composes a concert that, even without being intended, emerges from a multiple addressing and answering that links first-person allocutions to second persons, whose responses link them again to their first and other you's, without permitting any speaker to transcend the polylogical conversation by his or her private and final, self-owned synthesis. All our syntheses seem to be provisional only: summaries of adventures in more or less thoughtful communication; they must be followed by other proposals. What really counts, however, is how those who offer their proposals *deal* with them and with one another in light of their shared and unique destinies. Obviously, the question of truth demands rethinking. Is any hope or faith of any help in this?

Affection

The fundamental structure of reflection in dialogue and conversation is not restricted to the dimension of intellectual reflection and conceptuality. It shows already on the level of human affectivity.

Nothing emerges at all, and we cannot be aware of anything, unless it affects us in some way. That affection is not confined to impressions received through five senses is obvious. What Heidegger wrote about *Befindlichkeit,* for example, is easily recognized by anybody who is not completely unaware of the incessant attunement and emotional adjustment that forms the underground of all experiences. Philosophy will not be able to renew itself if it does not explore the layers and elements of human affectivity with more finesse and accuracy than ever. For it is in this dimension that the decisive determinations of our stance find their roots and nourishment. Our entire affective, poetic, and spiritual heritage must be reintegrated into philosophy if we want to overcome the barren scene of modern philosophy—and theology.

To show the relevance of affections for thought, we might begin by considering their structure and then ask how the affective dimension founds, permeates, and stylizes all other dimensions of our lives. Let me try to illustrate this by giving a rough sketch of the microcosm that is contained in one affective experience.

A phenomenology of affectivity could analyze such an experience as a synthesis of the following elements:

- Something (x)—an event, an encounter, a person, a landscape, a thing—affects (touches, addresses) me.
- I experience myself as being affected by x, which precedes my awareness of it and comes to me as a surprise: surprising, amazing, shocking, delighting, frightening, or soothing me.
- Through its surprising character, x summons me to pay attention to it and to receive it as intervening in my life and self-experience, even if it is only for a moment.
- X urges me to adjust myself to it, so that it "fits." At the same time, x provokes me to an affective response.
- My reception and adjustment to the affecting x are the beginning of my responding.
- I feel that my response should be appropriate, and this is made possible by the manner in which x contains suggestions for my appropriation.
- To respond implies that I integrate the affecting x into the entirety of my life. While undergoing x, I make it mine, a part of my own corporeal, mental, and spiritual being, even if it—for example, as a pain—remains to a certain extent strange or alien. As belonging

to me, x receives a human meaning. Affection is an event of human history, not a symptom of animality.

- I experience myself as affected by the union of the affecting x and my own more or less appropriate integration of it. Thanks to my way of receiving and responding, my affectedness by x reveals itself as being at the same time a form of self-affection.

- I experience my self-affected affection not only as a fact and a task, but also as a double question: "What does it mean?" and "Is my mode of experiencing (or 'having') it as my own appropriate?"

- As affected—still remaining on the level of affection—I evaluate my (self-)affection through an *affective* (self-)reflection and evaluation.

- Affective self-evaluation implies that I, within the dimension of affectivity, am darkly aware of a profound "sense" that distinguishes appropriate from inappropriate feelings. Human affection thus contains the source of all valuation in morality, art, philosophy, and religion.

For example, when I listen to Beethoven's third concerto for piano and orchestra, this music not only touches me, but also invites me to get into an attentive, receptive, and appropriate attunement to it. I am aware of the emotional change that issues from the encounter of this music with the mode in which my sensibility responds to the affective challenge. To enjoy the music (i.e., to allow myself to get and remain attuned), I do not focus on that awareness; on the contrary, the music urges me to focus on its melodic lines, rhythms, harmonies, and so on, so that it can permeate me. While listening, I taste, and while tasting, I integrate my affectedness. When I emotionally respond to the music, the music itself becomes an element of my own body. I thus sense my affected self-affection (my enjoyment of the music), and I probe its preimaginative and preconceptual meaning within the "space" and time of my momentary and ongoing existence. I thus evaluate my experience as a more or less adequate answering to the music and as a moment of my life in its eagerness to experience (accept and realize) meaning on all the corporeal, affective, and other levels of my life.

As when I listen to words addressed to me, I respond to music by a peculiar mode of receiving and adjusting to it, for example, by evoking a background of deep silence in my body and soul, such that nothing else interferes, or by concentrating on melodies, harmonies, contrasts, rhymes, reminiscences, colors, and so on. My responses to music might seem less active and less original than those in a spoken dialogue, but we should not underestimate the responsive effort performed by affective participation in musical re-creation. Similar analyses can be given of other dimensions of affectivity, such as the search for ultimate meaning and desirability in philosophy, religion, and faith.

With regard to the relevance of affectivity for the development of human lives, including the lives of philosophers, we should reconnect with a long tradition that seems lost in the main streams of modern and postmodern philosophy: the tradition of purification, maturation, and authentification. According to this tradition, truth and knowledge are not granted without a preparatory and accompanying process of emotional *katharsis* and *askesis,* during which one's own life is at stake as a unique, lifelong, and central experiment.

Intellectual life is impossible without rootedness in appropriate emotions. Experience is not a collection of empirical data that are obvious for everyone. To be discovered and appreciated, important facts demand not only openness, but ongoing exercise in more appropriate tasting, feeling, welcoming, undergoing, and union. In order to think well, one must learn to sense well. Refined sensibility and good taste condition contemplation.[11]

Faith

If we may understand faith as that in us which determines a person's basic stance, no life is possible unless it is rooted in faith—even if this faith is interpreted by some in an agnostic or skeptical language. Faith—for example, faith in history, faith in God, or faith in Reason— is always an affair of the heart. It can be neither confined to nor entirely displayed within the rational theater of egological self-knowledge, because it permeates all the elements and relations of acquaintance that position a person with regard to God, the others, humanity, the world, and history, insofar as all of these play a decisive role in a person's life story—including one's philosophy, if one happens to be a philosopher.

One must choose between faith in God and faith in the Totality, Nature, Reason, History, the Will to Power, Libido, Oneself, or other quasi-Absolutes. But no philosophy or metaphilosophy is possible without a descent into the faith by which such a philosophy is—or desires to be—inspired. A philosophy that declares itself autonomous and autarkic with regard to faith is too superficial to be serious and truly interesting. Such a philosophy is a fable without lesson, a heartless exercise in possibilities without roots, a hovering and wavering that can only be provisional. A philosophy that recognizes its roots might be risky; it needs time to discover how much light its faith might shed on the inherited and provisional worlds we share within the republic of thought. However, such a philosophy is true to thinkers who risk their thinking not only within the brackets of undecided abstractions, but from the heart of their committed lives. Such thinkers show who they are, while addressing their interlocutors without hiding behind the personae of their masks.

AFTERTHOUGHTS

The above notes were written and presented in the spring of 2006 as an introduction to discussion. Many statements should be founded and developed more elaborately. To indicate along which lines I would like to do this, I add here a few theses that seem defensible to me.

1. Without affective inspiration and integration, nothing in life, action, thought, or language is (humanly) real. An ethics that does not pay attention to the affective and emotional transformation of individual persons in search of amelioration does not speak to anyone. When the heart remains indifferent or "hard," an ethics of correct deeds leaves the speaker, the listener, and the thinker cold.

2. That affectedness generates not only an affective response but also an affective self-evaluation of that response is caused by our desire (the desire of becoming good), which transcends all our responses by its orientation toward the good itself. Diotima presents each stage of the discovery (of what "good" means) as a step toward a new appearance, which at the same time is a stage of self-transcendence (because the newly discovered phenomenon of "good" challenges our former attachments and provokes a shift to a new constellation of love). Plato/

Diotima stylizes the itinerary in a particular way according to his/her dominating perspective: beauty.

3. The greatest danger of emphasizing the role of affectivity lies in a prolonged and self-sublimating narcissism. The Greek way of loving *kalokagathia*,[12] for example, can easily become a form of self-glorification and self-divinization. Even quasimystical self-perfection within a Christian context can be practiced in a narcissistic manner.

The crucial discovery occurs when it becomes clear that the originary desire is not primarily a desire for self-satisfaction, but instead for the realization of a unique destiny, that is, for the realization of what each one is *meant* to be/become/receive/accomplish/suffer/enjoy— which includes that one gives what one has and is and does with regard *to* others, the society, friends, church, humanity, God. To the extent to which the meaning of an every-time-unique destiny is realized, that meaning will make the individual person happy, but it does not enclose this destiny in the self-enjoying solitude of a centralized interiority.

Desire is the desire to open, unfold, and coaccomplish the destination of one's life, as it "is meant to be." The ultimate desideratum remains partially hidden, but life itself, as having a past and memory, has a style and a direction, and it contains many hints for concretization— even if one still must go through one or more conversions.

4. Conversions are necessary, but how are they possible? We need models and exemplary analyses that do not overlook affective changes in dealing with the world and oneself. However, even within the dimension of affections, we must recognize the impact of the *word*—the addressing, greeting, appealing, calling word that challenges, provokes, and summons. (Cf. the various conversion stories from biblical and Greek antiquity until today.)

5. Converting words are accompanied not only by supportive actions, but also by the joy that beams from the more desirable stance to which the words provoke (and sometimes also by the horror caused by resistance to the call). The symbolization (picture, parable, dream, drama, sermon, prophecy) of the *better* life that becomes possible at the next stage must touch and pierce one's heart in order to make advancement possible. I must be brought to "feel differently" about "things."

Feast of All Saints, 2006

Notes

1. Bonaventura, *Itinerarium mentis in Deum*, ch. 1, n. 6.

2. Ibid., prologue, n. 3. To characterize the motivating desire, Bonaventura refers to Dan. 9:23 and Ps. 37:9.

3. Cf. Emmanuel Falque, *Saint Bonaventure et l'entrée de Dieu en théologie* (Paris: Vrin, 2000); idem, "Vision, Excès et Chair: Essai de lecture phénoménologique de l'oeuvre de Saint Bonaventure," *Revue de Sciences philosophiques et théologiques* 79 (1995): 3–48.

4. A more detailed and more personal attempt at conversion of philosophical modernity can be found in Adriaan T. Peperzak, *Thinking: From Solitude to Dialogue and Contemplation* (New York: Fordham University Press, 2006).

5. Cf. Adriaan T. Peperzak, "Life, Science, and Wisdom according to Descartes," in *The Quest for Meaning: Friends of Wisdom from Plato to Levinas* (New York: Fordham University Press, 2003), 123–48.

6. Ibid., 125–44, commenting on Descartes's *Discours de la méthode*, AT 6, pp. 22–29, and 9 B, pp. 2–17.

7. G. W. F. Hegel, *Gesammelte Werke* (Hamburg: Meiner, 1968–), 18:18. About the power of reason to prove the truth that is contained in the initial faith, see pp. 25–31, esp. 31.

8. That "the cat is on the mat" is one of the most ambiguous phrases that one can choose as an example in epistemology, I have tried to show in *Aanspraak en Bezinning* (Kampen: Klement, 2007), 13–61.

9. Cf. Immanuel Kant, *Kritik der praktischen Vernunft*, Ak. 5, pp. 74–82 (or first edition, pp. 131–47).

10. Cf. Peperzak, *Thinking*, chs. 2 and 3, esp. pp. 25–37.

11. See also the afterthoughts with which this essay concludes and Adriaan T. Peperzak, "Affective Theology/Theological Affectivity," in *Philosophy between Faith and Theology* (Notre Dame, IN: University of Notre Dame Press, 2005), 155–67.

12. To become "good-and-beautiful," that is, to be and to act as someone who is at the same time *kalos* (beautiful) and *agathos* (good), cannot be defined as either morally correct or aesthetically admirable, because it expresses an excellent union of both.

2 | *Naturae Desiderium*

The Desire of Nature between History and Theology

PETER J. CASARELLA

To attribute some form of desire or yearning to the natural world is hardly a new proposition. The proposition alone has for a long time been seen as a fount of diverse but unmistakable controversy. For example, Aristotle, in a woeful misreading of Empedocles of Acragas, chastises the Presocratic thinker for championing an original state of nature in which bodies are separated and in movement. "Empedocles," he writes, "omits the period when Love was gaining ascendancy."[1] Likewise, much of what Rémi Brague terms "the wisdom of the world" that has been lost with the rise of the modern cosmological anthropology and anthropological cosmology is also the loss of an ability to listen for a hidden desire in the most basic cosmic structuring of things.[2] Even more revealing in this regard is the disparaging judgment of the eminent literary historian E. R. Curtius regarding Bernard Silvestris's cosmological poem *De mundi universitate*: "The whole is bathed in an atmosphere of a fertility cult, in which religion and sexuality mingle."[3] The very idea of a desire of nature is not only ambiguous but inflammatory.

This essay will render neither a dismissive nor an exculpatory judgment on the idea. The point rather is to investigate its role in the unveiling of a trajectory of thought about religious and secular reason whose influence is still felt today. We will get a view of that trajectory only by examining its force in a particular juncture and examining that historical appearance of secular reason from a particular angle. The full force of the trajectory can be brought to light only if one holds in abeyance certain standard preconceptions about how to gain access to ideas in the past.

To be more specific, I will look at how a problem in thinking about the history of thought presents us with a problem for thinking about thinking. The focus is on the Middle Ages, but my approach is not designed to tout the medievals as superior to the moderns. In short, I will argue that the historical passage of Christian thought through the Middle Ages still counts as Christian *thought* precisely in its character as a passage. The point will be to show that the demarcation between the history of theology at a certain point in the past and what we conceive of as actual (or, to employ an even more telling term, "constructive") Christian thought need not become a divide.

To elucidate this point, I reexamine in this essay a question of periodization of history that lies at the cusp of the putative apex of the Middle Ages. The ramifications of this periodization, it will be argued, extend beyond the confines of the two periods in question and even beyond the confines of history. In other words, the close scrutiny of what constitutes the epochal divide between two supposedly distinct periods of medieval intellectual history is of more than antiquarian interest. The period under study in this essay, namely, the movement from the twelfth to the thirteen century, is intensely fascinating in terms of the how the thinkers in the later period viewed their relationship to the previous century and also in terms of vital questions in philosophy and theology today.

The essay has four parts. The first deals with a few elements of a new history of medieval philosophy as a framework for assessing the contemporary debates about religious and secular reason. Here I lay out the fundamental genealogical questions that are sometimes ignored in some prevalent presentations of the thought of the High Middle Ages.

The second part looks more closely at a specific question, namely, the concept of nature. Here I attempt to look in a new way at some aspects of the twelfth-century theology of nature that have been either overlooked or unfairly characterized in certain standard versions of the history of medieval Christian thought. The originality of these conceptions, I argue, lies elsewhere than what has normally been assumed.

The third part looks at how an influential contemporary exponent of the critical rediscovery of medieval thought configures this epochal transition. Specifically, I turn to theologian John Milbank, focusing on the brilliant but also highly problematic way in which he approaches one important strand in the thinking of Henri de Lubac in his book *The Suspended Middle: Henri de Lubac and the Debate Concerning the Supernatural.*[4] The demystification of scholastic thinking about nature presented in the first two parts parallels and strengthens a critique that I level against Milbank. The rediscovery of a scholastic theology of nature that precedes the beginning of the thirteenth century is the perfect point of departure for classifying some strengths and weaknesses of Milbank's *Suspended Middle,* even though Milbank's focus is on St. Thomas and the Italian Renaissance. In sum, Milbank fails to appreciate the rich heritage of twelfth-century thinking about nature and ignores support that his own theses about the Middle Ages would receive from paying more attention to these sources.

I conclude by looking at the implications of this combined historical and systematic analysis for the theme of religious and secular reason.

EPOCHAL TRANSITION AND THE HIGH MIDDLE AGES

More than one conception of reason and of natural reason emerged in the High Middle Ages, and this plurality precedes the formation of the cathedral schools and the debates that surround their formation. Recent research into the concept of nature in the twelfth century has confirmed the need for a reexamination of paradigms used to approach medieval Christian thought and to assess its overall significance. The issue under examination here is how, if at all, to mark the beginning of a new era. In Steven P. Marrone's *The Light of Thy Countenance: Science and Knowledge of God in the Thirteenth Century* (2001), it seems that the innovations of twelfth-century authors are taken as a seed that reaches its mature form only in the "Augustinian school" of the thirteenth century.[5] In his view, twelfth-century works that do not contribute to the advent of a "scientific" model for knowledge (such as Bernard Silvestris's highly allegorical *Cosmographia*) "must be described as largely symbolic and animist, organizing or communicating their thoughts primarily by means of interpretation or textual exegesis."[6] Given Marrone's focus on the course of illuminationist epistemology in the thirteenth century, it is no wonder that he gives twelfth-century attitudes towards nature such short shrift in his otherwise exhaustive volumes.

To his credit, however, Marrone is aware that a corrective view is in the process of being developed and acknowledges the artificiality of asserting a radical cultural divide between the twelfth and thirteenth centuries.[7] Marrone distinguishes between two avenues of investigation, "one tracing the boundaries of divergent currents and the other searching for the fault line of high-medieval change."[8] In the first case, twelfth-century views are virtually ignored, as when with seeming approval John Quinn cites Fernand Van Steenberghen's characterization of the whole period as one "of assimilation rather than of synthesis."[9] In this view, the focus is exclusively on the shape of Christian thought after the rise of the universities. The arguments focus on the so-called schools of that period (Aristotelian, Augustinian, Latin Averroist) as if they belonged to a self-contained historical unit. In the second case, which is basically that of intellectual historians writing in the wake of the research of Charles H. Haskins and R. W. Southern into twelfth-century humanism, scholars "speak of the metamorphosis from a subjective and highly literary or hermeneutical mentality in the twelfth century to a more empirical and discursive one in the thirteenth." In this view, "rationalism" still comes into its own only in the thirteenth century, but not without building upon earlier humanistic developments.[10]

In the end, neither of these approaches does justice to the new theology of nature that arose in the twelfth century. Among contemporary interpreters of medieval thought, Andreas Speer deserves much credit for recognizing the still positive contribution of the twelfth century to the *scientia* of the thirteenth century.[11] Speer builds upon the earlier work of Marie-Dominique Chenu, especially his *La théologie au douzième siècle,* a book in which Chenu coined the phrase "discovery of nature"

(*nature découverte*) and applied it to the twelfth century.[12] According to Chenu, not one Christian thinker in the twelfth century turned away from the idea of God and then suddenly "discovered" a natural world lying lifeless at his or her feet. Chenu's artful phrase includes the notions of "uncovering" and "unmasking," both of which support the twelfth-century idea that nature is a multilayered *integumentum*.[13] This discovering points to a new reality and a new form of knowledge. Chenu is quick to distinguish the reality uncovered from both the poetic evocation of a feeling and the plasticity of sculptural representations:[14]

> Our concern is with the realization which laid hold upon these men of the twelfth century when they thought of themselves as confronting an external, present, intelligible, and active reality as they might confront a partner (and in fact they personified this partner in their allegories) whose might and whose decrees called for accommodation or conflict—a realization which struck them at the very moment when, with no less shock, they reflected that they were themselves caught up within the framework of nature, were themselves also bits of this cosmos they were ready to master.[15]

The uncovering is thus a depersonalization and desacramentalization, a flattening of the symbolic meaning of things into something more literal.[16] There was an equally surprising range to the external realities being viewed in this way, for example, flora and fauna, erotic love, politics, the nascent commerce of the urban artisans, world history, and legal reasoning.[17] The theological contribution highlighted by Chenu concerns not so much the questions of sanction or blame (although these impulses were present) as the search for the universal element in the emergence of a new consciousness.

Drawing upon the work of Wolfgang Kluxen and George Wieland on the medieval notion of science, Speer then employs the term "paradigm shift" to describe the novelty. In most general terms, one should not look for a complete break with tradition but rather counterpose the emergent "scholastic" reality with the dissolution of a genuine twelfth-century "renaissance."[18] In other words, Speer's characterization allows one to examine the simultaneous presence of old and new while still charting a pattern of growth. Medieval concepts of nature did not change quickly or even progress linearly, but the *emergence* of a new paradigm is still clearly discernible in the course of the twelfth century. What dissolves is the authority of either an encyclopedic or an otherwise harmonious unity of the seven liberal arts and theology in which pride of place was accorded to the *trivium*. What intellectual forces lie behind this breakdown? Even before the inauguration of the University of Paris, signs of a new "scholastic" approach to nature can be clearly identified. In terms of how learning was accomplished, one need only point to the literary form of the *quaestio* that had been forged in the cathedral schools and the consequent rise of disputation as a pedagogical ideal. In terms of the investigation of nature itself, Speer highlights the search for causal explanations that are arrived at in relative independence from the traditional *auctoritates*.[19] In the foundation of a new knowledge and eventually a science of nature (*scientia naturalis*), Chenu's *nature découverte* is both the object of investigation and a process that leads to the emergence of new insights into the real.[20]

Speer's framing of the historical question may give the misleading impression that there was one predominant synthesis of the *artes* circulating in the twelfth century. This is not the case, and it is impossible to chart the transition to the approach to *universitas* at the universities without considering the potent diversity that preceded the foundation of the university. In an article surveying "the renewal of theology" between approximately 1075 and 1224, Jean Leclerq first posits two extreme poles: the hermits (e.g., the Carthusians) and the city dwellers (e.g., the masters of cathedral schools).[21] Regarding the many forms of learning that arose between these poles, one can differentiate between traditional monasticism (Rupert of Deutz, Peter the Venerable, Peter of Celle, and Arnold of Bonneval), Cistercians (e.g., Bernard of Clairvaux and William of St. Thierry, who defend the radical witness of a monk, albeit in public and highly influential ways), and regular canons (including the inhabitants of the monastery of St. Victor). The range of options between cloister and city is not, strictly speaking, socioeconomic or based on the differentiation of theory and praxis. Both ends of the spectrum include sophisticated theory, and both groups exhorted their followers to adopt concrete practices and new frameworks for pastoral care. The differences that allow the spectrum to unfold are, rather, methodological. Although the differences between different forms of monastic communities sharpened in the twelfth century, the theology that emerged from these diverse centers was in a real sense marked by the daily experience of praying, conversing, and reading in the cloister.[22] By the same token, the "schools" traveled, dispersed, and were reconstituted in new places. The constant was not so much fixed curricula as the beginning of a method of ordering and compiling that resulted in *sententiae* as a theological genre.[23] Even before the *summae* of the second half of the century, the schools had produced encyclopedic systematizations that "dealt with *all* the problems raised by Christian dogma and morality, faith and action."[24]

The differences between monastic theology and that of the schools sharpen if one considers their divergent approaches to the text. Leclerq continues: "The *intellectual methods* of monastic theology were based on the *lectio divina,* that is on reading accompanied by meditation and prayer; the methods of the schools were based on a *lectio* followed by a *disputatio.* In the cloister, there were 'conversations,' not debates."[25] Accordingly, the monks explored the states of the soul in the growth of the spiritual life. By contrast, the "psychology of the [urban] intellectuals strove rather to deduce logical consequences from principles related to the composition of the human being."[26] Thus, both sides contributed to the humanism of the age. Interaction and borrowings were not ruled out. The presence and perduring influence of the entire spectrum is determinative for understanding the rest of the medieval period, and even for its *longue durée* in the Italian Renaissance and beyond.[27]

NATURE PERSONIFIED IN THE MIDDLE AGES

The notion of nature as a fecund, maternal source has often been mistaken to be a purely modern innovation.[28] Goethe, for example, claimed that Mother Nature lives clandestinely in her innocent children:

She is the only Artist and she fashions the most simple matter to the most subtle and lofty contrasts; with no sign of exertion she raises the matter to the highest perfection, even the most exquisite distinctness, and her work is forever clothed in softness and executed with ease. Each of her children is unique in being; each of her appearances is alone in meaning and yet together they form but one. . . . She has reasoned and she continues to mediate, but never as a man mediates, but rather as Nature Herself. She holds within her being a unique and embracing tenderness which no amount of observation can steal from her.[29]

One need not embrace Goethe's well-known gender dualism to grasp the maternal sense of fecundity he sees emerging from the realm of the biological. Another modern view of Mother Nature that lies even closer to the medieval one can be found in an inscription composed by Pietro Bembo (1470–1547) that still stands on the tomb of the painter Raphael in the Roman Pantheon: "Here lies Raphael, by whom the mother of all things feared being conquered while he was alive, and while he was dying she herself feared death."[30] Bembo's Petrarchan humanism exalted the apotheosis of the artist, and the Renaissance cardinal was proud to allow the artist's work to equal or surpass divine generativity in the natural order.

The naturalists of the Middle Ages were seldom as confident as either Goethe or Pietro Bembo, but they did give voice to nature, regarding it as invested with its own creativity and not just as a product of God's artistry. Here we will treat this question from the vantage point of nature as a birthing process and as a *persona*. In doing so, one should still keep in mind that the new concept of nature in the twelfth century is as much a physics, theology, metaphysics, moral theory, and epistemology as an artistic achievement.

The history of Mother Nature in the Middle Ages takes a decisive turn in the twelfth century. Here a range of views can be found. Hugh of St. Victor, for example, writes, "All of nature is pregnant with sense, and nothing in all of the universe is sterile."[31] This view actually places little emphasis on the labor of the birth process and focuses instead on the upbringing of the new child, *ratio,* through the paternity of God's book, Scripture. It leads to the analogy of creation to a book, which is a teaching common to Hugh, Alan of Lille, and Bonaventure.[32] But even more daring formulations of the cosmic birthing arise in what scholars frequently, if somewhat misleadingly, term the school of Chartres, that community in which the revival of a Platonic world soul (*anima mundi*) became the signature of the new theology of nature.[33] The Platonic demiurge fashioned the world after the model of a living creature, which gives Ralph McInerny occasion to refer to the concept as "a cosmic animal" in order to show that the Platonists of the twelfth century wished thereby to express the creative causality of God.[34] William of Conches defended this idea. He was also the first to acknowledge its many meanings and see the difficulty of squaring the philosophy of nature in Plato's *Timaeus* with the Christian doctrine of the presence of the Holy Spirit in the world.[35] There is no reason to believe, contra William of St. Thierry, that the Platonists sought thereby to deny any distinction between creator and created. Regarding nature's subservience to the activity of the creator, Alan of Lille, a considerably more cautious but equally Platonizing author, writes:

> His activity is simple, mine multiple; his work stands of itself, mine is lacking; his work is a thing of wonder, mine mutable. He is unborn, I am a child; He is a maker, I made; He is the craftsman of my work; I the work of the craftsman; he acts from nothing; I beg work from something; he acts in his own name, I act under his name; . . . And so that you recognize that my power is impotent with respect to divine power, know that my effect is defective and consider my vigor worthless.[36]

Accordingly, at least some adherents to the new theology of nature recognize that nature is not a divine force. She is for Alan of Lille a decidedly creaturely activity, albeit one invested with an all-encompassing breadth of activity.

Whether or not the *anima mundi* is to be identified with the Holy Spirit and whether or not William consistently held to the notion of animated nature, he significantly "energized" the notion of nature.[37] William still used "nature" to refer to the specific property of a thing, but also and quite frequently used it to refer to the intrinsic dynamism of things. His view of a *natura operans* is not that of merely mechanical activity. It refers to the idea that nature works as an organic force permeating the whole fabric of reality or, as Speer writes, like a "causal network that receives its necessity from the final cause and whose final cause has the character of a first principle."[38] Among William's favorite definitions of *opus naturae* is the following: "The work of nature is such that like things are born of like things, from a seed or from a sprout. And nature is a power inserted in things that activates like from like."[39] The assimilative power of the world soul begets a form of unity that hearkens back to the *Timaeus.* In the *Timaeus* the creator forms the physical universe from within the world soul and unites the two "center to center."[40] Unceasing movement then begins in which the soul, "interfused everywhere from the center to the circumference of heaven, of which she is the external envelopment," invisibly permeates the visible spheres partaking of reason and harmony.[41] Commenting on this, William highlights that the soul is engendered as "a whole substance" rather than as several substances.[42] More precisely, the soul is whole in the individual parts of the world.[43] The wholism of the world soul for William is "virtual" because it arises in the potencies and powers of nature. For this reason, the whole is not to be seen as either universal or integral.[44] This creates an interesting problem for interpretation. The indissoluble unity of things in the spiritual nature of the world stands in stark contrast with the "mixed" character of the physical world. In highlighting this *aporia,* William has identified a fundamental ambiguity in Plato's concept of nature.[45] Materially, nature represents an aspect of a classificatory scheme based upon visible appearances (i.e., a species). Spiritually, nature represents a distinct kind of thing whose qualities are not visibly apparent (i.e., a genus). In the first sense man and horse share sensible natures. In the second sense, only man has a rational nature.

William of Conches's defense of the *anima mundi* marks a break with Augustine's theory of creation. To illustrate this point, Tullio Gregory cites two passages from the *Didascalicon* of Hugh of St. Victor, whom he takes as a reliable exponent of Augustinianism for the twelfth century. Hugh's own definition of the work of nature as "bringing forth into act that which lay hidden"[46] contrasts with the Ciceronian view he himself attributes to the *Physici*: " 'Nature is an artificer fire coming forth from a certain force in order to beget sensible things.' For the naturalists say that all things are begotten from heat and moisture."[47] Gregory maintains that the first definition lends support to Augustine's theory of seminal reasons, a notion whereby the simultaneous creation of all things by God could be reconciled with the daily occurrence of rebirth in the natural order.[48] William, on the other hand, is seen by Gregory as proposing a scientific vision of the world because he allows secondary causes to maintain their own proper efficacy. Gregory's standard for judging scientific progress could be questioned, but the fact that twelfth-century Augustinians such as Hugh wanted to keep their distance from a theory of nature defined by the *anima mundi* is beyond dispute.[49]

The revival of Platonic cosmogony in the twelfth century is mirrored in a very different way in the *Cosmographia* (also known as *De universitate mundi*), which Bernard Silvestris composed sometime between 1143 and 1148.[50] The book, literally a Platonizing "cartography" of the outer world and the human *microcosmus,* commences with a discussion of the musical harmony of nature and man. It continues a twelfth-century revival of the genre of the encyclopedia, which is also found in the *De eodem et diverso* of Adelard of Bath (ca. 1116) and the *Philosophia mundi* of William of Conches, which he wrote between 1135 and 1145.[51] Although the work is replete with knowledge of the natural world and history, Bernard clothes much of that knowledge in a mythical garb, a form of disclosure that he calls *narratio fabulosa.*[52] Although from our vantage point the *Cosmographia* may seem like an eclectic assemblage of medieval science, ancient myth, and moral philosophy, it remains one of the most important artistic achievements of the Middle Ages.

Nature is not a minor character in the *Cosmographia.* She has a dramatic role which, according to Bernard Silvestris, was aptly named *mater generationis* by Abu Ma shar, an astronomer from the eighth and ninth centuries.[53] Echoing Chenu's idea of dis-covery, Bernard's goddess *natura* takes on the all-determinative task of initiating cosmic reform and revealing the secrets of the universe.[54] Nature is introduced as a daughter of divine providence, "well endowed with intelligence"[55] and capable of conceiving the world "by sacred and blessed instincts and in accordance with a higher plan."[56] She is still primarily receptive, as we see when providence greets her with a Marian epithet: "O Nature, blessed fruitfulness of my womb."[57] As nature emerges from this state of untutored innocence, so too does the reader of the *Cosmographia* pursue a path of progressive enlightenment. Like nature, the reader is eventually sent in search of "Physis," the maternal fount of wisdom regarding how things work. Not surprisingly, Physis dwells in the very bosom of the earth alongside her daughters, Theory and Practice.[58]

Before embarking on this cosmopoetic journey, we need to begin where Bernard begins.[59] The fable starts with a dramatic plea: "Nature, as if in tears, makes complaint to Noys, or Divine Providence, about the confused state of the primal matter, or Hyle, and pleads that the universe be more beautifully wrought."[60] The plea reflects a desire to inaugurate a new stage in the history of the world, one in which the old elements will be rebuilt into a more harmonious form: "Desiring to escape from her ancient tumult, [*Silva,* i.e., formless chaos] asks for craft-bearing numbers and the bonds of music."[61]

What doctrines are ascribed to nature in this process? The creative model of the universe exists in God, and the sensible universe is born from this intellectual one, "perfect from perfect."[62] The eternal shaping of cosmic life proceeds cyclically from divine wisdom, a radiant light and "face inscribed with the image of the Father."[63] A living source of matter preexists its created form, although this must be seen as an eternal vitality established by God alongside the eternal exemplars.[64] Roundness is considered the perfect form and thus determines the shape of the universe.[65] Nature enters into a partnership with Noys to give shape and order to the chaos. Even in the protouniverse, a form of organized complexity arises in which the comprehensiveness of the system is sensitive to the activity of each part: "Now, if in the course of the work a single particle, however small, had been left out of this synthesis of matter, the cosmic order which was about to be realized might thereby have been subject to disruption and damage, since it would manifestly have been liable to assault from outside by foreign bodies."[66]

"Endelechia," the figure representing the Platonic world soul, emanates as a fountain-like intellectual substance to assist Noys in the cosmogony. In a nod to the goodness of the sensible world, the high priest Noys produces her only after the framework of Nature's elements is established and creation has assumed a beautiful outward form.[67] Although Bernard holds in common with Thierry of Chartres and William of Conches the Neoplatonic notion of creation as craftsmanship, Bernard's allegory may contain, as Brian Stock has suggested, a relatively unique insight. For Bernard it is not the case that *Deus fabricator* simply leaves on matter an imprint of a design that conforms to the divine mental image. Throughout the *Cosmographia* Bernard highlights matter's need for form.[68] The creative act of God is likened to *ars* but is not mechanical in the sense of an exterior force imposing itself on a foreign substance. The nonactualized state of prime matter fascinates Bernard, for he considers its privative character, namely, its primitive role as a chaotic and disordered substrate, as potentially creative.[69] This has significant repercussions for his view of the creator. As Stock puts it, Bernard's God is "god-in-matter, informing the world directly through matter's latent creativity."[70]

The text of the *Cosmographia* is woven from myth, science, and philosophy with a view to a new reading of history.[71] In this he was supported by the authority of Boethius and Martianus Capellanus, and by Macrobius's reading of the *Dream of Scipio,* but Bernard Silvestris famously felt that he had to defend his use of myth. His theory of myth making is noteworthy as an illustration of how seriously theologians of the twelfth century took the relationship between form and content. Bernard revived the Platonic notion that mysterious truths regarding the nature of the world and of God sometimes need to clothed with the form of myth, a covering he designated by the terms *involucrum* and *integumentum.* One cannot assume that for Bernard, as for moderns, myth represents a retreat into a prescientific universe, although a conscious program for demythologization had also been articulated *avant la lettre* in the twelfth century, usually in the name of prioritizing what these figures called the *quadrivium* or *scientia Arabica.*[72] As a Platonic metaphor the notion of intentionally veiled discourse functions at several levels, according to Brian Stock.[73] First, Bernard held that teachings from Virgil, the *Timaeus,* and other ancient cosmogonies could be taught equally well in either a philosophical (i.e., nonallegorical) or poetic guise.[74] Second, the refashioning in a cloaked form of key concepts of natural philosophy (sometimes derived from Hermetic sources) shows that nature's intrinsic mystery cannot be exhausted by the still untested and recently discovered scientific methods or Aristotelian learning.[75] Finally, and in light of the suspicions that surrounded the new discovery of nature, allegorization allowed Bernard to venture beyond what antinaturalists considered the prudent bounds of speculation while claiming (to use Alan of Lille's metaphor) only to twist the wax nose of authority.[76]

Bernard's personification of nature did not stand alone. As Chenu intimated, the "dis-covery" made by Christian thinkers of the twelfth century revealed nature as alive, involved in the unfolding of God's plan and human folly, and ready to express her opinions about the state of the world. In contrast to the openly ironic allegorizations that arise in the thirteenth century, the words attributed to nature in this period frequently still extol the ideal of *universitas*.[77] But a more realistic grasp of the ideal and also the distantiation of satire also make an appearance in the twelfth century. This problematic brings us to the reworking of the character of nature in Alan of Lille's *De planctu naturae* ("The Plaint of Nature"), a work influenced by the *Cosmographia*.

Although the outright identification of the representation of *natura* with "The Goddess Natura" has been rightly questioned, there is no question that the diverse ideas of nature employed by Alan—that is, *vicaria Dei,* a crowned and elegantly dressed bride, and the essence of a thing—manifest personal attributes as well as the conceptual rigor appropriate to quadrivial (i.e., scientific and mathematical) knowing.[78] Alan does not confuse nature's productivity with God's creative act. Nature is, strictly speaking, *obstetrix,* a midwife. Regarding man's second birth—what in the language of the Fathers was known as deification—nature even appears to renounce this ancillary role: "Man is born by my work, he is reborn by the power of God; through me he is called from non-being into being, through Him he is led from being to higher being; by me man is born for death, by Him he is reborn for life. But my professional services are set aside in the mystery of this second birth. But rather, I nature know nothing regarding the nature of this birth."[79] Nature's alleged ignorance of the *nature* of the birth obviously contains a hint of irony, for the midwife remains very aware of all God's designs.

Accordingly, nature remains active and in fact endowed with a quasidivine role of evoking man into being and forming him in God's image.[80] But God alone creates, and God alone restores man to new life. The two movements, that of God and that of his humble disciple,[81] are demarcated, but beyond that the relationship of God and nature is difficult to specify in purely conceptual terms. Nowhere in the *De planctu*, for example, does one find a discussion of man's natural endowment as a graced potency or other such terminological distinctions that dominated the scholastic period.[82]

How is the *De planctu* relevant to the study of thirteenth-century thought? The high level of dependence on the *Timaeus* and the mixing of metered and prose forms differentiate Alan's *De planctu naturae* from the style and substance of later scholasticism. More significantly, figures like Bonaventure and Aquinas inhabit a world that looks beyond Alan's largely Platonic and Boethian cosmos to the virtue theory of the *Nichomachean Ethics* and the commentaries written thereupon, especially that of Roger Bacon.[83]

But there is more continuity between Alan of Lille's *De planctu* and scholastic thought than is allowed by Van Steenberghen's problematic notion of "assimilation rather than synthesis." First, Alan not only puts the *trivium* to work in his theology but contributes to the new relationships between grammar and ontology being forged at the time. His figurative use of terms points to a multilayered reality. Alan is thus trying to see the essence of language as part of the newly discovered nature and at the same time to point to a new vision of the world and of moral order that is reflexively linguistic. The term *theologia sermocinalis* was used in the twelfth century by Peter Abelard to refer to the revival of the *trivium* within a theological compass.[84] Alan not only contributes to this development in the twelfth century but has forged an implicit metaphysics of language that rivals the efforts along these lines of Bonaventure, Meister Eckhart, and Nicholas of Cusa in the succeeding centuries.[85]

Moreover, Alan's philosophy of nature falls in the encyclopedist tradition (especially in the *Anticlaudianus* and *Regulae theologicae*), but it also manifests early signs of the emergence of an autonomous *philosophia naturalis*.[86] Alan, standing on the shoulders of the giants of the past, caught wind of the trumpets of new Aristotelian learning (*aristotelica tuba*) and tried to take this novel outburst into account.[87] If, as Speer has argued, Alan only adumbrated the groundbreaking principles of a new natural philosophy without developing its constituent parts, then it fell to the next century of Christian naturalists to work out these details.[88]

Alan studied human nature as a microcosm. With regard to the moral life, it seems clear in light of Alan's microcosm that the *De planctu* has moved beyond a simple catalog of virtues and vices to a consideration of their place in the overall fabric of reality. Later generations, especially in the wake of the controversy generated by Jean de Meun, tended to focus narrowly on this dimension of the work, but Alan saw virtue not only as a mere stamp of nature but also as a *habitus, dispositio,* or *qualitas.*[89] In other words, Alan's moral allegory was intended to be reduced neither to the thin gruel of moral maxims nor to a value-free description of human behavior. He saw human nature all at once as a marvel of creation, indigent, prone to error, and reformable.

A CASE IN POINT: THE READING OF *NATURAE DESIDERIUM* IN JOHN MILBANK'S *SUSPENDED MIDDLE*

This rediscovery of the polyphony of voices in the High Middle Ages regarding faith, reason, and the person of nature seems pertinent to the discussion of religious and secular reason. Manifold implications could be drawn from this new, post-Enlightenment illumination of what were once considered "the dark ages." I would like to focus on a more limited set of questions, namely, ones raised by Milbank's book *The Suspended Middle.* The work includes at least two intricate arguments. The first concerns the defense of the embattled theologian Henri de Lubac. The second consists of a reading of de Lubac's comprehensive vision, which Milbank takes to be (together with that of Sergei Bulgakov) the closest approximation to his own radical orthodoxy as was achieved by any theologian in the twentieth century. Not only is de Lubac, alongside von Balthasar, "one of the two truly great theologians of the twentieth century," but his breakthrough *in philosophy* can be considered absolutely groundbreaking. Rather than survey the whole of the contents of *The Suspended Middle* (which has been treated extensively in the book reviews), or even its general strengths and weaknesses, I will begin by stating some theses defended with typical erudition and verve by Milbank. These are not necessarily the theses that have attracted the most attention in the critical literature that the book has generated. They are all, however, central concerns of the text.

First, Milbank takes de Lubac to be a novel theologian—better yet, the only truly novel theologian—of finite spirit. The unique character and breadth of this praise is summarized in this provocative remark: "Indeed, it can now be seen that the *Surnaturel* of 1946 was almost as important an event of cultural revision as *Being and Time* or the *Philosophical Investigations*."[90] Milbank's return to the late essay "Tripartite Anthropology," as well as his underscoring of the Jesuit's debt to both Maximus the Confessor and Maurice Blondel, shows that Milbank's focus is on what he dubs "the metaphysics of pneuma."[91] Milbank takes de Lubac to have surpassed even Heidegger on the question of the "ontological difference," and the founder of Radical Orthodoxy thereby betrays the not-so-orthodox vantage point from which he makes judgments about the Catholic theologian.

Second, Milbank emphasizes throughout *The Suspended Middle* the *cosmic* orientation of the world to the supernatural order. When one examines Milbank's interpretation of de Lubac simply in terms of standard debates such as those generated by the promulgation of the encyclical *Humani Generis* (Pope Pius XII, 1950) or the question of nature and grace, then one can easily miss this point. But it is here that Milbank's *The Suspended Middle* most closely approximates the intent of the twelfth-century theologians examined above. The chapter entitled "Supernatural, Spirit, and Cosmos" focuses on de Lubac's real but ignored debt to Renaissance humanism. Here Milbank maintains that de Lubac's "apparent endorsement of the fundamental positions of Pico, Cusa, and Bérulle surely speaks volumes." Leaving aside (for the moment) the specific claim as it regards both history and theology, it seems that Milbank's interest is cosmic in at least two senses. First, he does brush aside (for they would be indeed anachronistic) the important questions regarding the theological status of nonhuman intellectual creatures.[92] Second, and even more decisively, Milbank offers a human-istic endorsement of the notion of man as a microcosmic entity. Take as just one barometer of this view Milbank's loud (and not unjustified) praise for the "heliocentrism" of Nicholas of Cusa and Cardinal Bérulle. In line with this tradition, Christ, the sun of creation, is the one medi-ator who, from within, elevates the entirety of the created order to its supernatural end: "Earth and man are elevated, but only as more radi-cally receptive."[93]

Third, Milbank considers de Lubac to be the theologian of the gift par excellence. The specific gift that he highlights is not a thing. It is a process that maintains a reduplicative character, namely, the gift of the anticipation of the gift as a rendering of the "elicited desire." The clever, albeit truncated and not entirely convincing, theses proffered by Mil-bank regarding the strategic decisions made by the Jesuit in the light of *Humani Generis* and the critiques of the conservative Neo-Thomists in France fall into this category as well. Wherever de Lubac anticipates a more radical orthodoxy than Pius XII, Milbank reveals that the guid-ing thread is that of the (Thomistic) model. No one doubts that de Lubac plotted carefully his every move. Given the spirit of his times, he would have been foolish to have done otherwise. On the other hand, Milbank's suggestion that de Lubac radically revised his thesis regard-ing the orientation of finite spirit to the supernatural in his later writ-ings is lacking in firm textual evidence.

Fourth, Milbank elaborates his praise for de Lubac in terms of the Jesuit's largely Thomistic recourse to the analogy between art and grace. Milbank devotes seventeen dense pages (out of a total of 108) to re-hearsing familiar arguments about the lack of a truly dramatic charac-ter to von Balthasar's theology of beauty. His Gadamerian critique of the lack of an element of play in Balthasar's predominantly "spectacu-lar" approach to theo-drama is without foundation. Furthermore, he simply ignores two key texts written by the Swiss theologian in praise of Nicholas of Cusa when he suggests that the difference between Bal-thasar and de Lubac is epitomized by the former's claim that the Cardi-nal from Kues lies at the root of modern titanism. If one abstracts from Milbank's wearying polemics with both Balthasar and contemporary schools of French Thomists, it seems that the analogy of art can be summarized this way: "For de Lubac (and von Balthasar much of the time) the approach of God lay in beauty because God was eminently beautiful."[94]

Fifth, *The Suspended Middle* represents yet another noble attempt by Milbank to write the definitive theological interpretation of Christian Neoplatonism. Mention has already been made of the currents from the Renaissance that received much praise from the side of Cardinal de Lubac and become one of the central paths to Milbank's reappraisal of de Lubac. Milbank also has some fine remarks about the living heritage of Neoplatonism that passes through both Thomas and Bonaventure. Based on Jacob Schmutz's work on scholastic theories of causality, Milbank pinpoints the decline of Proclus's influence on the specific matter of divine *influentia* in the thirteenth century, a decline which Milbank himself dubs "the de-metaphorization of 'influence.'"[95] Here is where Milbank comes very close to Speer in indicating the precise, multilayered, and determinative novelty of the theology of the thirteenth century. Accordingly, whereas the earlier (i.e., pre-thirteenth-century) model was predicated upon the Proclean idea that a cause remains in that which is caused, thirteenth-century accounts of divine influence begin to leave this principle behind in favor of either the divine general concursus or special interventions of God in a natural order that lies outside of the divine essence. The paradox of a "unilateral exchange" that Milbank attributes to Thomas owes much to this Neoplatonic doctrine of creative causality.[96] When seen in this light, the theological metaphysics of the Angelic Doctor is much easier to square with the Russian sophiology (above all, Sergei Bulgakov) that constitutes another building block of Milbank's own account of the supernatural.

On all five of these points, Milbank has certainly identified a strand of medieval theology that was truly kept alive by de Lubac. De Lubac, Milbank notes, was not just a collector of these ancient relics but a theoretician of the real. This generosity towards de Lubac is thus combined with a genuine anxiety of influence whereby Milbank rereads his own theological theses into the texts of de Lubac. Here I would cite just three of the more obvious interpolations. First, Milbank interprets de Lubac's Christological rendering of analogical paradox in terms of an aporetic "non-ontology." Milbank says, for example, that the natural desire for the supernatural is neither nature nor grace. It is "rather like the problematic plane between two and three dimensions in fractal geometry."[97] The translation of De Lubac's notion of paradox into the idiom of postmodern scientific inquiry would surely meet with the Jesuit's approval. On the other hand, the imputation of a "non-ontology" to the thought of de Lubac seems like a palpable residue of later German idealism quite foreign to de Lubac's more Blondelian metaphysics. Second, through his elevation of the analogy of art, the entire created cosmos becomes for Milbank (as for Vico) an infinite artifact supplemented by spirit, one whose natural givenness is never static. Milbank's otherwise fascinating rearticulation of a cosmic *poiesis* results in a seemingly willful ignorance of de Lubac's biblical hermeneutics. Milbank, for example, treats de Lubac's tropological mysticism as a variant of his own cosmic allegorization of the world.[98] It is difficult to see how such an assertion corresponds in any real way to de Lubac's monumental efforts in this field. Third, in his final chapter Milbank undertakes what appears to be a wholesale critique of the foundations of de Lubac's ecclesiology.[99] While the issues that he mentions (male priesthood, the office of Peter) are in fact among the most controversial ones in contemporary Catholicism, Milbank's further anachronism lies in his overt substitution of his own preferred Russian sophiology for de Lubac's view of a eucharistic, Catholic unity rooted in the *corpus mysticum*. He would have been better off exploring the more careful attempts at rapprochement between Eastern and Western ecclesiologies mediated, for example, by Louis Bouyer or Paul McPartlan.[100]

What can be said about the treatment of the Thomistic "desire of nature" in Milbank's *The Suspended Middle*? In order to respond to this question, we will examine a single passage in de Lubac's 1965 work *The Mystery of the Supernatural*. The new genealogy of medieval thought that I sketched above could illuminate the passage and supplement Milbank's reading. Milbank himself alludes to this passage but passes over the salient point.[101] In the passage, de Lubac defends the "magnificent and severe" Bérulle on the natural, hidden, and gratuitous inclination of the soul to God:

> Such a being, then, has more than simply a "natural desire" to
> see God, *desiderium naturale,* a desire which might be interpreted

vaguely and widely, which might, as a later commentator on St. Thomas has said, simply be "*desiderium conforme naturae,*" or as another says, "*juxta naturam.*" St. Thomas is most clear that such is not the case. The desire to see God is, for him, a "desire of nature" in man; better, it is "the desire of nature," *naturae desiderium*: this expression, which he uses on several occasions, should be enough to do away with any tendency to fancy interpretation. It therefore remains necessary to show how, even for a being animated with such a desire, there still is not and cannot be any question of such an end being "owed"—in the same sense in which the word rightly gives offense. It remains to show how it is always by grace—even apart from the additional question of sin and its forgiveness—that God "shows himself to him."[102]

Why does de Lubac call attention to the phrase *naturae desiderium*? Is there any real difference between "a natural desire" and "a desire of nature"? The Jesuit theologian is well aware that Thomas does not support the robust personification of nature envisioned by twelfth-century authors. At the same time, de Lubac's remark brings into relief a missing element in the standard readings of the Angelic Doctor's position on nature and grace. The main point of de Lubac is that grace remains wholly gratuitous. God owes us nothing, and the gratuity of the supernatural order cannot be reduced to the noninterference of two separate realms (what A. Gardeil terms a desire of "mere 'complacence'").

A more interesting question concerns the subject of desire in *naturae desiderium*. The common reading, which is endorsed by the translator of the above passage and may also be the most plausible, is that *natura* signifies human nature even though this is not expressed as such. The fact that human nature as such is not indicated by the words does not preclude the possibility that Thomas would abbreviate *human nature* as simply *nature*. De Lubac's stress leaves little room for a bifurcation between man and nature. De Lubac's reading sees grace within the internal dynamism of human nature without broaching any form of a-cosmism. His highlighting of *naturae desiderium* invites the question of whether there is some way to read the phrase used by St. Thomas as indicating either a desire of nature *tout court* or, more likely, the human desire rooted in its cosmic context. If one followed this latent possibility, then one still could not assimilate the position of St. Thomas on nature to that of Alan of Lille. One would, however, be stating that the subjective desire of a human nature is imbedded within an ontological *élan* that extends into and permeates the entire realm of the natural order. Interpreted in this second sense, Milbank's cosmic rendering of Thomism reveals both its real merits and its real difficulties. Human nature and its desire for God cannot be torn from the fabric of reality. On this point, Milbank's cosmic Augustinian version of Thomism is quite in line with de Lubac's more severely Augustinian Thomism, which in this case is mediated by Bérulle.

Milbank has highlighted a critical and previously ignored element in de Lubac's interpretation of St. Thomas. Milbank's misprision proves once again the ancient elusiveness and volatility of the idea of endowing nature with desires. A fuller examination of that idea within the Thomistic corpus unfortunately lies outside the scope of this inquiry. In any case, the highlighting of a pivotal and crucially overlooked problem in grasping the religious cosmology of the Angelic Doctor brings us back to the central question of how misplaced bifurcations between nature and desire place unnecessary strictures on reason itself.

HEARKENING TO A REPRESSED POLYPHONY: IMPLICATIONS FOR RELIGIOUS AND SECULAR REASON TODAY

Raúl Fornet-Betancourt, a Cuban philosopher of culture teaching in Aachen, has spoken of the need to recognize a polyphonic presence of voices of reason.[103] This phrase, which derives from Habermas, brings to the surface one of the main problems concerning the way in which the medieval heritage on faith and reason is generally received. Scholars, even when they overcome the modernist idea that the period between Aristotle and the Renaissance was lying dormant until the light switch of modern rationality was activated, continue to impose categories derived from late medieval or scholastic schools upon the whole of the medieval tradition. To recover Thomism or Augustinianism or even a novel amalgam of the two (like Milbank's) serves the ideological ends of those still interested in promoting the hardened lines of old and new schools. The cathedral schools from the twelfth century need further study, but this undertaking should not proceed in terms of the equally modernist dichotomy of school and cloister. Here I have merely outlined the *longue durée* as that notion was handed down from theologians in the twelfth to theologians in the thirteenth century. This partial presentation of what is a more complex narrative was intended to illustrate the absence of a single epochal shift. Fornet-Betancourt's notion of a polyphonic presence of voices of reason highlights the possibility of hearkening to the harmonic concordances that supersede the overt strife of school debates. The true polyphony of medieval thought is neither a forerunner of the theological pluralism of the contemporary academy nor a new grand narrative. The exercise of attending to the plural voices of reason with their distinctively medieval rhythms is a necessary part of the task of writing a living history of philosophy. We need to recognize the plaint of nature as it emerges in varied historical and cultural centers in order to contribute decisively to a genuinely philosophical genealogy of philosophy.

How does the genealogical dis-covery relate to the question of nature's desire? No one historical inquiry as such can validate a philosophical principle about reality. But history and nature often mirror each other in novel ways. The sum and substance of the historical point just made might be displayed in St. Thomas Aquinas's defense of the Aristotelian dictum *anima quodammodo omnia* ("the soul is in a sense all things"). There is nothing unsurprising about Thomas's approach to this ancient heritage. His position offers rich resources for confronting the dual challenge of an autonomous reason and an exclusivist, a-cosmic faith. Milbank alludes to this principle as the lacuna that distinguishes Neoscholastic modernism from Thomas's own thinking.[104] Milbank more generally bases his interpretation of de Lubac's Thomism on this very principle. In a sense, Thomas's reading of Aristotle on this question brings us very close to the real intent of Milbank's understanding of the medieval tradition of Christian thought. Milbank insists against de Lubac's detractors that the human desire to know God is an ontological élan, not a mere epistemological curiosity.[105] Milbank, as we have seen, embraces a Proclean-inspired notion of the causality of grace as a paradoxically conceived unilateral exchange.[106] While this clever insight lies far afield from any plain sense of de Lubac's texts, the claim for a Neoplatonic Thomism of unilateral exchange takes on new meaning in light of Milbank's own defense of the Aristotelian dictum in question. In other words, the "somehow" in the dictum suddenly becomes the key to the Christian interpretation of Aristotle and perhaps even to the epochal transition sketched above.

How, exactly, *is* the soul all things? Naturalists old and new might point out the insights gained from the constitution of the human body. Could the soul include parts of the outer world just like the body? The "somehow" in the dictum makes the naturalistic interpretation highly implausible. The things are not contained in the soul in the same way as they reside in a material container, even one so beautifully ordered as the human body. For Thomists like Milbank an additional, metaphysical point must be made. There is something other than the objects of the world to be discovered in the soul. The mystery of the world lies in the mystery of the human creature, and the soul is the focal point of these intersecting mysteries. *Quodammodo* certainly does not mean that only certain faculties of the soul are microcosmic. The adverbial qualifier is a clear reminder that the being of finite spirit is a cosmic cipher. Herein lies the path to the rediscovery of the openness of reason to all of reality. Because of the singular achievement of Henri de Lubac, we can say that the *anima* that is *quodammodo omnia* is penetrated to its core by the gift of the anticipation of the gift of grace. To introduce the question of grace at the end of these reflections is not to add a new element to the mix. It is rather for St. Thomas and de Lubac the rediscovery of nature's ownmost desire.

Notes

1. Aristotle *De caelo* Γ2, 301a14, quoted in G. S. Kirk and J. E. Raven, eds., *The Presocratic Philosophers* (Cambridge: Cambridge University Press, 1957), 347.

2. Rémi Brague, *La sagesse du monde: Histoire de l'expérience humaine de l'univers* (Paris: Fayard, 1999).

3. E. R. Curtius, *European Literature and the Latin Middle Ages* (Princeton: Princeton University Press, 1953), 112, quoted in George D. Economou,

The Goddess Natura in the Medieval Literature (Notre Dame, IN: University of Notre Dame Press, 2002), 60.

4. John Milbank, *The Suspended Middle: Henri de Lubac and the Debate Concerning the Supernatural* (Grand Rapids: Eerdmans, 2005).

5. Steven P. Marrone, *The Light of Thy Countenance: Science and Knowledge of God in the Thirteenth Century* (Leiden: Brill, 2001), 1:11.

6. Ibid.

7. Ibid., 1:4n10, 1:12n21.

8. Ibid., 1:5.

9. Fernand Steenberghen, *Aristotle in the West: The Origins of Latin Aristotelianism* (Louvain: Nauwelaerts, 197), 23–28, quoted in John Francis Quinn, *The Historical Constitution of St. Bonaventure's Philosophy* (Toronto: Pontifical Institute of Medieval Studies, 1973), 46.

10. Cf. R. W. Southern, "Scholastic Humanism," in *Scholastic Humanism and the Unification of Europe,* vol. 1, *Foundations* (Oxford: Blackwell, 1995), 1–13. According to Marrone, Southern characterizes the humanism of the thirteenth century in this essay "as contentious and authoritarian" but points to 1270 as the starting point of the transformation (Marrone, *Light of Thy Countenance,* 1:4n10). Marrone himself takes the divide between the prescientific inquiry prior to the twelfth century's discovery of nature and theology in the twelfth and thirteenth centuries to be greater than that between the scientific revolution of the seventeenth century and the period before it (1:13).

11. Andreas Speer, *Die entdeckte Natur: Untersuchungen zu Begründungsversuchen einer "scientia naturalis" im 12. Jahrhundert* (Leiden: Brill, 1995).

12. Marie-Dominique Chenu, OP, *La théologie au douzième siècle,* 3rd ed. (Paris: Vrin, 1966), 21.

13. I am thinking here of Bernard Silvestris's notion of nature as *integumentum.* Willimien Otten is quite instructive on the general historical problem here. See her essay "Nature and Scripture: Demise of a Medieval Analogy," *Harvard Theological Review* 88 (April 1995): 257–84.

14. This insight into the nature of "dis-covery" came through a reading of Enrique Dussel, *El Descubrimiento de America,* which makes the point that every uncovering is also a covering over of another reality.

15. Chenu, *La théologie au douzième siècle,* 5, as translated in M.-D. Chenu, *Nature, Man, and Society in the Twelfth Century* (Toronto: University of Toronto Press, 1997), 4–5.

16. Alexander Schmemann ties this flattening to the loss of the true meaning of the symbol in high medieval Western theology. He claims that between the Carolingian Renaissance and the Reformation, symbol becomes identified with a means of knowledge, so that the total (sacramental) experience of knowledge *of* reality is reduced to rational discourse *about* reality. In the eucharistic controversy of 1059, Schmemann claims, *neither* Berenger of

Tours *nor* those who condemn him seem to be aware that this radical transformation of the symbol has already taken place. Alexander Schmemann, *For the Life of the World* (Crestwood, NY: St. Vladimir's Press, 1973), 142–43.

17. In other words, Chenu uncovers the world of human making as a constitutive process within nature, a theme quite central to the work of John Milbank.

18. Andreas Speer, "Wissenschaft und Erkenntnis: Zur Wissenschaftslehre Bonaventuras," *Wissenschaft und Weisheit* 49 (1986): 169; idem, *Triplex Veritas: Wahrheitsverständnis und philosophische Denkform Bonaventuras* (Werl/Westfalen: Dietrich-Coelde-Verlag, 1987), 26.

19. Speer, *Die entdeckte Natur,* 289.

20. Ibid. Cf. Andreas Speer, "'Agendo phisice ratione': Von der Entdeckung der Natur zur Wissenschaft von der Natur im 12. Jahrhundert (insbes. bei Wilhelm von Conches und Thierry von Chartres)," in *"Scientia" und "Disciplina": Wissentheorie und Wissenschaftspraxis im 12. und 13. Jahrhundert,* ed. R. Berndt and M. Lutz-Bachmann (Berlin: Akademie Verlag, 2002), 157–74.

21. Jean Leclerq, "The Renewal of Theology," in *Renaissance and Renewal in the Twelfth Century,* ed. Robert L. Benson and Giles Constable (Cambridge, MA: Harvard University Press, 1982), 68–87. If one sticks simply with the chronological century, then one must omit from consideration the most important theological works of, for example, St. Anselm of Canterbury (at the end of the eleventh century) and Alan of Lille (at the beginning of the thirteenth).

22. Jean Leclerq, OSB, *The Love of Learning and the Desire for God: A Study of Monastic Culture* (New York: Fordham University Press, 1982).

23. Ibid., 72.

24. Ibid., 77.

25. Ibid., 82–83.

26. Ibid., 83.

27. Milbank highlights Henri de Lubac's rewriting of the distinction between the Middle Ages and the Renaissance. More will be said about this below.

28. See, for example, Romano Guardini, *The End of the Modern World* (Wilmington, DE: ISI Books, 1998), 36.

29. From the fragment "Nature," written in 1782 for the *Tiefurter Journal,* quoted in Guardini, *End of the Modern World,* 37.

30. Ille hic est Raphael, timuit quo sospite vinci rerum magna parens, et moriente mori. See also his *De imitatione* (1512).

31. Hugh of St. Victor *Didascalicon* 6.5: "Omnis natura rationem parit, et nihil in universitate infecundum est." Jerome Taylor finds echoes of Asclepius in this passage (*The Didascalicon of Hugh of St. Victor* [New York: Columbia University Press, 1991], 224n23). Ivan Illich makes the more probable connection to Augustine *De Genesi ad Litteram* (PL 34, 245): "God has written two books, the book of creation and the book of redemption" (Ivan Illich, *In the*

Vineyard of the Text: A Commentary on Hugh's Didascalicon [Chicago: University of Chicago Press, 1993], 123).

32. Alan of Lille: "Omnis mundi creatura / quasi liber, et pictura / nobis est, et speculum" (PL 210, 579).

33. Tullio Gregory, *Anima Mundi: La Filosofia di Guglielmo di Conches e la Scuola di Chartres* (Florence: G. C. Sansoni-Editore, 1955); Speer, *Die entdeckte Natur,* 151–62. Not all the theologians who espoused these views were affiliated with Chartres.

34. Plato *Timaeus* 30bc; Ralph McInerny, *A History of Western Philosophy,* vol. 2, *Philosophy from St. Augustine to Ockham* (Notre Dame, IN: University of Notre Dame Press, 1970), 171.

35. Chenu, *La théologie au douzième siècle,* 33; idem, *Nature, Man, and Society in the Twelfth Century,* 22. For more details, see Gregory, *Anima Mundi,* 123–74, and especially Speer, *Die entdeckte Natur,* 151n64, which references a study that claims support for this idea in saints Basil, Ambrose, and Augustine.

36. Alan of Lille *De planctu naturae* 6, prosa 3 (PL 210, 445): "Ejus operatio simplex, mea multiplex; ejus opus sufficiens, meum deficiens; eius opus mirabile, meum opus mutabile. Ille innascibilis, ego nata; ille faciens, ego facta; illa mei opifex operis, ego opus opificis; ille operatur ex nihilo, ego mendico opus ex aliquo; ille suo operatur nomine, ego operor illius sub nomine. . . . Et ut, respectu potentiae divinae, meam potentiam impotentem esse cognoscas, meum effectum scias esse defectum, meum vogrem vilitatem esse perpendas." English translation from idem, *The Plaint of Nature,* trans. James J. Sheridan (Toronto: Pontifical Institute of Medieval Studies, 1980), 124.

37. Bonaventure rejects the Neoplatonic thesis regarding the *anima mundi,* but his rejection is directed at the Avicennist rather than the twelfth-century version. Although William defends the *anima mundi* in his commentary on the *Timaeus,* the notion disappears from the *Dragmaticon,* a later work on natural philosophy. Regarding the identification with the Holy Spirit, William writes in *Glosae* (in *Timaeum* 34B) 71 (ed. É. Jeauneau), 145: "Hunc spiritum dicunt quidam esse Spiritum Sanctum, quod nec negamus nec affirmamus" (quoted in Speer, *Die entdeckte Natur,* 155n76).

38. Speer, *Die entdeckte Natur,* 206.

39. William of Conches *Glosae* (in *Timaeum* 28A) 37 (ed. É. Jeauneau), 104: "Opus nature est quod similia nascuntur ex similibus, ex semine vel ex germine. Et est natura vis rebus insita similia de similibus operans" (quoted in Speer, *Die entdeckte Natur,* 206n229). See Speer, 205–21, for more details.

40. Plato *Timaeus* 36de.

41. Ibid., 36e–37a.

42. William of Conches *Glosae* (in *Timaeum* 36D) 91 (ed. É. Jeauneau), 172.

43. Ibid.: "eadem enim anima tota est in singulis partibus mundi."

44. Ibid. (in *Timaeum* 35B), 89 (ed. É. Jeauneau), 156: "est enim anima totum quoddam non universale nec integrum sed virtuale . . ."

45. Speer, *Die entdeckte Natur,* 209.

46. *Didascalicon* 1.9 (PL 176, 747c): "Opus naturae, quod latuit ad actum producere."

47. *Didascalicon* 1.10 (PL 176, 748d): "Natura est ignis artifex, ex quadam vi procedens in res sensibiles procreandas. Physici namque dicunt, omnia ex calore et humore procreari." Cf. Cicero *De Natura Deorum* 2.22. For a more favorable reading of Mother Nature in Hugh, see *Homilia in Ecclesiasten,* hom. 2 (PL 175, 136), in which he says we can accept "occultam naturae vim . . . quae universa invisibiliter nutrit et vegetat."

48. Gregory, *Anima Mundi,* 181.

49. Below, I consider an even more severe objection raised by William of St. Thierry.

50. Bernard Silvestris, *Cosmographia,* ed. Peter Dronke (Leiden: Brill, 1978); idem, *The Cosmographia of Bernardus Silvestris,* trans. Winthrop Wetherbee (New York: Columbia University Press, 1983). The dating here follows Stock, as cited below.

51. Brian Stock, *Myth and Science in the Twelfth Century: A Study of Bernard Silvester* (Princeton: Princeton University Press, 1972), 21–22; John Marenbon, *Early Medieval Philosophy (480–1150): An Introduction* (London: Routledge & Kegan Paul, 1983), 125–26.

52. Silvestris *Cosmographia* 1.2.9, p. 5, ed. André Vernet, quoted in Stock, *Myth and Science,* 45.

53. Stock, *Myth and Science,* 65.

54. Ibid., 63.

55. Silvestris *Cosmographia* 1.2; Wetherbee, p. 69.

56. Ibid.

57. Ibid. Later in 1.2 (Wetherbee, p. 72), the four elements (fire, earth, water, and air) spring from the womb of the mother of life.

58. Silvestris *Cosmographia* 2.9; Wetherbee, pp. 111–12.

59. Cf. Giuseppe Mazzotta, *Cosmopoiesis: The Renaissance Experiment* (Toronto: University of Toronto Press, 2001).

60. Silvestris *Cosmographia* prologus; Wetherbee, p. 65.

61. Silvestris *Cosmographia* 1.1, quoted from the Vernet edition in Stock, *Myth and Science,* 69n13: "cupiens exire tumultu / artifices numeros et musica vincla requirit" (translation mine). Cf. Wetherbee, p. 67. More quadrivial elements emerge in 1.2; Wetherbee, p. 71.

62. Silvestris *Cosmographia* 1.4; Wetherbee, p. 89.

63. Silvestris *Cosmographia* 1.4; Wetherbee, p. 87: "Noys and the divine exemplars live eternal; without their life the visible creation would not live everlastingly. Hyle was in existence before it, preexistent in substance and in

the spirit of an eternal vitality. For it is not to be believed that the wise creator of insensate matter did not first establish a basis for it in a living source."

64. Silvestris *Cosmographia* 1.4; Wetherbee, p. 88.

65. Silvestris *Cosmographia* 1.4; Wetherbee, p. 89. Cf. "The Phenenomenology of Roundness," in Gaston Bachelard, *The Poetics of Space* (Boston: Beacon Press, 1964), 239–40.

66. Silvestris *Cosmographia* 1.2; Wetherbee, p. 73.

67. Ibid. Cf. Stock, *Myth and Science,* 123–25.

68. Stock, *Myth and Science,* 98–117, esp. 114.

69. Ibid., 117.

70. Ibid., 125.

71. See, for example, what is disclosed with the unveiling of the world soul in 1.2; Wetherbee, p. 74: "There were the tears of the poor and the fortunes of kings, the soldier's strength and the happier discipline of the philosophers, all that the reason of angels or men may comprehend, all that is gathered together beneath the dome of heaven." Cf. Stock, *Myth and Science,* 86.

72. On the question of *integumentum/involucrum* in the twelfth century, I follow Stock, *Myth and Science,* 31–62, an approach that accentuates the medieval path to Italian humanism and then Vico.

73. Ibid., 59.

74. On Virgil's poetic theology of nature, Bernard writes: "Scribit enim in quatum est philosophus humanae vitae naturam. Modus vero agendi talis est: sub integumento describit quid agat vel quid patiatur humanus spiritus in humano corpore temporaliter positus. Atque in hoc scribendo . . . utrumque narrationis ordinem observat, artificalem poeta, naturalem philosophus. Integumentum vero est genus demonstrationis sub fabulosa narratione varitateis involvens intellectum, unde et involucrum dicitur." Bernardus Silvestris, *Commentum super sex libros Eneidos Virgilii,* ed. G. Reidel (Greifswald, 1924), 3, quoted in Stock, *Myth and Science,* 42n51.

75. Stock, *Myth and Science,* 97–118.

76. According to Stock, Peter Abelard employs the terms *involucrum* and *integumentum* to show that what on the surface may be lacking in sense may on closer inspection be found to be full of great mysteries. Stock, *Myth and Science,* 53, citing Petri Abelardi, *Introductio ad Theologiam, in libros tres divisa* (PL 178) 1021C. See also Stock, *Myth and Science,* 228–37, for the similar pattern in Bernard of Silvestris's *Cosmographia.*

77. See, for example, the second half of *Roman de la Rose,* which was composed in 1270 by Jean de Meun as a deliberate inversion of the moral cosmology in *De planctu.* Cf. Johannes Köhler, "Natur und Mensch in der Schrift 'De Planctu Naturae,'" in *Mensch und Natur im Mittelalter,* ed. Albert Zimmermann and Andreas Speer, Miscellanea Mediaevalia 21 (Berlin: Walter de Gruyter, 1991), 1:65–66; J. Huizinga, *Über die Verknüpfung des Poetischen mit*

dem Theologischen bei Alanus de Insulis (Amsterdam: N.V. Noord-Hollandsche Uitgevers-Maatschappij, 1932), 15–16.

78. Lille *De planctu naturae* 6, prosa 3 (PL 210, 446c): "Et, ut familiarius loquar, ego sum natura, quae meae dignationis munere, te meae praesentiae compotem feci, meoque sum dignata beare consortio." Cf. Köhler, "Natur und Mensch," 58–61. See 58n4 on the debate.

79. Lille *De planctu naturae* 6, prosa 3 (PL 210, 445d–446a): "homo mea actione nascitur, Dei auctoritate renascitur. Per me, a non esse vocatur ad esse; per ipsum, ad melius esse perducitur. Per me enim homo procreatur ad mortem, per ipsum recreatur ad vitam. Sed ab hoc secundae nativitatis mysterio, meae professionis ministerium ablegatur; nec talis nativitas tali indiget obstetrice; sed potius, ego natura hujus nativitatis ignoro naturam." Here I follow the translation in Alan of Lille, *The Plaint of Nature*, trans. Sheridan, 124–25, except for the last line. On the relationship of deification to Alan's theology, see Andreas Speer, "Kosmisches Prinzip und Maß menschlichen Handelns," in *Mensch und Natur im Mittelalter*, ed. Zimmerman and Speer, 1:120–21.

80. Cf. Köhler, "Natur und Mensch," 60.

81. Lille *De planctu naturae* 6, ed. Haring, p. 129.

82. Cf. Joseph Ratzinger, "Der Wortgebrauch von natura bei Bonaventura," in *Die Metaphysik im Mittelalter*, ed. Paul Wilpert, Miscellanea Mediaevalia 2 (Berlin: Walter De Gruyter, 1963), 494–98.

83. Bonaventure and Roger Bacon overlapped in Paris in the thirteenth century, although the exact lines of influence have not yet been traced. Jeremiah Hackett says that Bacon is in general agreement with Bonaventure's *De reductione artium in theologiam*, although Bonaventure may have set limits on Bacon's work in the period from 1267 to 1273. See Jeremiah Hackett, "Roger Bacon," in *The Cambridge Companion to Medieval Philosophy*, ed. A. S. McGrade (Cambridge: Cambridge University Press, 2003), 617.

84. Cf. Peter Casarella, "Language and Theologia sermocinalis in Nicholas of Cusa's 'Idiota de sapientia' (1450)," in *Old and New in the Fifteenth Century*, ed. Clyde Lee Miller (Binghamton, NY: CEMERS, 1993), 131–42. On grammar and ontology in the medieval context, see Jean Jolivet, "Eléments pour une étude des rapports entre la grammaire et l'ontologie au Moyen Age," in *Sprache und Erkenntnis im Mittelalter*, ed. Jan P. Beckmann et al., Miscellanea Mediaevalia 13 (Berlin: Walter De Gruyter, 1980), 1:136–39; Jan Ziolkowski, *Alan of Lille's Grammar of Sex: The Meaning of Grammar to a Twelfth-Century Intellectual* (Cambridge, MA: Medieval Academy of America, 1985). For a more systematic approach, heavily influenced by Wittgenstein, that also takes into account the medieval developments just discussed, see the intriguing study of Thomas Schärtl, *Theo-Grammatik: Zur Logik der Rede vom trinitarischen Gott* (Regensburg: Pustet-Verlag, 2003).

85. Cf. Ewert Cousins, "Bonaventure's Mysticism of Language," in *Mysticism and Language*, ed. Steven T. Katz (New York: Oxford University Press,

1992), 236–57; *Maître Eckhart: Métaphysique du verbe et théologie négative,* ed. Emilie Zum Brunn and Alain de Libera (Paris: Beauchesne, 1994); Frank Tobin, *Meister Eckhart: Thought and Language* (Philadelphia: University of Pennsylvania Press, 1986).

86. Speer, "Kosmisches Prinzip und Maß menschlichen Handelns," 126–28. See, for example, Alan of Lille *Regulae theologicae* (ed. N. M. Häring) 115, 1 (217).

87. Alan of Lille *Quoniam Homines* (ed. P. Glorieux) prologus 1 (119), as cited in Speer, "Kosmisches Prinzip und Maß menschlichen Handelns," 110n19.

88. Speer, "Kosmisches Prinzip und Maß menschlichen Handelns," 127–28. See G. R. Evans, *Alan of Lille: The Frontiers of Theology in the Later Twelfth Century* (Cambridge: Cambridge University Press, 1983), for a thesis that supports that of Speer.

89. Speer, "Kosmisches Prinzip und Maß menschlichen Handelns," 123.

90. Milbank, *Suspended Middle,* 63.

91. Ibid., 62.

92. Cf., for example, ibid., 62.

93. Ibid., 54; see also 88–103.

94. Ibid., 87.

95. Ibid., 94.

96. Ibid., 91.

97. Ibid., 39.

98. Ibid., 57.

99. Ibid., 104–8.

100. See, for example, Louis Bouyer's *Cosmos: The World and the Glory of God* (Petersham, MA: St. Bede's, 1988) or Paul McPartlan, *The Eucharist Makes the Church: Henri de Lubac and John Zizioulas in Dialogue* (Edinburgh: T&T Clark, 1993).

101. Milbank, *Suspended Middle,* 16.

102. Henri de Lubac, *The Mystery of the Supernatural* (London: Geoffrey Chapman, 1967), 75–76.

103. *Hacia una filosofía intercultural latinoamericana* (San José, Costa Rica: Departamento Ecuménico de Investigaciones, 1994), 19, quoted in Miguel Díaz, *On Being Human: U.S. Hispanic and Rahnerian Perspectives* (Maryknoll, NY: Orbis, 2001), 115n14.

104. Milbank, *Suspended Middle,* 63.

105. Ibid., 25n10.

106. Ibid., 91.

3 | Athens, Jerusalem, and . . .

Overcoming the Exclusivist Paradigms of the Past

KEVIN CORRIGAN

I have chosen this broader title to think about the split about reason and faith or the gap between secular rationality and religious sensibility, particularly in university life, not only because of Tertullian's famous question, what has Jerusalem to do with Athens?[1] but because for me it sums up a good deal of my upbringing and my later experience at universities in England and North America. This will also give me a chance to introduce myself and my present understanding of things past, present, and future to you. I grew up, as it were, in Jerusalem, in the midst of a sea of individual faces in my hometown parish, just about all of whom evinced the same brand of basic North of England Christian piety: daily services, visit the sacrament, indulgences, and the convictions, at times overwhelming, that the faith is really all there is (except perhaps for education, but this meant top grades ultimately) and that to marry outside the fold, for example, was a terrible misfortune. No one in my world then could articulate that bridge between learning and reverence that Alfred North Whitehead had already seen as a major challenge to the British system of education.

Instead, I was, of course, aware of other faces somewhere on the horizon of my pre-adolescent consciousness: through snatched glimpses of a television program called *The Brain's Trust,* which I was not allowed to watch, the unforgettable, but rather puzzling and utterly assured, faces of the philosopher Bertrand Russell and astronomer Fred Hoyle compelled me to realize that *per impossibile* some people—mostly the "university crowd"—did not believe in God. So, in the absence of voices already in the world but not near me—alas—I realized dimly that there were two certainties, each utterly opposed to the other, and while I loved one face and was puzzled by the other, I was afraid of the certainty of both, the tenacious vulnerability of Jerusalem and the aristocratic superiority of Athens. But if you had asked me when I was eleven, "Can there be a Jerusalem without an Athens?," I should have answered haltingly, expecting to discover that it was a trick question whose answer was that while there probably must be both on earth, people might well do without smug, superior, arid intellectualism in heaven.

And then, to cut a long story short, I discovered Athens myself, first at school in isolated moments—a sudden and real glimpse that Virgil was actually a human being (and not just lines), that Plato's Greek could take your breath away (if you forgot to treat it as work), and above all, one morning when I was twelve, that Alphonse Daudet's use of the word *étincellant* to describe wine in his "Letter," *Les trois messes basses,*[2] was perfect somehow under any conditions—and then even more so at university, where I became deeply committed to the love of learning for its own sake, its profound nobility; for what I took to be its deeply civilizing and humanizing power; and, probably too, for the inherently "universal" nature of the university ideal, that is, its apparent commitment to the freedom of a universe, and more, and to the responsibilities of civilization which accompany such freedom. But I found no institutional context that could embrace and ground this vision.

Instead, in my twenties, when I ran into the more homogenous faces of Christians, I tended to recognize different "types" and secretly breathed a sigh of relief that I could escape again into the fresh air of university life. When I say "types," I mean this pejoratively, probably because I became incapable of really seeing individual faces, since an ideology or a group mentality seemed to obscure individual identity: I disliked traditional authoritarians (and their opposites) for their lack of generosity, social libertarians (and their opposites) for their ideologies, intellectualist Christians (and their opposites, like Bertrand Russell) for insisting that belief is a matter of quantity (e.g., "you must have a certain amount of *definite* belief before you have a *right* to *call yourself* 'a religious being'"[3]), and martyr-complex believers for making reality the very difficult business it doesn't always need to be.

The problem of faith without doubt or reflection might have made me despair altogether but for Sophocles' *Antigone,* which presented to my mind one of the major problems of reality, namely the problem of determining between two conditions which resemble each other—in this case, the problem of determining whether Antigone is a fanatic or a sane, intelligent human being when she says to Creon that there are divine laws made by no one—unchangeable.[4] For nineteenth-century German editors, in the scene just before Antigone exits to her death, she should not reconsider or break down, because this is inconsistent with her otherwise strong character. They therefore excise her final lines, which seem to indicate a radical weakness in the whole of her existence.[5] Yet, for me, such reconsideration was additional confirmation of her intelligence and humanity, so tragically and dramatically alone, in the face of an always unknown, existential reality.[6] So when I met apparently invulnerable believers who could not be dissuaded by any arguments (people, unfortunately, who might resemble some of our ancestors or, indeed, our own selves), then I did not despair of the possibility of authentic martyrdom, but instead was merely frightened of the ambiguity and incommunicability of being. So Athens in this case helped me to overcome the deficiencies of Jerusalem.

But what of Athens itself? And here I am coming closer to the central problem I wish to examine. After delighting in the fresh air of an open Athens, I began to realize that this Athens I had discovered in universities in England and North America was really another exclusive center. Religion and the moral and spiritual life had been more or less excluded from consideration except by splinter groups or in special, and not very frequented, classes. But at the same time, the "thing-in-itself,"[7] research, was so often just self-interest, an excuse not to be human, or the graveyard of dreams in the context of a competitiveness that stopped real conversation altogether. At a conference I attended some time ago on "value and the university," a conference at which most of the major disciplines were represented, I was, of course, not looking for the word "divinity" in the general vocabulary, but I was disconcerted to discover that not one of the speakers at any of the talks mentioned love, feeling, or passion! How is it possible for there to be an Athens where love, even love of wisdom, stops being a value and where the great classics of the spiritual traditions of humankind, together with the history of spirituality and mysticism, are not even read or understood with any empathy (except perhaps by the tiniest proportion of students or faculty) and much less practiced (*askēsis*)? The problem has deeper roots. If one could access these treasures by what Plato calls a "divine chance,"[8] one would be simultaneously confronted by their almost complete excision from any curriculum. Our children grow up with no sense of the real thing, eternally preparing to meet it one day, but ultimately waiting for Godot. At what point then can one explain to our students that even the ancient philosophical traditions, as Pierre Hadot and others have shown,[9] cannot be understood without the realization that they are also meditative, or spiritual, exercises, exercises that in some significant sense refuse to split human life into the dichotomies of subjectivity versus objectivity or rationality versus feeling?

So, for me, the problem of the split between Jerusalem and Athens is not just the ancient problem of somewhat bigoted thinkers like Tertullian or much more enlightened individuals like Kierkegaard or Dostoevsky. It has informed my experience of the meaning of modernity. It is a condition I rediscover every day in the classroom in the spontaneous responses of my students, and a condition I discover when I look at the poverty of so many university curricula. Yet the poverty of Athens is mirrored by the poverty of Jerusalem—in some ways the latter is a much more desperate poverty. When I first went to senior school at the age of eleven, I was fortunate to join a superb choir under whose aegis I was nourished on the music of Palestrina and Perosi and came to feel the musical rhythm of the liturgical year with its birth, death, and weekday plain chant. I remember vividly the choirmaster telling us that when we returned home, we would be appalled at the state of music in our own dispensations (which we had never hitherto appreciated for what it really was), but never to look down on it. I was impressed by his admonition then, and I have always lived that way till now, but sometimes the present state of liturgy masquerading as community enlight-enment is (almost) too much for me to bear. No; in truth, I can bear it, but I cannot altogether bear it for my children. So, of course, there is no way back to the simple piety of my childhood, even if I could stand it anyway. Worse still, in a world in transition, the sanctuary itself has become the battleground of competing ideologies, drawing off all en-ergies, and leaving issues of formation/education that have to do with beauty and reverence far behind. Like a lecture in which of four hun-dred students each takes copious pages of notes and in which there is possibly not one thought, so Jerusalem seems the pallid shade of what it might be and, worse still, divided by irreconcilable differences. Our contemporary geographical Jerusalem is unfortunately a vivid example of this, where not simply ideological difference, but deeper division and violent death are the order of the day, with no resolution in sight. Such, of course, in a material sense, is the whole history of thought and spirit.

So the point I want to make is the simple one that the split between Jerusalem and Athens which I have experienced in a personal way in my own life is a pressing contemporary problem which merits our at-tention and which may occur in many different forms, some of which I shall take up here; and the reason I have couched this problematic in autobiographical form is that I cannot pretend that my own face—with its inscrutable ambiguity—is not an integral part of the picture I paint or the crossroads at which I stand. So I am comforted by Dante to find myself "nel medio del cammin di nostra vita,"[10] and I am going to follow his example in part here insofar as I intend to enlist the help of a few sensitive, urban pagans and their descendants to help me with my problem.

THE ATHENS-JERUSALEM SPLIT

First, the question itself: can there be a Jerusalem without an Athens? Let me give an answer up front which will serve as part of my thesis. No, there cannot be a Jerusalem without an Athens (except in the trivial sense that one can always find oneself shipwrecked and marooned on an island), or vice versa, and even both are insufficient, not least because they are finally and only territorial determinations, and geography alone should not be the ultimate or exclusive distinction of any face, religious or academic. Jerusalem is still only a place on earth, and not the happiest or most generous. Here I no longer mean only the Jerusalem of my childhood, but the actual geographical Jerusalem where three major religions vie for exclusive hegemony. And the same goes for Athens and its preoccupation with the "thing-in-itself" and its committees, external reviews, self-definitions, and mission statements. There must somehow be a perspective beyond each, but present to each, which is capable of including and transforming both. This may seem fairly obvious, but the problem is, in my view, that Athens and Jerusalem cannot be telescoped into each other thereby. In the aftermath of recent events, there seems no other way to overcome the actual divisions in the world than by the remilitarization of power and the extermination of the enemy. The instinct for self-preservation is on full alert, since it teaches one to cede spaces to those who want to occupy them. We too readily recall the admonition of W. B. Yeats: "The best lack all conviction, while the worst / are full of passionate intensity."[11] And yet the long-term survival of humanity also demands something much deeper, for there is surely no other way finally of overcoming error and terror than by a deepening of the spirit and a process of ennoblement and understanding along the trajectories of tolerance, coexistence, and a communication between different values, a communication which is not submersion or extermination of the other, but confrontation between values or disvalues of crucial importance, but without wanting to kill. It involves believing that the errors of the past do not obliterate all of the realities that have given life to and have nourished the spirit: "Garlic and sapphires in the mud. Clot the bedded axle tree," as T. S. Eliot put it.[12] So if there is to be another perspective, it must be one in which distinctiveness and difference are capable of emerging and we can linger in its warmth without the need for instantaneous or procrustean resolution. And this leads me to a somewhat different claim about the nature of thinking itself, whether inside or outside Athens or Jerusalem.

I do not believe that there can be a living form of experience without the world in which it came to birth and continues to have its life, and to which it also looks forward. Such a thesis may appear to commit me to a relativistic view of truth, but this is certainly not my intention. What I want to argue is this: just as our universities desperately need (and now more than ever) intelligent, more holistic perspectives in order to carry out their mission, but without turning those perspectives in any sense into new ideologies or quasireligious systems, so does religious thought itself require not only many different points of view but a viewpoint or viewpoints as big as or bigger than itself without reducing religion to a parochial, relative activity in the *banlieu* of the Milky Way or without religion losing its capacity to be distinctive. But this is too big a thesis to tackle all at once, and so I am going to set about the problem in a more restricted fashion in terms of the Jerusalem-Athens split.

OVERCOMING THE SPLIT

In order to begin to overcome the split, this so-called binary opposition that includes no "other" viewpoint, we need to shatter the arrogance of a single paradigm. History provides many examples of dogmatic paradigms in both spheres. The nineteenth century rejected religion, but canonized physics. As a part of this process, we have deified "science," as though all the sciences shared a single paradigm, that of dispassionate scrutiny of the "facts." But there have always been dissenting voices. Heidegger emphasized how even our preoccupation with the "facts" was already pervaded by the nihilating power of the "nothing" ("science wishes to know nothing of the nothing . . . how is it then with the nothing?"[13]). Michael Polanyi argued that even if physics and chemistry were the sole dominating disciplines, themselves dominated by the overwhelmingly mechanistic paradigm of eighteenth-century science, we should not have been able to predict the existence even of machines themselves on the basis of these two sciences alone. We need, he suggested, all the sciences in an open-ended way to question each other's assumptions, shatter the straitjackets of each paradigm, and, therefore, open up the sciences, arts, and the humanities to their own possibilities for the future.[14] Thus, as we go into the future we return in a sense to deeper resonances in our past, for this is to develop an insight of Pascal, namely that a mind correct in its own domain will be wrong in another domain.[15] Intelligence is multidimensional, spatially and temporally pervaded by difference, and not susceptible of the straitjacket of any one science or art. Can Christian (or Jewish or Islamic) higher education, as we know it today, embrace such a vision—can it look for friends across dividing lines and not simply enemies who remain not sufficiently pure according to this or that ideology?

But it is precisely this understanding that makes us despair, and there are, of course, serious problems with any supposed retrieval or development of a more holistic vision. There is never any way back into the supposed bedrock of a more foundational time, and there is no quantitative way forward past the threshold of one's own desire, for if we have learned any lesson over the past century, it is a lesson of doubt and despair that ultimately paralyzes hope and will.

Moreover, when we look at the last four hundred years of thought, we see unfortunately how all the symbolic forces of history for a more holistic way of thinking have been systematically eradicated or annihilated. There is nothing to animate an organism: the soul is apparently dead, the word *soul* only a ghostly afterlife in the common tongue or a New Age label on the display shelves at Borders. And there is certainly no community of souls or saints, no larger presence or absence animating even the earth, planets, or stars.[16] Even "Mother Earth" (operative in generally marginalized New Age thought) is yet another abstraction formed to illuminate, however dimly, the vast graveyard of galactic and intergalactic dust which we suppose to be all that is—except, that is, for the brief epiphenomena of individual and civil liberties. By contrast, I should like to quote Whitehead on education:

> The present contains all that there is. It is holy ground; for it is the past, and it is the future ... the communion of saints in a great and inspiring assemblage, but it has only one possible hall of meeting, and that is, the present; and the mere lapse of time through which any particular group of saints [Whitehead mentions Shakespeare, Molière, Sophocles, and Virgil] must travel to reach that meeting-place, makes very little difference.[17]

And yet our world still rests implicitly upon a scientific illusion of ancient heritage: atomism, that is, the belief, not that there are atoms, but that the ultimate building blocks of meaningfulness are indivisible (un-cuttable) facts, material solidities, and nothing else (except the void). And yet atomism is the one scientific theory, however appropriate at its own level, to have been utterly disproved as a general theory of everything in the early twentieth century. Caught, therefore, between our desire for a more holistic framework or understanding and our residual but so firmly engrained belief that material solidities in the vacuum of space are the only realities of our world, we are stretched upon a rack that, finally, can only tear us into pieces, if we let it. Yet the rack is purely illusory in a sense, except that we live so much of our lives tormented by its phantas-magoric force. This rack, this yoke, we have to shed somehow. But how?

The only power we have, paradoxically, is a power of active recep-tion which involves a new form of receptivity, the power of the whole (and I do not mean the whole as a closed logo-centric system), the power of the dialogical idea as opposed to the destructive, reductive force of the manipulative ego, namely, that single paradigm or discipline in whose image everything is fashioned, or the postulating of atomistic facts per-vaded inevitably by nothingness. What do I mean by this power of the whole, the power of an idea which is never entirely our own? Perhaps the greatest oxymoron of the later years of the twentieth century is the no-tion of intellectual property. Ideas or concepts can become properties or commodities only when they are lodged primarily as purely mono-logical solidities in the mind of one individual, where essentially they have lost their activity as ideas to animate and to be shared, where they become dim images of ideas, tokens to be traded in a commodities mar-ket. The idea, by contrast, really is the property of no mind, for it is born as the in-between; it is discovered in the conversation *between* minds as the property of none, but as shared by both, by all, by neither entirely, by none altogether. A real idea, therefore, is a living, dialogical activity, living not even because it is by nature to be shared, but self-living in its own right and, consequently, able to be shared. This notion of the idea, which literally snatched Mikhail Bakhtin from a world of total oblitera-tion in his native Russia and from the deterministic forces of history,[18] is still alarmingly absent in our own times, so pervaded, as they are, by a more commercial, sound-byte mentality—and absent from spaces in the university, where our students never or rarely hear us in dialogue with each other: we present, but we so rarely talk.

But this self-disclosing power of the idea is particularly important for any institution which claims to live by the freedom of ideas, namely the university, for one of the central problems of the contemporary university is the lack of an adequate animating principle, or "academic vision," as we tend to put it. The modern problem of the idea is the reductionist tendency itself, useful and pragmatic in delimited areas, but potentially fatal outside of these, since certain forms of reductionism transform the very idea of a university—*universitas*—either into abstract humanism or into an equally abstract pluralism in which individualistic market forces are merely given the appearance of disinterestedness and universality when they are really only little atomistic centers of pure self-interest. Scholarship and the academic enterprise as a whole always stand in danger of devolution. And so the central problem for all the sciences and the arts is that they not be made in the image and likeness alone of the individual minds or gods who think and play within them. In other words, a collection of animating I's or egos is not an academic vision. And this is even more so at a time when the research engine of so many academic institutions is driven not by the principle of discovery for discovery's own sake, but rather—and in increasing proportions—by outside corporate interests, so that the success of universities can even be measured by how much external (corporate) funding the institutions are capable of attracting. This is not to deny the practical use of such funding or even its theoretical benefits, but rather to point to the even greater need for academic vision in the future. For the flourishing of humanity, we seem to need a much larger view of what it means to be "selves" in a universe, a universe that is partially entrusted into our care and radically bigger than ourselves, and yet not to be measured purely by size or quantity. Otherwise, as Bertrand Russell observed, an elephant or a whale would be of much "bigger" importance than a newt or a human being.[19]

Not only, then, do we need to shatter the paradigms of a single science or of a select group of sciences or, again, of a single form of rationality; we also for the above reasons (among others) have to confront the problem of the overwhelmingly objectivist paradigms in epistemology which have become so engrained in our thinking over the past four hundred years, that is, the view more or less that knowledge is a question of knowing objective things in which either the knower (inevitably only a human ego) is set apart from the objects he or she knows or else the knower simply disappears, as it were, into his or her own knowing, so that cognition is only a matter of internal consistency, not adequation, correspondence, or even multidimensional interplay. Consistency, a notion of truth so often associated with Kant's first two *Critiques* and the *Foundation of the Metaphysic of Morals,* is not all that Kant had in mind in his works (especially when the three *Critiques* are considered as a whole), yet the notion of truth as only a question of consistency is what is so often attributed to a Kantian, Neo-Kantian, or Post-Kantian epistemological or moral standpoint.[20] It is possible to be completely consistent and yet quite mad. The worst forms of bureaucracy and also of tyranny possess their own quite devastatingly unavoidable logics. In the modern university, poststructuralism was moved by the desire to escape from this straitjacket, to stop looking at ideas as constructed out of individual blocks that couldn't be moved, to deconstruct the whole idea of immovable construction, but in the process it has unfortunately created its own straitjacket with its hidden preference for authoritative over dialogical discourse; instead of favoring conversation that goes to the heart of differences, we tend to privilege discourse only between people who accept each other's assumptions and preferences, and often in a metalanguage that terrifies the fervent and naïve newcomer into lifelong submission.

So one of the major challenges for Athens, as I see it, is that the trouble with real ideas is that they don't fit single paradigms, objectivist rationalities, or purely dispassionate scrutinies. Meaning and feeling do not come prepackaged with the right directions for assembly or contempt. Sometimes the best thing about experiencing meaningfulness is the feeling we have about it that leads us far beyond our original point of entry into a meaning. Meaning and feeling—for I want to see both together—are messy, untidy:[21] they stick out, as it were, in an infinity of directions, always involving more than we bargained for, namely, more than our own individual or even human perspectives. Sometimes the most important thing about a meaning is that we *fail* to capture it. What is crucial for Athens, then, might well be this: that it be open, certainly, to admitting the inadmissible, the unsayable, the not yet thinkable—as well as muons, newts, and antelopes—for their own sake (and not just for *our* own interests), to admitting even Jerusalem and its interests, but that it also *fail* to resolve it all to system, order, and tangibility, and that its failure be a genuine measure of its success. According to Wilamowitz, this was one of the real meanings of the Delphic Commandment, *Gnōthi seauton:* know yourself not to be a god; know one's own limitations.[22] Again, Whitehead seems to see the implications of this for education rather clearly. "In education, as elsewhere," he observes, "the broad prim-rose path leads to a nasty place. This evil path is represented by a book or set of lectures which will practically enable the student to learn by heart all the questions likely to be asked at the next external examina-tion."[23] Instead, Whitehead thinks, education should be an intensely personal experience; he deplores standardized exams as "educational waste" and even envisages an academic forum radically open to Jeru-salem. The "essence of education," he insists, "is that it be religious"; and what does this mean? According to Whitehead, "A religious education is an education which [inculcates] . . . reverence in this perception, that the present holds within itself the complete sum of existence, backwards and forwards, that whole amplitude of time, which is eternity."[24]

JERUSALEM WITHOUT ATHENS

But what about Jerusalem, on the other side of this equation/disjunction? Let me take up here one of the most famous criticisms of Western Christianity, Dostoevsky's challenge to the Western church in Ivan Karamazov's "Grand Inquisitor." Dostoevsky's Inquisitor provides a perfect version of a modern Tertullianism, or in other words, a church of sheep directed by the cardinal archbishop of Seville, but split irrecon-cilably from real spirit. According to the "fantasy" Ivan relates to his brother Alyosha (and we don't need to be Christians to appreciate this), Christ returns to earth to visit his people the day after nearly a hundred heretics have been burned at the stake.[25] He comes unobserved, but everyone flocks around him, drawn irresistibly by the sheer power of life that flows from him and that expresses itself superabundantly. A blind man is cured, a dead girl comes back to life; there is a sense of celebration and exchange not sanctioned by the structure; the Grand Inquisitor sees immediately what is happening and has him arrested. In the subsequent conversation in prison (a monologue, for the Inquisitor is the only one who speaks), the Inquisitor takes Christ to task for refusing the three temptations in the desert. The people, especially the weak, do not need to be free; they need to be fed and led by those who will take upon themselves the burden of such freedom: the demands of bread, power, and ultimate security overwhelm the freedom of thought. To keep Jerusalem pure, a thoughtless Jerusalem necessarily comes to be animated by the clear-sighted atheism of an altruistic Athens. The origins of modern atheism, the leadership of the Grand Inquisitor, are to be located in the very triumphalism of the church.

One can see in a nutshell the force of Dostoevsky's criticism. What is it the church lacks? According to Dostoevsky, as a structure animated by an alien principle, it lacks precisely the uncontrollable mystery of life itself, or, as Yeats so powerfully phrased it, "the uncontrollable mystery on the bestial floor."[26] In the presence of the silent, atavistic stranger, what is genuinely new and always recognized, but invariably suppressed, springs up spontaneously. The blind see, the dead walk, the people begin to live a new life, and the intellectual cardinal recognizes the cause directly, but in its very presence knows the superior rationality of his own very old, superior case. Whether or not this is a correct diagnosis of a certain kind of religious structuralism, the chilling partial accuracy of Dostoevsky's diagnosis should at least give us pause. Even if there cannot be a Jerusalem without an Athens, nonetheless neither Jerusalem nor Athens, it would appear, could serve as an animating principle to the other, for neither is capable of catching the individual yet universal reality of life itself that emerges, as it were, out of the utterly unexpected—the improvised of Jazz or *unvordenklich* of modern German thought—a reality that cannot be sufficiently contained by any of the normal structures of life, especially those which hear only the sound of their own voices.

My overall argument, then, is this: if we are to think of a future which includes as much as we can put there or find there of what it is to be human, and more besides, and if we are to participate in a future of the humanities, arts, and sciences which does not radically restrict the questions that need to be posed, we can no longer divide the spheres of human life into mutually opposed, armed fortresses which have nothing whatever to say to each other; nor can we substitute one sphere for the other or animate one sphere simply from the perspective of the other.

We cannot find in Jerusalem what Athens fails to provide, and we cannot redeem the failure of Jerusalem by appealing to Athens. The Athens which naturally wants to question dogma becomes itself a dogmatic secular church, receptive only of the differences which the flavor of the month or year valorizes. The major issues of the past, and this includes the past's form-creating texts as well, can then be discarded like so many primitive scientific theories, and in order to protect students from their primitive impact we can so easily come to trust our own puristic devices much more than any free, open-ended interaction with a text. Something of this eliminative method is perfectly reasonable in some of the sciences where a pragmatic focus is called for, but it is possible that in art, in the humanities, as well as in science and technology in a broader sense, a different approach is long overdue: here there is a need for a greater inclusiveness, a new expansion, even, and especially, a training for empathy with perspectives one does not hold (that perhaps should be one mark of an undergraduate education). Most of the major issues of any time (e.g., the nature of good and evil, soul, substance, technology, etc.) do not need to be eliminated beforehand or stigmatized simply as forms of a lie, or as the erasure of absence (no matter how important privation and nothingness might really be). Equally, the Jerusalem which wants to offset rationalism and materialism can tend to be herded into extremes of its own making: towards either blind fanaticism or dull fundamentalism, or new pitiless radicalism which neither brooks nor knows another viewpoint, upholding only its own intellectual case, into which the untamable religious spirit of a transfigured Moses or a silent Christ cannot be fitted.

So my wish for the future of the humanities and the university, in particular, and for their potentially transformative effect upon the major questions of our age, is that they develop an environment in which each of us could be encouraged, and even trained, to inhabit *at least* two different universes of discourse, universes which, preferably, may at first

sight appear to be mutually exclusive, but that we approach both as fragmented and as wounded bodies. Such an attitude, I believe, expands
the human soul, and such an expansion is not a question of quantity. It
seems to me that human beings need *at least* two souls, as well as a sense
of bigger souledness altogether, in order to entertain, without wanting
to exterminate, genuinely different lived experiences, viewing them not
as exclusive domains, but as fragmented and suffering realities of human
experience.

Dialectic (including those of Plato, Hegel, and Marx) has had a
very checkered later history, so transformed has it been in Kierkegaard,
Nietzsche, Sartre, Foucault, Derrida, de Beauvoir, Adorno, Irigaray, and
so on.[27] Yet if that dialectic is understood not as a tool with which to
beat everybody over the head, that is, to explain everything to one's own
satisfaction, but rather as an open-ended, dialogical heuristic device,
which admits failure and error as intrinsic to its provisional process,
then I don't believe we have outgrown the need for this dialogical vision.
Things grow into their opposites so very quickly, so unconsciously. The
dogmatic religious bigot and the opinionated atheist may have much
more in common than their official dividedness proclaims. The most
privileged members of the most privileged society can be so very close
to those who reject and wish to destroy everything that society has to
offer. The three stages of Hegel's unhappy consciousness, the Epicurean,
the Stoic, and the Skeptic, may be three contiguous faces not only of a
certain historical period (namely, the Hellenistic world) but also perhaps
of the same person.[28] So when I talk of the need for other "souls" in us, I
consciously use a word that is not valorized in contemporary discourse,
because I do not mean quantity or individualisms somehow united and
homogenized. Rather, I mean something of what Jean-François Lyotard
seems to me to have meant by his use of the term "différend," that is, an
incommensurability between two faces for which words do not yet exist,
a condition that obtains "when human beings who believed they could
use language as an instrument of communication learn by this feeling
of pain which accompanies silence (and of pleasure which accompanies
the invention of a new idiom) that they are required by language, not to
increase for their own benefit the quantity of information communi-
cable through existing idioms, but to recognize that what there is to be

put into words exceeds what they can presently do and that they must be allowed to institute idioms which do not yet exist."[29] The phenomenon of Lyotard's vision should, I think, be seen more carefully. A postmodern thinker, he left behind his own meditations on Augustine, which his wife published after his death to the surprise of so many of his friends and students.

Lyotard's writings on Augustine are visited by the notion of a present/future incommensurability which exceeds language, imagination, and thought, emerging out of the wounded or lacerated body (and spirit) of the past, and this seems to me to be so very fruitful for any consideration of the humanities, and preferable, too, to the tendency at the end of both the nineteenth and the twentieth centuries to consider that science has discovered everything there is to discover about the mysteries of the universe and that all we need now is to dot the i's, cross the t's, and catalog the vast chains of available information so that we can forever thereafter manipulate them for the good of human beings. We do not know everything there is to know, and we shall never be in a position where we could ever do so. A lifetime's research finds the problem to be infinite, to comprise so many more questions than one could even have dreamed of when one began to notice that there was something there worth looking at in the first place. Homer's *Iliad*, for instance, is more than any one mind might grapple with for a whole lifetime, but you wouldn't know this unless you started looking in the right way.

In negative or apophatic theology, that is, a theology which resists the temptation to make the experience of the divine into one's own image and likeness, one has to be trained to cancel the assumptions of one's own being in the hope of becoming radically open to an experience that one does not manipulate, systematize, or catalog. Such forms of discourse are therefore all about the discovery of other souls and, particularly, about the incommensurability of the infinite and the finite not as a lost origin or an end in itself, but as what is closer to us than either. In *La confession d'Augustin,* published posthumously[30] and, perhaps appropriately, never completed, Lyotard undertakes, as it were, his own confession of Augustine's confession, that is, not an intellectual stratagem or a philosophical treatise, but an attempt to articulate through the mind, imagination, and heart the "fissure" of the infinite with which Augustine's conversion is saturated. On the face of it, we could not find two more different thinkers than Lyotard and Augustine, and it is significant how far against his own grain Lyotard was prepared to go to pursue the hidden possibilities of the *différend.* At times we are unsure in this work that never appeared in the author's lifetime who it is who so directly addresses the subject, so deeply does the fissure Lyotard locates in the "grain" of Augustine's conversion reach into his own living meditation. What is striking, however (and all the more so in the case of a postmodern thinker not particularly noted for religious sensibility or for any proclivity for Augustinianism), is that the postmodern concept of the cut, impregnated with a surplus of potential and the possibility of the infinite, becomes a means of entering into a profound understanding of Augustine's religious sensibility, of his passionately erotic selfhood, and of the complex, genuinely postmodern character of this confessional writing—which is not in any way linear or simplistically factual—together with its vibrant semiology of Scripture. One or two examples will have to suffice here. On Augustine's famous *interior intimo meo,*[31] Lyotard sees Augustine turned inside out: "With this body being punctured and penetrated by the other sense, the soul can assume bodily form, be incarnated, flesh find its soul, your presence reside in the inner human" (9). What is this "flesh visited, co-penetrated by your space-time, disturbed and confused with this blow, but steeped in infinity, impregnated and pregnant with your overabundant liquid" (11)? The originality and immediacy of Augustine's response, in Lyotard's view, anticipates (and outstrips) much later discoveries of "cuts" and "n-dimensional space theory": "To conceive the logic of these transformations of space, Augustine cannot rely on Dedekind and Poincaré's geometry" (10). Instead, Augustine has to invent his own images: "The body, sponge-like in its permeability to the other space-time, exceeds its *sensoria.* Lifted are the blindness waiting for vision from the other side of the visual field, the deafness at the edge of hearing, the anorexia threatening taste. . . . If the human being, thus bestowed with grace, is declared to be inner, it is simply because the secret of such an ecstasy remains kept, because the words to express it are lacking. Not easily does grace let itself be revealed" (11). The silent, atavistic stranger or Christ of Dostoevsky, sentenced to death and yet walking out into the unknown, is not far from this vision.

Lyotard's meditation is resonant with his sympathetic and close understanding of Augustine's view of the soul-body relation, and his foregrounding of the primal fissure or puncture of the finite in the sea of the infinite is highly original as it is put into the context of modern geometry and physics, and more generally imbued with the sense of a wounded, lacerated body, an image, I believe, we should accept most carefully in the twenty-first century. And he is equally worth reading on other important resonances in Augustine's work. My claim and my point then are this: we must accept the woundedness of the frameworks that we inherit and that we hand on to our children; in the face of this we need open-mindedness, courage, and a new sense of the *différend* (and not an ideological community of sameness) in order to break down the often too artificial divisions of academic territory; we need also to be open to the nonacademic, to those ways of life which may not be ours, including the cultural and mystical spirits of other places and times, as is Lyotard in this profoundly innovative work; and we need to do this if for no other reason than to avoid making the university into its contrary, a monoversity, where most of what may be relevant to the human (and inhuman) mind and spirit—faith, hope, love, imagination, and feeling—is excluded. We thus need in the face of this woundedness never to leave hold of the great classics of the past (from the Bible to Homer) or to exclude a priori the possibility of electrifying, highly original and necessary in-readings or rereadings of the form-creating texts which are capable of lighting up our "bestial half-light" in an infinity of new ways. Lyotard, with an intertextual/intratextual hint of Kant's third *Critique*,[32] puts this in the following way: "A writing sparkles under the vault of the skies, the glow of the verb in our bestial half-light. This streak of light, far from growing weak, appears all the more bright, its intensity all the more 'sublime' since the great mortals, your servants who have given us the eternal script, have been extinguished." In the words of W. B. Yeats, who was also profoundly aware of the fissure or woundedness of a life, nonetheless impregnated with all-souledness, a new sailing for Byzantium: "An aged man is but a paltry thing, / . . . unless / Soul clap its hands and sing, and louder sing."[33]

Notes

1. See Tertullian, *Prescription against Heretics* (*Adv. Haer.*) 7, where Tertullian argues that philosophical methods of inquiry have nothing to do with teaching by the authority of Scripture and goes on to draw an absolute, broader distinction between the Academy and heretics, on the one hand, and Christians and the "porch of Solomon," on the other.

2. *Les lettres de mon moulin* (Castelnau-le-Lez: Climats, 1997); or *Les trois messes basses* (Paris: Hachette Jeunesse, 1986). Translation in *Letters from My Mill and Letters to an Absent One* (Freeport, NY: Books for Libraries Press, 1971).

3. Bertrand Russell, *Why I Am Not a Christian* (New York: Simon and Schuster, 1957), 3–4.

4. *Antigone,* lines 454–45.

5. Lines 904–20 of *Antigone* have been excised on the grounds that they are an interpolation, alien to the character of Antigone, either by Sophocles' son or some actor. See, for example, R. C. Jebb in *Sophocles Part III: The Antigone* (Cambridge, 1891), 164, 258–63, and compare C. D. Whitman, *Sophocles* (Cambridge, MA: Harvard University Press, 1951), 92–93; 263–64; note on lines 942–57.

6. Antigone goes to her death isolated (from Ismene, Creon, and Haemon, who has not yet appeared in the play) and dramatically alone, a woman among a chorus of men who do not understand her, intelligent and clearsighted about her real fate by contrast with the mythical spectacles through which the chorus tries to glorify her destiny (808–943; esp. 839–40). In such a context, her ability to think open-endedly and even to reconsider radically is poignant evidence of her isolated intelligence (and ultimate lack of any real fanaticism).

7. This is Hegel's phrase "die Sache Selbst," from the subsection "The Spiritual Zoo and Humbug, or the Affair-on-Hand Itself" ("Das geistige Tierreich und der Betrug, oder die Sache selbst") of the larger section "Reason," in the *Phenomenology of Spirit* (see, for example, the translation by A. V. Miller [Oxford: Oxford University Press, 1977], 23 ff.).

8. Plato *Republic* 6, 492e–493a.

9. Pierre Hadot, *Exercices spirituels et philosophie antique,* 2nd ed. (Paris: Études augustiniènnes, 1987). English translation, Michael Chase, ed., with introduction by Arnold I. Davidson, *Philosophy as a Way of Life: Spiritual Exercises from Socrates to Foucault* (Cambridge, MA: Blackwell, 1995).

10. These are the first words of bk. 1, canto 1, the *Inferno* of Dante's *Divine Comedy*: "In the middle of the journey of our life I found myself in a dark wood, for the direct way was lost." For text, translation, and commentary, see

Dante Alighieri, *The Divine Comedy: Inferno,* trans. Charles S. Singleton, Bollingen Series 80 (Princeton: Princeton University Press, 1970).

11. W. B. Yeats, "The Second Coming," in W. Harmon, ed., *The Classic Hundred Poems* (New York: Columbia University Press, 1998).

12. T. S. Eliot, "Burnt Norton," sec. 2 in *Four Quartets,* in *Collected Poems, 1909–1935* (London: Faber and Faber, 1936).

13. Martin Heidegger, "What Is Metaphysics?," in *Martin Heidegger: Basic Writings,* trans. David Farrell Krell (New York: Harper and Row, 1997), 98; originally published as *Wegmarken* (Frankfurt-am-Main: Klosterman, 1967).

14. Michael Polanyi, *Knowing and Being: Essays,* ed. Marjorie Grene (London: Routledge and Kegan Paul, 1969); idem, *Science, Faith, and Society* (Chicago: University of Chicago Press, 1964).

15. See Pascal, *Pensées,* trans. W. F. Trotter (New York: Random House, 1941), sec. I, 1–3.

16. See Kevin Corrigan, "Being and the Eclipse of Soul: Plato and the Philosophical Tradition," *Diadoche: Revista de Estudios de Filosofiá Platónica y Cristiána* (2001): 8–17.

17. Alfred North Whitehead, *Aims of Education* (New York: Free Press, 1967), 4.

18. Mikhail Bakhtin, "Discourse in the Novel," in *The Dialogic Imagination,* trans. Caryl Emerson and Michael Holquist (Austin: University of Texas Press, 1981), 112 (originally published as *Voprosy literatury I estetiki* [Moscow: Khudozhestvennaya Literature, 1975]); and, especially, *Problems of Dostoevsky's Poetics,* ed. and trans. Caryl Emerson (Minneapolis: University of Minnesota Press, 1984), 237.

19. Bertrand Russell, "The Expanding Mental Universe," in *Adventures of the Mind,* ed. R. Thruelsen and J. Kobler, 275–84 (New York: Knopf, 1959).

20. For a more holistic view of the three *Critiques* see R. A. Makkreel, *Imagination and Interpretation in Kant: The Hermeneutical Import of the Critique of Judgment* (Chicago: University of Chicago Press, 1990); also Werner S. Pluhar, introduction to *Critique of Judgment,* by Immanuel Kant (Indianapolis: Hackett, 1987).

21. For a recent treatment of the "intelligence of the emotions," see Martha C. Nussbaum, *Upheavals of Thought: The Intelligence of the Emotions* (Cambridge: Cambridge University Press, 2003).

22. Ulrich von Wilamowitz, *Der Glaube der Hellenen* (Berlin: Akademie Verlag, 1932), 123.

23. Whitehead, *Aims of Education,* 7.

24. Ibid., 23.

25. Fyodor Dostoevsky, *The Brothers Karamazov* (San Francisco: North Point Press, 1990), 248.

26. W. B. Yeats, "The Magi," in *Responsibilities* (New York: Macmillan, 1916).

27. For a partial history of this complex issue see Howard P. Kainz, *Hegel's Phenomenology, Part I: Analysis and Commentary* (Tuscaloosa: University of Alabama Press, 1976), 146–51; also Judith P. Butler, *Subjects of Desire: Hegelian Reflections in Twentieth-Century France* (New York: Columba University Press, 1987).

28. See G. W. F. Hegel, *Phenomenology of Spirit,* sections on Self-Consciousness, the Freedom of Self-Consciousness, and the Unhappy Consciousness.

29. Jean-François Lyotard, *Le Différend* (Paris: Éditions de Minuit, 1983), 30, sec. 24.

30. Jean-François Lyotard, *La confession d'Augustin* (Paris: Galilée, 1998). I cite from Jean-François Lyotard, *The Confession of Augustine,* trans. Richard Beardsworth (Stanford: Stanford University Press, 2000).

31. Augustine *Confessions* 3.6.11: *Tu autem eras interior intimo meo et superior summo meo.*

32. This is especially in the light of Lyotard's own long-standing interest in the third *Critique,* an interest which finally saw the light of day in his *Leçons sur l'analytique du sublime: Kant, Critique de la faculté de juger* (Paris: Galilée, 1991), 27–29.

33. W. B. Yeats, "Sailing to Byzantium," in *The Classic Hundred Poems,* ed. Harman.

4 | Kant

Boundaries, Blind Spots, and Supplements

CYRIL O'REGAN

Kant's project of defining the relations and differences between reason and faith is as urgent now as it was at the end of the eighteenth century. What to do with Christianity, given its depleted or rapidly depleting authority in modernity, when the background conditions are religious tensions and wars, the oppressive and repressive behavior of religious institutions, continuous squabbles over a host of esoteric theological subject matters, lack of certainty as to the status of the biblical text and what constitutes an adequate or proper interpretation, and absence of assurance as to the right relation between the Bible and critical reason and as to their relative authority?

Kant's project rests on three basic assumptions. The first assumption is one that Kant shares with the *philosophes,* that is, that modernity is a *novum.* Kant's boast in his introduction to the *Critique of Pure Reason* (1781, 1787; hereafter CPR) to the effect that his "critique of pure reason" is a "Copernican Revolution" (second preface, 22, 25) represents a particular expression of the Enlightenment's general attitude toward Christianity, while both exploiting and inflecting a particular trope, indeed in a certain sense pulling it in a more Ptolemaic direction by dint of the anthropological or anthropocentric turn.[1]

The second, and obviously related, assumption is that the particular view of reason advanced squares with what is operationally supposed by science, indeed, legitimates it. Kant is prepared to accept the consequence that this has a negative effect on philosophical theology as traditionally practiced, especially in the German sphere of Leibniz and Wolff, which has an inadequate view of the limits of reason and an equally inadequate view of reason's relation to faith. The third assumption is that the basic aim of critique is not the destruction of Christian thought, but its philosophical justification in which Christianity will have to pay the price of being more ascetic in its claims. Although Kant need not be taken at his word, his critical program as a whole gives good reason to believe that his aim is indeed "to deny knowledge, in order to make room for faith" (CPR, 29). Most certainly, Kant is not the "all destroyer" (*Allzermalmende*) that Moses Mendelssohn announced him to be. On the one hand, to call him such is to reduce Kantian philosophy to the skepticism of Hume, which, as he clearly states early on in the first *Critique* (CPR, 32, 57), he intends to overcome. On the other, it is to confound Kant's relatively moderate German version of the Enlightenment, which has its context—if not origin—in German Pietism,[2] with the supercritical French forms, first of Voltaire and later of Diderot and d'Alembert, which never made much headway in Germany.

These three assumptions define one side of the Kantian project, or, to change the metaphor, present one of its faces. The other, and complementary, side of the project, or the project's other face, consists of what might be called Kant's form of the "logic of supplementarity," which is both more local and more exoteric than Derrida's version.[3] Although reason is the standard by which philosophical theology, in the first instance, and theology, in the second, are judged, reason is neither as deep nor as comprehensive as it can be, even as it remains indelibly a finite form of knowing. Happily, according to Kant, significant aspects of the insufficiency of reason can be overcome in and through an interpretation or reinterpretation of Christianity. This view is prepared for rather than exhibited in Kant's ethical work, which involves the practical or ethical analysis of such foundational Christian beliefs as the reality of freedom, immortality, and God. As is well known, the *Critique of Practical Reason* suggests that while neither the freedom of the self, nor the immortality of the soul, nor the existence of God is strictly provable or demonstrable, all three must necessarily be postulated if moral action is to make sense.[4]

The supplementary or compensatory view is most certainly exhibited in *Religion within the Boundaries of Mere Reason* (hereafter Rel),[5] in which Kant not only justifies key biblical symbols, but also avails of these symbols to clear up deficiencies in philosophical interpretation of the self and its fundamental orientations, deficiencies from which even his own critical philosophy is not immune.[6] As Kant both licenses a hermeneutical detour and performs it, he points to a revision of the Enlightenment model of philosophy as an autonomous discipline. While both the *Critique of Pure Reason* and the *Critique of Practical Reason* suggest that the autonomy of philosophy is a self-evident given, since autonomy is itself coextensive with reason in its most reasonable deployment, *Religion* comes to suggest that autonomy is in some measure a result that involves at least preliminary concessions to another discourse as having alethic properties that philosophy does not immediately have. Hegel's expanding of this insight to include art as well as other discourses,[7] with his deepening of Kant's hermeneutic frame, very much deserves the kind of sustained reflection that it has recently received.[8] The basic conviction that drives this particular essay is that it is Kant's rather than Hegel's exercise in hermeneutics, especially as this refers to the Bible, that enjoys by far the greater contemporary currency and prestige. It does so because it supplies a grammar of the architectonics, dynamics, and symbolics of supplementarity found to be much more attractive than the Hegelian version, which, culminating in absolute knowledge, is deemed invidious from a moral as well as an epistemological-metaphysical point of view. Indeed, Kant's logic of supplementarity, which sets limits to both the range and the depth of critical reason, can be exploited by modern and postmodern thought with a view to trimming Hegel's promethean ambitions.

I am aware of the need to define each of my three terms, "architectonics," "symbolics," and "dynamics," whose discussion provides the basic architecture of the paper. I will define my terms in due course, but only as the need arises. What I will focus on for the moment is Kant's project more narrowly defined in its relation to Scripture, and how especially this involves making crucial decisions regarding the interpretation of the biblical text that place him in opposition to influential cultural forces in Germany in the latter half of the eighteenth century. Kant makes no bones about the biblical text enjoying a status not granted any other text in the Western tradition. If the incommensurability of the text is marked by the adjective "sacred," Kant does not mean by this that he is accepting anything like a doctrine of inspiration, not to mention inerrancy. The point is descriptive; although the text is challengingly obscure in places, it is in a universe of one when it comes to revealing human aspiration and accomplishment (Rel, 61, 64, 136−41). It outbids all other religious texts. In a move that suggests continuity with the fundamental principles of the Reformation, Kant judges the biblical text to have leverage over tradition, doctrine, ritual, and, of course, ecclesiastical authority. While, of course, many Protestant sects have exhibited one or more of these features, the entire battery especially mark Catholicism (Rel, 156−59).[9] With respect to recommended interpretive practice, first, Kant stipulates that the interpretation of Scripture ought not to stray far from a plain reading of the text. As *Religion* (bk. 3) makes clear (136−38; also 198), Kant does not suppose that a moral reading is other than a plain reading. By no means does he think that it amounts to allegory (Rel, 143).[10] Second, Kant does not recommend that biblical discourse be replaced by another discourse, which proposes principles of justification that are more obviously epistemic than those found both in the biblical text and in its standard Protestant exegesis, what Kant variously refers to as "dogmatic" (e.g., Rel, 145; *Conflict of the Faculties* [hereafter C], 286) and "ecclesiastical" (C, 267; Rel, 138, 144).

Kant's options for the plain reading of the biblical text also represent decisions against influential alternatives. In the first case, it is obvious both from *Conflict* (bk. 1) and *Religion* (bk. 3) that Kant has decided against the group of religious thinkers whom he refers to as "enthusiasts" (*Schämerei*), who provide a mystical-allegorical interpretation of the biblical text (Rel, 162−63; C, 270). While Kant's scruple inhibits polemicizing against individual thinkers, nevertheless, more than occasionally he mentions names. Not surprisingly, given his demolition of the claims of the eighteenth-century theosophist Emmanuel Swedenborg in his *Dreams of a Spirit Seer* (1764),[11] the name of Swenden-borg is tendered (C, 270). Kant, of course, is aware that Swendenborg is simply the most egregious instance of a larger movement which, in his view, also includes Pietists such as Bengel and Oetinger (C, 282–83), who improperly interpret the biblical text by literalizing and allegoriz-ing it at the same time.[12] In the second case, Kant wishes to disassociate himself from Romantic Intuitionists such as Herder, Hamann, and Ja-cobi, who adopt an "apocalyptic tone" and essentially displace the prose of argumentation by the poetry of vision.[13] Of course, Kant has not separated out tone from content; apocalyptic tone implies a content accessed by intuition that does an end run around conceptual knowing (*Vernunft*), which the first *Critique* has laid down as the only legitimate form of knowing. Kant is just as hard on this group as Hegel is in *Faith and Knowledge* (1801),[14] and castigates them as "mystery mongers" (*Ge-heimniskrämer*).[15] In his reconstructive enterprise these differences make a difference. Against the second group he stresses the opportunities provided by the biblical text, especially in the form of its central nar-rative of creation-fall-renovation-eschaton, to say more than what rea-son can say without leaving reason—now in interpretive deployment—behind. He proceeds to stress the incentive provided by the thoroughly exoteric character of the biblical text, which, nonetheless, offers as com-prehensive an account of human being in its tensions and ultimate goals as can be imagined. Against the first group, Kant insists that the Bible does not provide its own legitimation procedures, nor can such proce-dures be extrapolated from the Bible; they must necessarily be supplied by philosophy as the organon of moral reason.

ARCHITECTONICS

By "architectonics" I mean not so much what Kant means at the end of the first *Critique*, where he refers to the idea of a "whole" of knowl-edge which is intended in and built up by forms of knowing that oper-ate within the "bounds of sense" but which is never complete. Rather I am referring to Kant's notion of "boundary" (*Grenze*) in *Religion*, where the notion is intended to mark off one discursive space from another that is contiguous to it,[16] on the grounds that these discursive spaces are defined by different assumptions and protocols. In *Religion* and *Conflict* Kant accepts the de facto reality of a plurality of discourses. His refusal, however, to think of reason's relation to other discourses, and especially religion, as a zero-sum game does not preclude some irritation with the fact that the contiguous discourse of religion is a mixture of reason and unreason and some anxiety concerning the prospect of competing discursive authorities that spells disaster for philosophy as well as science. The frame of reference of *Conflict* is fairly general; it distinguishes between disciplines, marks their protocols, and delimits the domain of application, marking where the rule of one ends and that of the other begins. Crucial also is the argument as to which discipline provides the mapping of such boundaries. It does not come as a surprise that the cartography for all the disciplines—law, medicine, theology—is itself supplied by philosophy. The truly critical issue, however, is the relation between theology and philosophy, which is addressed in book 1. Here Kant faces a conundrum similar to what he faces in *Religion*; although theology deals with such things as doctrine, history, law, the boundary between it and philosophy cannot be marked off cleanly. The reason is that both theology and philosophy make claims to interpret the biblical text, and that on philosophy's behalf Kant is not prepared to cede interpretation of the Bible to the theology faculty and concede that this discipline is likely to provide an authoritative interpretation. Indeed, he is of the view that practical philosophy provides a more adequate interpretation of the Bible than biblical scholarship so-called.

Now, the very general nature of Kant's brief prevents him from exploring what is at stake for reason in making this claim about a discourse that is not obviously a work of reason, and which as a matter of fact has essentially been the property of theology for the better part of two millennia (C, 269). By contrast the task of *Religion* is more focused (Rel, 62–63). Concerned with the contiguous space of religious discourse, which seems to be a mixture of reason (narrowly understood) and unreason, Kant attempts to draw a clear boundary between what is reasonable and what is unreasonable by filtering out the sense from the nonsense in religion, or, more specifically, the sense from the nonsense in Christianity and its basic text. Of course, this is essentially to redraw the de facto boundary, the one assumed for the sake of discussion, and which marks off the discourse of reason from the discourse of revelation. In any event, drawing the boundary means that the area of "mere" (*blosse*) reason has expanded, and correlatively the area of "religion" has shrunk, and in fact now becomes uniformly an area of unreason, however procedurally polite Kant is prepared to be. The consequence for philosophy itself as reason should not, however, be ignored. In getting to draw or redraw the boundary, reason has not simply expanded its domain; it has also brought about a sea change in it. Reason, which has been defined as criticism, essentially becomes hermeneutical. There are, then, more than simply lexical reasons to refuse to translate *blosse* as "pure," as is observed by the editor in the new English translation. Although *blosse* does connote "pure," as in "unmixed" and "undiluted," it also has the legal sense of an action performed by a person without reference to anything else (Rel, 53). The legal sense provides a note of dynamism that is lacking in the sense of reason being "pure." Should the old translation of "pure" continue to be used, it risks being ironical in some fundamental respect. For precisely as interpretive, reason is no longer "pure" in the sense of working according to its own critical procedures in splendid isolation from other discourses, indeed defined over against them. Now it is doing anything but minding its own business and is in fact reaching out and extending itself into a discursive "gray area" where its task is to extract what is reasonable from a mixture rather than assume it or presume against it.

Now before I turn to the interests served in marking a boundary, or in tracing one—which is a remarking or retracing—I should observe just how much Kant's topological scheme differs from other schemes in the Enlightenment. Speaking in general, these schemes can be reduced to two. First, the deist or the *philosophe* scheme supposes the existence side by side of two homogenous discourses of totally different value. The recognition of their contiguity, however, is merely a concession to social reality; in principle the relation between spaces is vertical. Reason has absolute value; religion—defined by superstition, authority, and fanaticism—essentially has none. Moreover, among expressions of religion, Scripture proves to be the rule rather than the exception; it has proved itself to be a social bane, a seedbed of argument and violence. Here the hierarchical dimension of the topology is firmly in place from the beginning. Second, the more moderate theist tends also to think of the discursive spaces of philosophy and religion as both separate and internally relatively homogenous, but recommends rational policing of religion rather than excising it altogether. There are some features of religion in general and especially of Scripture that show a modicum of rationality. There is huge variation among theists as to what in religion is rational, and where in the biblical text it might be found. Locke and Rousseau provide two very different examples. Whether the text is *The Reasonableness of Christianity* (1695) or *Profession de foi de Vicaire savoyard* (1752?), what sense can be found in the biblical text can exhaustively be translated into reason, which thus remains the same after such critical vetting. These forms of moderate theism proceed, then, on different lines from what we have called Kant's logic of supplementarity. In the case of moderate theism, there exists a definite hierarchy, but one a little less absolute than the first version. Kant's particular topology comes closer to this model than that of the deist, but is identical with neither. It resembles the position of the theist (1) in thinking that as a discursive space in the encompassing space of social and discursive interaction, religion cannot, or at least need not, be defined solely by superstition, heteronomy, and fanaticism, and (2) in ruling out the kind of exaggerated hierarchy characteristic of the strong deistic position. Kant's position distinguishes itself from the moderate theist position both in the degree of engagement with religion it requires of reason, especially when it comes to Scripture, and in how it comes to inscribe hierarchy. In fact, reason comes to see that there are secure and insecure hierarchies. An insecure hierarchy—also thereby one that is not secured—is a hierarchy that has left some good outside itself in the discursive space of religion that it does not regulate. As long as this situation maintains itself, the hierarchy is purely stipulative. Recognizing this good, and thus in a sense allowing the discursive playing field to become more level, is a necessary first step in what will turn out to be a complicated interpretive process in which reason will gradually assert itself. From the point of view of *Religion,* which breaks with the two Enlightenment paradigms and points the way towards what becomes commonplace in German Idealism, only that kind of hierarchy that is both end and means of a respectful interpretation of religion is secured and assured.

A number of interests are served in the actual making of a boundary between reason and unreason in the space of religion, which, unlike deism and theism, Kant understands to be more nearly heterogenous than homogenous. The first of these relates crucially to the requirements of definition, which demands determination and thus negation, to invoke the Spinozist formula of *omnis determinatio est negatio.* Definition may be ready at hand, or may need to be produced by distinguishing the real boundary from the apparent boundary between reason and unreason. Only an operation of definition in which the boundary between reason and unreason gets produced essentially seals the border of reason from a discourse which threatens to contaminate it even if it does not actually do so. The second is that in a complex situation in which the integrity of reason is, on the one hand, guaranteed only by its self-limitation and, on the other, stimulated by a related but different kind of reason to be found in religious discourse, which is a mix of reason and unreason, reason is at once encouraged to reach out beyond itself and by so doing to create a buffer zone between it and unreason. As a text *Religion* is the dialectical outcome of the problem generated by the ascetic purity of the first *Critique,* where Kant tries to secure the integrity of reason. Themselves responses to the first *Critique,* the *Critique of Practical Reason* and the *Critique of Judgment* represent graded attempts to see how far reason can extend beyond the limited preserve to which it has been assigned, a preserve that is, nonetheless, consistent with its maintaining its integrity and not falling into antinomy and other sorts of contradiction. In the case of the former, this leads to a supplementary account of human freedom and responsibility as lying outside the network of causation, and the generation of postulates regarding human freedom, the immortality of the soul, and the existence of God required to adjust merit with happiness. In the case of the latter, it involves an authorizing of aesthetic judgment that allows the universality of its claims, while at the same time suggesting that, unlike the universality of scientific judgments, that of aesthetic judgments lacks objectivity in the sense Kant gives it in the first *Critique.*

In *Religion* one comes upon reason in its most conspicuous and most significant extension, that is, its extension into the area of religion as this area is ambiguously marked by nonsense as well as sense. The rules for extension, which are at the same time the rules for adjudication and sifting of reason and unreason, are provided by practical rather than theoretical reason. The rules are decidedly not a third thing agreed on by the philosophical and theological parties who share a positive estimate of the biblical text. These rules are in effect legislated by philosophy. In any event, as practical reason plays referee with, and brings definition to, the ambiguous discursive space of religion, something important happens to the space. Essentially it is divided into two subspaces, more specifically into the discursive subspace that is redeemable by practical reason and the discursive subspace that is not, and which accordingly must be placed outside reason's border. Long before it appears in Derrida,[17] in Kant there is a construct of an outside, in fact the Outside, which functions as the "remains" of a process of discursive adoption. Kant does not simply imply that something like this category is in use; he deploys it, even if he hedges it with quotation marks. Memorably—if not felicitously when speaking of Judaism and the Jewish element of Christianity in *Conflict*—Kant invokes the apothegm of Cicero to the effect that "these remains weary us" (*nunc istae reliquas non exercent*) (263). In *Religion* (bk. 1) Kant speaks to the "outside" or "extra-territoriality" under two different rubrics with Greek names, that is, *parerga* (Rel, 96–97) and *adiaphora* (Rel, 89; C, 271). The meanings of the terms are clear, even if this clarity does not lead to transparency in Kant's use. *Parergos* is essentially a rhetorical term that means "subordinate" or "beside the main subject," whereas *adiaphoros,* which has a number of contexts in the ancient world, means "negligible" or "making no difference."[18] It is clear enough what different phenomena these terms are to cover. Falling under parerga in religion in general, and the Bible in particular, are miracles (Rel, 157), and "mysteries" such as satisfaction (Rel, 147–49, 168), election (Rel, 168), and Trinity (Rel, 166–68, 170–71), which by definition are "beyond reason." On grounds of the first *Critique,* since we cannot make an appeal to direct divine agency, we are prohibited from making an appeal to particular agency that is involved in election, disqualified from describing the mechanisms in and through which God saves, a point made all the more neuralgic by the unlikelihood that the means of salvation would fly in the face of the axiom of human autonomy and human responsibility. Similarly, the appeal to the triune God as mystery is at best obscurantist, at worst deceitful, since we are declaring that we know a great deal about what we are and at the same time saying that we are unable to know. Furthermore, a religious system which talks casually about grace and its means also can be included as a parergon. As Kant makes clear later on in book 3 of *Religion,* however, we have to add the proviso that in this case it might be possible to deploy the concept of grace in a way that does not disturb—as it appears to disturb—the axioms of freedom and responsibility. By contrast, Kant speaks of adiaphora when he is concerned to define those elements of religion, and specifically of the Bible and its interpretation, which are disposable coverings for its true meaning and message. This is Kant operating in terms of the Reformation version of the contrast between letter and spirit as that is historically disseminated in and through German Pietism. Now, although Kant in *Religion* illustrates these different outsides, he does not explicitly give a particular ranking, nor gauge their relative distance from reason.

Reason's hermeneutical extension evinces a paradox: at once demonstrating a kind of humility towards the discursive other that is unusual in modern philosophy, yet proudly insistent on the rule of reason, at once generous in granting the good of the other discourse—something that is in excess of its own critical accomplishment—and convinced that much of it can be ignored or discarded, at once responsibly recognizing the plurality of discourses and the distinct value of Christianity, and exhibiting nonchalance in transgressing the de facto borders between reason and revelation. The question arises whether in its turn to interpretation reason presents a simulacrum of kenosis; that is, whether, far from relenting from its own prerogatives in reaching out towards the other, it is even more insistent on them. Kenosis is less a form of emptying than of filling or fulfilling, thus of plerosis. The question also arises whether in its reaching out towards the discursive other—which might very well be a reaching for—reason does not betray its pathological character: reason is disturbed by, or endures the pathos of, its own limitations; reason "suffers" the other discourse in its openness and hospitality for it; and reason enacts an interpretation of religious discourse in which it not only performs a humane service, but makes itself more than it would have been had it remained within its own borders.

The third and final interest in *Religion* is to bring the "good news" of modernity to the those who speak in and with the "unwashed" discourse of the Bible, to tell religious believers in particular that they are not prohibited from becoming members of the "ethical" and rational commonwealth of which Kant makes so much in the text. More specifically, it is to invite religious believers and worshipers to look at themselves in the mirror of reason and become members of the "invisible church" (Rel, 134–35, 152), and if not actually to secede from, to at least become a preeschatological leaven in the visible church. The acceptance of this invitation justifies the self-regard of those who commit themselves to a certain way of reading Scripture, while leaving without excuse, however, those who continue under the old rules of theological and/or historical interpretation.

SYMBOLICS

Religion does not make sense without the general assumption that there is something wrong with the "seeing" of reason as this is enacted especially in the first *Critique,* and even to a certain extent in the second *Critique.* What is wrong is that, counterintuitively, the "seeing" of reason in its critical mode lacks sufficient focus and depth. Religion points to a number of interrelated deficits. Here I mention only five; many more could be adduced. (1) Critical reason in neither its theoretical nor its practical deployment is able to capture adequately the dimensions of freedom and responsibility of a self that enacts a life in a world that is materially and temporally conditioned. (2) Critical reason is unable to account for the continuity of such a self, how the self is an enactment of a particular character. (3) Critical reason is unable to present a persuasive picture as to how such a self admits of a radical change that can be attributed to her rather than to factors in the material and historical environment. (4) Critical reason is unable to come to terms with the concept of moral exemplarity, and critically to assess what role it can or cannot play in moral renovation. (5) Critical reason has difficulty thinking richly about the relation between the individual self and the community as a whole, and how the improvement of one is related to the improvement of the other.

As is well known, Kant's overall solution is to require that reason turn hermeneutical; more specifically Kant demands of reason that it engage in an interpretation of the biblical text. If in one sense hermeneutics represents a deferral or delay of understanding, in another, it is the indispensable means towards the most adequate "seeing" possible, where this "seeing" is resolutely that of a finite self and in no way the seeing or knowing of absolute knowledge (*absolut Wissen*) which intercalates a subject, that is, essentially calls it into being. Now, Kant's interpretation is not focused on individual passages, nor is it interested in microscopic analysis across the entire biblical text. For Kant, the biblical text reduces to a schematic narrative of creation-fall-redemption-eschaton with Christ playing a pivotal role in bringing about that renovation of character that constitutes conversion. In a sense, then, the Bible reduces to kerygma, and pushes aside all else as external. In particular, Kant judges severely those aspects of the biblical text that emphasize law, ritual (sacrifice), and miraculous intervention. It so happens that these elements are dominant in Hebrew Scripture (Rel, 154–56); their presence in the New Testament—and Kant admits their presence—is put down to anachronism. Hegel will essentially repeat Kant's Marcion-like culling of the biblical text in such early efforts as the essays "The Positivity of the Christian Religion" (1795) and "The Spirit of Christianity and Its Fate" (1799).[19] How the biblical text is interpreted is related to what is interpreted. If the what is the kerygma, and the focus is on the event of redemption in and of the individual (Kierkegaard is Kant's successor here), then historical or positivist strategies of interpretation are essentially beside the point. For Kant this leaves standing only a mode of interpretation that will line up—as far as is possible at least—the biblical givens with practical reason, although a condition of "lining up" is that practical reason becomes more than it was in its native (unhermeneutical) habitat.

The interpretation of Scripture offers reason something of a seeing aid: in the very famous book 1 of *Religion* Kant argues that the "historical" or "mythological" account of the fall aids reason by showing the definite order between creatureliness and systemic fault (Rel, 87), an order that Kant proceeds to mark lexically by distinguishing between the "predisposition" (*Anlage*) towards the good and the "propensity" (*Hang*) towards evil, and insisting on the secondariness of the latter with respect to the former. Yet in the account of "radical evil," which provoked Goethe to claim that the hero of the Enlightenment had regressed to the dark side of Christianity,[20] Kant departs from his critical work by suggesting that the symbolic account of the fall in Genesis—although not necessarily any of its standard theological interpretations[21]—instructs us concerning the essentially nonrational nature of our fundamental option for good or evil. The instruction is necessary, for in his ethical works Kant had tied freedom (*Wille*) and reason (moral) so closely together that where reason is absent, effectively there is no choice. Now Kant is persuaded that this view is crucially mistaken: our choice of basic maxims is more fundamental than our correspondence to the demands of practical reason (the categorical imperative) and our failure to correspond given our acquiescence to nonmoral incentives. More, it is this fundamentally nonrational option that accounts for who we are over time, and thus our character. Kant's lesson is not lost on Schelling in his famous essay *On Human Freedom* (1809),[22] where Kant's account of fundamental option is transposed into a speculative, perhaps even theosophic, key.

The lexical mark of the advance brought about by hermeneutics in *Religion* is the shift from *Wille* (will corresponds to reason) to *Willkür* (will as more primordial than reason). The concept of *Willkür*, generated in dialogue with Genesis 1–3, enables us to address more adequately the first two issues, which critical reason seemed incompetent to try, and to contribute towards the third, in that radical change cannot be imagined without a fundamental change in the maxims we adopt. Kant redresses the imbalance in his critical treatment of morality when he addresses the role Christ plays in moral renovation in book 3. Having painted himself into a corner by reducing the foundations of morality into a choice between specifically moral and nonmoral incentives, he seems to have put exemplarity in a position that is ambiguous at best. Willing to imitate a moral agent is not the same as willing as a moral agent should, but neither does it seem unequivocally to be a concession to egoistic desire or need. Consistent with the first and second *Critiques*,

Kant does not allow Christ causally to effect redemption (Rel, 114–16, 121), and consequently he does not support justification in the same way as Luther and Melanchthon do (Rel, 116). Nevertheless, he does think that, as an exemplar of pure moral consciousness (an example of the "pure will"), Christ serves as a ground of the hope of redemption's realization (Rel, 104–5, 109). Without this hope morality might well flounder. Religion, therefore, overcomes a fourth deficit of the critical regime.

It also overcomes the fifth. In his critical thinking the emphasis falls so exclusively on the individual that Kant does not think through the relation between the individual and the community, nor the relation between the present community and the generations past and future. These relations have become important to him. Although there are undoubtedly philosophical influences at work in *Religion,* with, arguably, Rousseau being first among equals,[23] once again it is the biblical narrative, and especially its protology and eschatology, that suggests the need to think more broadly and more deeply about the issues. Thinking through these problems does not mean that Kant will compromise on the axiom that salvation primarily concerns the individual, and that salvation is essentially morally effected, whether we appeal to, or refuse to appeal to, the language of "grace." Nor does it mean that Kant's recognition of history as the milieu of moral agency and moral renovation makes him inclined to think of history as a determinant rather than a condition.[24] Hegel will, of course, think that Kant fails to be sufficiently radical on either front; and he suggests that Kant's *Moralität,* premised on the individual moral subject, be replaced by *Sittlichkeit,* premised in significant part on a more collective moral agency,[25] and that Kant's formal recognition of the role of history be replaced by a recognition in which history itself is an agent of human self-constitution and thus redemption.

This is simply the briefest of sketches concerning the achievements of the hermeneutics of reason. Each of the five elements I have isolated is worthy of a paper-length treatment. But these details are not my brief, nor is even a rounder view of the general achievements of this hermeneutics. Here my interest is in the supplement to seeing provided by hermeneutics, that is, in its capacity to correct for the "blind spot" of critical reason and thereby enable reason to see in a focused and three-dimensional way. Now the relationship between the three *Critiques* and *Religion* graphs onto an ocular grid. As the *Critiques* represent the overcoming of a blindness of a philosophical theology that masquerades as seeing, *Religion* addresses the blind spot that results from the correction to this blindness. Recall the image of blindness embedded in what is, arguably, the most famous passage in the first *Critique*: "Concepts without intuitions are empty, intuitions without concepts are blind" (CPR, 29). It follows necessarily that, as a discursive or conceptual enterprise, critical philosophy is in the business of overcoming the blindness that marks classical philosophy in general and philosophical theology in particular.[26] Pretending to see much, philosophy does not manage to see anything as it really can be seen. The purpose of the Transcendental Dialectic is to reveal as blindness the claims of philosophy to see truly the realities of substance and cause. The second and third *Critiques* do not break faith. Kant's discourse of practical reason not only represents a real advance with respect to understanding what warrants can be provided for human freedom, the existence of God, and the reality of divine providence, but it also overcomes deficiencies in traditional ethical discourse, which amounts, Kant is inclined to think, to little more than a confused compound of the distinct languages of obligation and description. In the second *Critique* Kant shows us how to "see" in a way that exceeds that of the first *Critique*. Similarly, his articulation of aesthetic judgment is intended to overcome the "nonseeing" that marks classical and contemporary aesthetics, the former tending towards an unjustifiable objectivism, the latter tending towards an equally unjustifiable subjectivism. It is possible, if we are to take such disparate witnesses as Despland and Heidegger into account, that the third *Critique* represents an attempt to articulate the synthesis beyond the synthesis of the transcendental unity of apperception, that is, the synthesis of imagination.[27] Nonetheless, although the critical discourses are, relatively speaking, forms of "seeing," the fact is that Kant comes more and more to judge that there is a blind spot in critical thought itself that leaves it somewhat at a loss when the truly deep issues concerning the self need to be faced—although part of the problem is that it does not fully see these issues until it encounters and comes to appreciate the biblical text.[28] Importantly, in terms of definition, a blind spot is a limit to seeing, a not-seeing that is internal rather than external to seeing. It seems to be nothing less than a self-limitation of reason; as such it cannot appeal to itself, but only to an outside, for assistance in making it see properly or adequately.

The appeal to the biblical narrative, then, belongs to the metaphorics of ocular correction. The most obvious and straightforward form of this is that the biblical narrative offers spectacles to critical reason that enable reason to see more comprehensively and deeply. Of course, the spectacle metaphor could be mined further with a view to deciding whether the correction is more nearly for myopia or farsightedness. I will avoid what might give the appearance of conceit by suggesting, without discussion, that in this instance it is best to think of the biblical narrative as correcting for both, since the biblical narrative permits vision of the greatest temporal and historical range, while at the same time permitting reason to have a sharper focus as to when and where reason breaks off and requires a supplement. Of course, the metaphorics of ocular correction is not wholly without irony. As the spectacles (determined by a hermeneutic of Scripture) correct for the blind spot of critical reason, which in turn corrects for the blindness of noncritical philosophy, these spectacles themselves require adjustment. This adjustment, as most commentators on *Religion* would agree, is provided by practical reason: not just any reading of the biblical narrative will do; indeed, only a reading conducted by, or at least vetted by, practical reason suffices. In this further correction, which involves a translation from biblical narrative and symbol back into an ethical-philosophical code, there is a limit to thought: we cannot think through the relation of grace to moral responsibility (Rel, bk. 3), for example, but the fact that we cannot think it does not mean that the connection is without value. Of course, we cannot think through a host of other things either, which are of no less value. Instructed by hermeneutics, reason knows that it cannot go further than the inscrutability of the ground of freedom that can adopt an evil as well as a good maxim (Rel, 73; also 80, 83, 85–86), nor can it go further than simply acknowledging the inexplicable continuity of the free and responsible self (Rel, 71), nor go further in its analysis of radical change than attributing it to a fundamental change in the maxims adopted by the transcendental self that specifies itself temporally. There is, then, a final limit to the entire process of correction, and thus an incurable blindness that seems to mark finitude itself. This is not the kind of result favored by Hegel, and his departure from Kant on this point seems not only to have the first *Critique* in mind, but also *Religion,* when he insists in the *Phenomenology* (secs. 7, 8) that the process of interpretation, and of the biblical narrative in particular, leads to a totally transparent mode of knowledge. Of course, there is more at issue here than the difference between a finitist and an infinitist. Hegel has a very different relation to the biblical text than Kant. Kant grants the biblical text a status that Hegel does not appear to grant, even if he reduces it to a narrative schematization which requires interpretation to remove its "story telling properties" with its misleading suggestions of before and after (Rel, 85–89).[29] If, undoubtedly, part of the reason is Kant's much deeper embedding in biblical culture, the rest is Kant's ethical concerns which make the interest in this case the application of the biblical narrative to an individual's particular situation and life.[30] Hegel is fundamentally interested in the biblical narrative as making a truth claim about the world that can be redeemed only within the precincts of philosophy.

Other less obvious forms of correction are also suggested in and by this ocular metaphorics, some of which will come to have their day in postmodern philosophy. It is possible to think of the biblical narrative and its key symbols as providing something like a third eye to the two eyes of critical reason, which turns out to be bedeviled by something like the "eyes wide-shut" syndrome. Here too, however, there is irony. Under no circumstances would Kant countenance something like the Hermetic eye—the eye of vision or intellectual intuition[31]—this smacks too much of the kind of enthusiasm and apocalypticism that he insistently condemned. In a sense, the third eye is cyclopean, in that it does not see what it sees or know what it knows. The biblical narrative, which now serves as a means of interpretation, is itself submitted to interpretation in order that its particular obscurity and blindness may be overcome. As is well known, it is Hegel rather than Kant who appeals to the figure of Ulysses.[32] The figure may well be in the margins of Kant's texts, yet it is the integration of this figure with the figure of Cyclops that is more concerted and more riveting. Neither the (non)seeing eye of the Cyclops nor the all-too-seeing eye of Ulysses is privileged; Kant seems to have them negotiate with each other, such that the cylopean eye is necessary for the philosophical Ulysses to see, while it guarantees that the Ulyssean eye never achieves full transparency.

Interestingly, this ocular metaphorics brings another metaphorics, that is, the metaphorics of *pharmakon,* into view. As Derrida has so influentially pointed out, *pharmakon* has the double sense of "cure" and "poisoning."[33] Although functioning more dialectically in Kant than it is in Derrida's own work, where the pair figures an antinomy, "cure" and "poison," nevertheless, are in both cases thought together. The spectacles or third eye of biblical narrative provides a cure for the poison that turned out to be latent in the cure effected by critical reason on the blindness of the philosophical tradition which pretends to see. Of course, as indicated already, unassisted by practical reason, the biblical narrative is in no position to offer a cure. Indeed, in all likelihood, itself left unassisted, it would only produce a poisonous obscurantism. It in turn, then, is cured by the seeing of practical reason as this enacts itself in interpretation of the biblical narrative. It only seems that movement is circular; in truth, the movement of ocular correction shapes a spiral that ends with, but is not closed by, a blindness that cannot be gotten over and for which there is no cure, since we have reached the bedrock of finitude itself.

DYNAMICS

The first two sections have indicated the benefit that accrues to reason as it turns hermeneutical, chief among which are its overcoming of insularity and its correction for a blind spot. But, of course, Christianity also seems to receive a credit that no other religion receives; its narrative and its symbols alone can serve a role in extending reason beyond its narrow province. As book 3 of *Religion* shows clearly, this is a compliment that is withheld from nonmonotheistic forms of religion such as Zoroastrianism, Hinduism, and the primitive religions, but also from Judaism and Islam as the two other forms of monotheism. When it comes to Islam, Kant proves that Lessing is the exception rather than the rule in thinking that it has value.[34] Kant could hardly have been more dismissive. Kant is particularly severe on Judaism. Indeed, he sets the pattern for much of German Romanticism and Idealism by excoriating its legalism and its incompatibility with autonomy (Rel, 154–60). Certainly, he does not accept Mendelssohn's attempt to argue the compatibility of law and reason.[35] At the same time, Kant also feels obliged in book 3 to insist that this narrative-symbolic construal of Christianity differs *toto coelo* from institutional, ritualistic, hierarchical, and doctrinal forms of Christianity. Obviously, Catholicism is here the main target (Rel, 140–41). Kant does not dot the *i* and cross the *t* with respect to the double exclusion, but in Kant's wake, Hegel will bring an inner connection between Judaism and Catholic Christianity: this lies not only in their formal similarity in that both side with heteronomy over autonomy, but that a heteronomous form of Christianity such as Catholicism represents at once a betrayal of the proper genius of Christianity and an introjection of the spirit of Judaism.[36] And again, Kant wishes to distinguish his position from the Romantic position, which, without Schleiermacher being yet in the picture,[37] he considers to be based on "feeling" (Rel, 145; C, bks. 1 and 2).

In Kant's rhetoric of justification, Christianity gains as much as philosophy from the encounter; it acquires higher cultural status that comes only with being in the "light" and exercising freedom, and gets to enjoy the Christian kernel that has shucked off the dogmatic and historical husks. The question is whether the gains are real, and what are the criteria by which one could make a considered decision? More particularly the issue is whether in and through interpretation of biblical narrative and symbols the emphasis falls primarily on spreading the empire of reason or on telling the story of reason's self-limitation. The question can be put in another key again: given that the determination of the boundary between discursive spaces of reason and what is outside of it is provisional, and that reason's talking to religion turns out to be but a preliminary to a talking about it; given also that recursive self-adjustment is an invariable feature of the fluency of a colonizing discourse and what makes it effective,[38] are we talking in the final analysis of the colonization of religion and Christianity in particular?

Now, I want to suggest that the evidence indicates that we are in-deed dealing with a form of colonization. Precisely in its negotiation with Christian discourse philosophy dismantles its would-be authority. Nevertheless, the accommodation critical reason makes with respect to Christian discourse is limited in scope; it applies, as we have seen, only to Christian discourse in its biblical narrative form. Moreover, a defini-tive hierarchy with respect to needs satisfied and gifts given seems to be in operation. It is true that the engagement with the biblical narrative answers a fundamental need of philosophy to be all that it can be. Yet the gift received from biblical religion is exceeded by the gift given, which is the gift of clarity with respect to what the biblical narrative says about human freedom and responsibility, about character and its reformation, and about our ultimate destiny. The gesture towards asymmetry is not in the slightest accidental. Kant's work shows clearly that the gratitude of philosophy towards religion is procedural; by con-trast ingratitude is structural. Philosophy not only will not, but cannot accept being beholden to another discourse. In particular, it refuses to accept that the cure of its blind spot by and in and through a reading of Scripture puts it as much in debt to Scripture as Scripture is to it be-cause of the perspicuity of Scripture's moral analysis. Indeed, it is not clear that it is not so blinded by its own gift giving that it essentially re-peals the acknowledgment of the assistance it gets from the biblical narrative towards enlarging the scope of reason and deepening it, even as it recalls that acknowledgment in *Conflict* and enacts it in *Religion*. Formally speaking, philosophy gets counted twice: first, as its own dis-cursive space separate from religious discursive space and vying with it for authority, and second, as a metadiscourse that provides the rule of translation for biblical discourse that brings the latter up to intellectual code. As a metadiscourse, reason dynamically extends well beyond its pregiven territory or space, thereby expanding its periphery, but also suggesting the lack of distinction between core and periphery. Under certain rules, there is no distinction between the outer province and the central executive hub. Kant's procedure bears a relationship—although it is much less inclusive—to the behavior of the Roman Empire with respect to the gods of the nations: these gods are accepted, while Rome, which will constitute the pantheon, reserves the right to interpret and translate the religions of those gods into an idiom which reveals what "really" is entailed in the claims and practices of religion.[39] It does not matter that these religions would not recognize themselves in their "official" description; this would be sheer stubbornness indicative of the disenlightened.

In any event, Kant redraws the map of the empire of reason, essentially changes the pregiven borders, and by so doing neutralizes religion in general, and Christianity in particular, as a potential and actual competitor. The hermeneutic of the biblical narrative engaged in by reason turns out to be at once bridge and prosthesis: bridge in that, at least in appearance, hermeneutics is the space of interlocution between reason and nonreason, prosthesis insofar as this interlocution in the end reveals itself as locution which extends reason over a region of discourse whose value is acknowledged at precisely the moment its sovereignty is violated. A significant portion of this discourse, or what is significant about this discourse, is annexed and essentially put under another rule, that is, the rule of practical reason. The Greek word for extension, *prosthēkē*, helps reveal an important aspect of what is going on. For in the extension of the rule of reason enacted by hermeneutics, reason functions like a prosthesis which creates a boundary line that was not there before between reasonable and unreasonable religion, specifically reasonable and nonreasonable Christianity. A hierarchy asserts itself as inalienable. In the act of extension in which rational religion is justified as a prosthesis, the pregiven border between discourses of reason and revelation is violated. But, as often with colonization, the issue of whether an extension in the strict, that is, the juridical sense, has occurred is more important than the factual change in boundaries. For there is always and everywhere dispute over the legitimacy of the boundaries. It is possible for Kant to be complacent in both *Religion* and *Conflict* as to whether a territorial violation has occurred. To cross the pregiven border is precisely not to cross the real line; to extend the boundary of one's reason's operation is not to extend the real boundary, but rather to (re)discover it. In a sense, Kant builds into his hermeneutics the erasure of all movement and all trembling of discursive space. Hermeneutics is the scene, then, not so much of a real happening, but of an oxymoron, that is, of a "nonhappening happening." Transgression is made invisible, even as the spread of the empire is touted.

This finds its complement in what is a second note of colonization, that is, the distinctly shifting identity of that which crosses the border; for example, not untypically, at first it is a liberation army, then the genuine voice of the citizens, or the true citizens who wish the yoke of repression and oppression to be removed. In the case of Kant, if in a very definite sense reason has crossed and crossed over, in another sense no crossing over has occurred; the prosthesis is passive rather than active, since the extension can be described as if it is an event internal to Christianity itself, the movement of its becoming self-aware, finding itself looking at itself in the mirror of reason, thinking of itself as within the circle.

Hermeneutics in Kant is a de-cision in the strict sense, that is, it makes a cut in the space of religion between what can be sanctioned by reason, on the one hand, and what cannot and must therefore be left outside, or named as outside, on the other. Quite literally, then, the space of religion, that is, the pregiven space, is de-vastated in that there is the construction of "waste" or "remains." *Waste* or *remains* names not what is of obscure or questionable value, but what has no value whatsoever. Kant's axiology then proceeds by a meontology; the remains of religion—creeds, dogmas, history, institutions, rituals, perhaps even historical or learned analysis of the biblical text—move towards a condition of nothing. Religion in this mode can be mapped only as a limit; it is a where that is nowhere, the distopic place of the absolute other to reason; it is unreason and nondiscourse. This is to make certain versions of Christianity (with Judaism and other religions) the site of the barbaric, for on analogy with the ethnographical studies that so fascinated the age of Kant,[40] the barbarian is one who deprives sense of any foothold. It is also to deepen the analogy with colonization, for one could argue that the spread of any empire is marked by the construction of the barbarian who represents the other to one's reason and value,[41] who cannot be brought in and thus represents the limit. The first question that emerges is who, from a religious perspective, is a barbarian. There are obvious referents; as an avid reader of travel adventures and ethnographical studies, Kant finds plenty of "candidates" in primitive societies whose whole social organization is determined religiously. But also a bevy of religions, historical and actual, are "candidates."[42] The most troubling of all candidates for barbaric status is Judaism, and in its wake certain fundamental ways of being Christian, of holding beliefs, and certain practices and ways of reading Scripture. The follow-up question is, what duties are owed to what is barbaric, to what is absolutely deprived of reason and thus of value? In particular, the question emerges, does the prohibition on repression extend only to that to which can be ascribed some value?[43]

I have read Kant's hermeneutic posture towards Christian discourse as showing evidence of the dynamics of colonization. There is nothing about this that is a "strong" reading; this reading fairly naturally forces itself on a reader of Kant who is not particularly well schooled in postcolonial theory. Still, it is interesting that the legitimation (such as we find in Kant) of the extension of a privileged discourse, the de-cision of a pregiven discursive field into what is savable and what is not, the construction of a univocal religious language, the concomitant construction of the barbarian who either cannot speak or refuses to speak this language, and the introjection of a laundered version of knowing and behavior that makes one fully human are, according to a postcolonialist theorist such as Edward Said, common features of the colonizing apparatus. My interest is different from and more narrow than Said's. For the purposes of this essay I am not interested in the mechanics of the dissemination of Western values and the cultural and human costs of those who play the role of host. Rather I am interested in the way the Enlightenment turns against Western culture as it once was, and against the modes of Christianity that made it possible, and in particular how the Enlightenment wishes to cleanse and arbitrate the correctness of Christian-speak, to unrubbish the old bulky grammar of Christianity and provide it with a lean new grammar which insists on the ethical and the practical.

In my remarks about religious colonization I did proffer something of an analogy with how ancient Rome dealt with religion or religions. The limits of this analogy could be teased out more. This analogy gains greater plausibility than it might otherwise enjoy when one keeps in mind Kant's recourse to Roman authors of Stoic complexion throughout his ethical works and also in *Religion*. This should not surprise, since the Roman authors, such as Cicero and Seneca, who are recurred to are moralists who are able to distinguish what is valuable from what is val-

ueless in religions and are ready to prioritize the rational and ethical.[44]
Still, it behooves us to recall a number of elements of Kant's colonization that mark his view as specifically modern. First, Kant's extension
of the empire of reason in and through the practice of protocols of
translation supposes the emergence of Christianity and its assumption
of world-historical importance, while at the same time presupposing
the contemporary crisis of its authority and validity. This introduces
stratification into the religious field that does not find an analogy in
Roman conjugation. More specifically, it makes the question of the relationship between Christianity and other religions secondary, just as it
makes the relation between practical philosophy and these other religions secondary. Second, Kant has a deep Protestant bias against ritual,
or what he calls in *Religion* "divine service." This aversion to the ritualistic elements of religion is far in excess of what is evident in the Stoic
philosophers he admires, even if their tolerance is in the main procedural and political. Admittedly Kant does not totally dismiss the procedural, which refuses to press the issue of adequacy even as its logic presupposes it. At the very least, Kant's proceduralism is interrupted in
Religion by a binary model of adjudication in which different religions
as well as various historical and contemporary forms of Christianity
are deemed to be inadequate. Third, while Kant fully subscribes to the
Stoic distinction between rational and cultural religion,[45] and thus between the esoteric and exoteric dimensions of religion, his Enlightenment commitment to the dissemination of knowledge much more exi-
gently forces the issue of the general social acceptance of knowledge,
practical as well as theoretical, that has claims to adequacy. Thus, while
the gap is accepted as a matter of fact, there is a demand that at least it
be narrowed both qualitatively and quantitatively, if not entirely overcome in the modern world. Fourth, finally, and relatedly, there is a sense
in which the Kantian mode of religious colonization bears a closer approximation to linguistic colonization than that expected by Stoic philosophers, who both buttressed Roman power and provided the means
of its critique. If all colonization is linguistic as well as institutional, it
is not the case that there is always the demand to speak in or move towards speaking in a common tongue, for instance, Latin or Greek. In the
case of Kant, while there is some concession to bad religious speakers,

and bad Christian speakers in particular, all things being equal it would be good if all Christian speakers spoke as Kant does, or were able to enact the kind of translation of the biblical text he performs in *Religion*.

SUPPLEMENTING THE SUPPLEMENT

It is undoubtedly true that what is provided here is at best the sketch for a kind of refiguration or reconfiguration of Kant that would demand not only much greater detail, but much greater conceptual sophistication. Still, to lay out, in however an inchoate form, the relationship between Kant's discourse and the discourse of Christianity in its architectonic, symbolic, and dynamic dimensions and to name Kant's hermeneutical, symbolic, and expropriating strategies is a necessary first step in coming to grips with what amounts to a revolution in modern thought,[46] whose influence has marked much of nineteenth- and twentieth-century Liberal Protestant thought from Ritschl to Harnack. In his survey of modern Protestant thought, Barth could decry Kant's legacy, even as he could praise Kant's genius in this as in other respects.[47] Moreover, Kant still provides a way for philosophers to embrace Christianity, for Christianity proves both transparent to reason and a supplement. As hinted in the introduction, arguably even more interesting is the fate of Kant's conjugation of faith and reason in postmodern discussions in which atheism is considered as philosophically uncouth as theism, and in which Hegel's conjugation is considered to be the ultimate dead end, precisely because it is the dead end of the ultimate. For example, one way of reading the work of Lévinas and the later Derrida is to see that their complex articulations of the relation between philosophical and religious discourse (now Jewish as well as Christian) essentially repeat the threefold form that we have extracted from an analysis of Kant's writings on religion. That is, both Lévinas and the later Derrida, precisely in their anti-Hegelianism, can be understood to present an architectonic in which philosophy and religion are assigned spaces that border on each other but do not mix, in which religion proves supplementary not only in that it gives philosophy something to think but also in that aspects of it function to cure philosophy of its blindness and its self-amputation, and in which, nevertheless, that supplement in seeing and prosthesis represents something of a hostile takeover of religious discourse.

In the case of Lévinas, it can be said that self-consciously Lévinas follows the lead of Kant in denying theological interest or competence. Lévinas's claim to work solely in terms of the discipline of philosophy is, however, complicated by the fact that he engages in Talmudic hermeneutics.[48] It is one thing to insist that religious and philosophical discourses proceed according to distinct protocols; it is another thing altogether to be assured that Lévinas obeys his own strictures against mixing. Although it is appropriate to ask this question of *Totality and Infinity*, the question becomes urgent in the context of *Otherwise Than Being*, given that the text generously borrows religious categories, even specifically biblical categories, such as "substitution," "prophecy," "inspiration," and "glory."[49] Although abstracted from their original religious context, even as their validity is confirmed by phenomenological analysis, these categories also direct and guide such analysis. At the very least implicitly, these categories function as supplements to what passes as "first philosophy."[50] Nevertheless, as a not fully competent reason is made to see better than otherwise it would, the tack taken is that the symbols or categories that are borrowed become fully transparent, and thus the means of transparency, only when they are phenomenologically reduced. If one substitutes phenomenological for transcendental analysis, then Lévinas can be understood clearly to repeat Kant with respect to the basic point that the supplement is itself supplemented. In any event, to procure biblical symbols as supplements effects a gaping wound on the biblical whole. By focusing only on the prophetic texts, Lévinas already makes a deep cut which removes the discourses of law, history, and wisdom. But even when we allow the limiting to prophetic texts, and Isaiah in particular, Lévinas manages to leave behind as dogmatic "remains" the conviction of a really real God who is Lord of history. The dynamics of Lévinas's implied hermeneutic of Scripture is colonizing in that it annexes and redraws the pregiven boundary of these discourses.

Admittedly, this analysis of Lévinas is too brief to be other than probative. Still, probation is justified, and not simply for those for whom religion is necessarily thicker and also capable of giving an account of itself, but also for someone like Derrida who, however influenced by Lévinas, does not rule against the possibility that Lévinas's ethical philosophy is more implicated with religion than the idea of a sealed border between them would imply. But, arguably, no thinker is more aware of the possibility in modern philosophical thought of the generation of "non-dogmatic doublets" of Christianity than Derrida. And, arguably, no thinker is more willing to accept that the charge of such production—what corresponds to what I have been calling "colonization"—is admissible with respect to his own writing. Needless to say, Derrida does not enter a guilty plea, even as, or especially as, he recognizes that he is involved in making many of the same claims and deploying many of the same hermeneutical strategies with respect to religion as Kant and major continental thinkers since Kant. Nor is Derrida unsympathetic to the motivations of Kant and his epigones, who wish to limit the intellectual toxicity of religion, and especially the damage it does in the social and political spheres. Of course, all of this functions as potential amelioration should the charge of colonization be sustained against him. Importantly, Derrida does not think that the charge is sustainable. Adducing the genetic consideration that Derrida's turn to religion is belated and, in consequence, that religion cannot play a constitutive role only does so much argumentative work. After all, the same could be said of the subject of this paper, Immanuel Kant. The burden of exculpation obviously has to be borne by Derrida's success in persuading that whatever the correspondence between his view of *khora* and the hyperousiological God of the negative theology tradition,[51] on the one hand, and his view of messianicity and the views of the Messiah and the messianic in Judaism as well as Christianity,[52] on the other, there is a fundamental asymmetry. Neither khora nor messianicity functions at the same level as its religious correlative. Indeed, to use the language of the much earlier Derrida, they both function in a quasitranscendental fashion, as other than but also as conditions of the possibility for these more concrete historical concepts.

Derrida's arguments might not amount to a convincing defense, but a fair trial would necessarily be complicated for the obvious reason that Derrida is always trying to correct for the errors of those thinkers with whom he enjoys an elective affinity. This is the subject of another paper, perhaps more than one paper. What I want to pursue here, however, is not so much the issue in what way Derrida's thought might be hoisted on the petard of "colonization," but in what way his work, especially his "later" work, helps both to confirm and to develop my analysis of Kant. The text I would like to speak to, but also in a sense abstract from, is "Faith and Knowledge,"[53] which represents one of Derrida's most concerted engagements with Kant. The very title of this essay points to the moment in European history—which may well be nothing less than an event—in which the claims of faith and reason are negotiated and in which reason, precisely as critical reason, plays the role of judge. In a sense this is a crux of what has come to be called the Enlightenment (46–48). There can be no caviling with the rectitude of its motivation, aimed at the overcoming of obscurantism and of the fanaticism and violence that it breeds and endorses (59–60). Even giving the prophets of suspicion their due, Derrida deems it reasonable to take the proponents of the Enlightenment at their word. Importantly, for Derrida, the proponents of the Enlightenment are various as well as plural. Looked at broadly, Kant is just one proponent, and his name stands for one strategy of adjudicating the claims of faith and reason. Voltaire is another (46–47, 59–60), and his name stands for another strategy.[54] For Derrida, then, there is a French form of Enlightenment as well as a German. Depending upon how one reads the following, Derrida is also admitting that there is an English version: "Pure attestation, if there is such a thing, pertains to the experience of faith and the miracle" (99). Even if other interpretations are possible, one way of reading this is to think of Locke's philosophical justification of the fiduciary in a text such as *The Reasonableness of Christianity* (1695).[55] Whatever the reading of this passage, the main point is that despite, or perhaps because of, Derrida's concentration on Kant, the Enlightenment is too complex to reduce to a single figure or even a particular movement.[56] Undoubtedly, however, in "Faith and Knowledge" Kant is enjoying certain privileges as a figure of the Enlightenment.

The question, which is easier to ask than to answer, is what reasons and/or what kind of reasons Derrida can produce. Although this is an un-Derridian way of proceeding, it might be said, on even the most superficial of looks, that Derrida's highlighting of Kant contains a pe-culiar mixture of description and recommendation. Perhaps because of preference and/or a sense of Kant's philosophical authority, Derrida sometimes rolls up all Enlightenment or indeed "modern" problema-tizing of the issue of the relation of faith and reason (and consequently the various strategies deployed) into Kant's specific way of handling the issue (45). Any raising of the question of relation, on Derrida's ac-count, represents essentially a "Kantian gesture" (45) and points to Kant's famous *Religion*. But recommendation is not absent. The very repre-sentative nature of Kant, which means that he can enfold the other En-lightenment (and post-Enlightenment) attempts to conjugate the rela-tion between faith and reason, implies some judgment of relative merit. This, plausibly, involves a critical assessment concerning relative com-prehensiveness of treatment and intellectual penetration, as well as clarity concerning the eschatological horizon (48) for the operation of critical or reflective reason (52–53). Even if this were to be sustained— and any straight-up comparison of *Religion* with Voltaire's *Philosophi-cal Dictionary* and Locke's *Reasonableness* might vindicate Derridian judgments—the fact is that the criteria are fairly generic. What more particular help does Derrida's text provide with respect to Kantian ad-vantage in parsing the relation between faith and reason? The short answer is the concept of "auto-immunization" (50–51). What Kant's critical negotiation with religion effects, in a way that the other forms do not, in sorting out what is admissible from what is inadmissible in religion is the immunization of critical discourse from criticism. Only this form of critical reason is sufficiently generous to grant something substantial to faith. It is this very generosity that allows a colonization that cannot be successfully executed within Voltaire's form of Enlight-enment reason precisely because in Voltaire reason is so obviously hos-tile to religion and so given to opportunistic condemnation; such a colo-nization is unlikely also within a Lockean scheme, which tends to grant to religion only the advantage of a push-start to what reason can essen-tially procure on its own. It is the hermeneutic generosity of the Kantian scheme that at once makes it unimpeachable and undefeatable. Even if it takes away more than it gives, and in a sense it takes away everything, critical discourse has outmaneuvered criticism (actual and potential) by constructing it as not only irrational and nonsensical, but also as inherently ungrateful.

This is what is confirming in "Faith and Knowledge" of the analysis of Kant I prosecuted under the rubrics of architectonics, symbolics, and dynamics, and especially the last. But in this complex essay, which is much more than a meditation on Kant, Derrida takes a step beyond and shows a way to broaden the lines of investigation. He does so under the auspices of globalization, that is, a reflection on how this temporally (eighteenth-century) and geographically (Europe) bounded parsing of the faith-reason relation plays in the contemporary world, which, because of communications and technology, is a vast interconnected web of relations. Either singly or in concert with other Enlightenment examples, and often implicated with the European history of its subsequent (dis)qualification, the Kantian view of critical reason is a machine of repetition which repeats its outbidding not only of Christian faith, but also any kind of faith, religious or otherwise. For its supporters this form of critical reason is just the opposite to hostility to forms of faith, and imputed to it is the benevolence of desiring faith to be all that it can be. They cannot comprehend how it can be read as hegemonic, and how, despite its rhetoric of tolerance, it can be perceived as violent (88). Critical reason is read as being without liabilities, as if the constructions of the barbarians were not at the very least a by-product of its operation, as if from the beginning Judaism and Islam were not both illegitimate (45, 52–53): systemically so in that they are both religions of the law, which, on Kantian principles, is the other to a pure moral religion that is embedded in Christianity, and historically so, since the one (Judaism) did not have the decency to cease once it was surpassed by Christianity, and the other (Islam) had the indecency to arrive and challenge its inexpugnable prerogatives.[57] For Derrida, critical reason is tied after all to Christianity, however Christianity gets worked over, and the strangeness of its beliefs and practices, and especially of its sacred text, gets reduced to the absolute minimum. The upshot is globlatinization, that is, the dynamic movement whereby a culturally and religiously specific Western discourse (Latin) works on or over other strangenesses in the interests of a reason that is justified as well as useful and tolerant. The messianism of this form of reason is only too apparent to Derrida.

Intimations with respect to how the operation of critical reason excites a messianic counterreaction are an important weave in Derrida's intricate text, and such intimations intrinsically merit discussion. For present purposes, however, it is more important to point out that "religion within the bounds of reason alone" has no apparent end, even if it has a beginning (although this is not routinely confessed). It reproduces itself and essentially has no borders. It affects all discourses that it comes in contact with and, depending on point of view, infects them. As it does so, its supporters (European and North American) presume that some losses in the erstwhile religious, ethnic, and social fabric of non-European cultures will be sustained, and equally presume that they are bearable.[58] For Derrida, the ongoing colonization is every bit as stipulative as it was in Kant's time, while now being more linked to instrumental reason and its communicative and technological products. It is also in a real sense out of control, and thus in a sense a monster. This monster has incredible regenerative powers, but it also creates other monsters, the monsters of reaction and fear, who believe in another kind of apocalypse.

Notes

1. Page numbers of *The Critique of Pure Reason* refer to the Norman Kemp Smith edition (London: Macmillan, 1968).

2. Kant's deep debt to German Pietism of the second half of the eighteenth century is well known and has been competently discussed, especially in the German literature. While it is not Kant's habit—as it is Hegel's—explicitly to align himself with particular forms of thought, he does refer to Pietism on more than one occasion throughout his work. One of the most conspicuous, as well as most relevant, pieces of evidence of Kant's acquaintance is to be found in book 1 of *Der Streit der Fakultäten* (1798), in which he speaks approvingly—albeit at a critical distance—of the major players, Spener, Frank, and Zinzendorf. See *The Conflict of the Faculties* in *Immanuel Kant: Religion and Rational Theology,* trans. Allen W. Wood and George di Giovanni (Cambridge: Cambridge University Press, 1996), 235–327, esp. 277–81.

3. The classical expression of Derrida's view of the supplement is to be found in *Of Grammatology,* trans. Gayatri Chakrovorty Spivak (Baltimore: Johns Hopkins University Press, 1976).

4. Supplemented by other of Kant's ethical works, such as *The Ground-work of the Metaphysics of Morals.*

5. The German title is *Die Religion innerhalb der Grenzen der blossen Vernunft.* A new translation by George di Giovanni can be found in Immanuel Kant, *Religion and Rational Theology,* vol. 6 of *The Cambridge Edition of the Works of Immanuel Kant,* trans. and ed. Allen W. Wood and George di Giovanni (New York: Cambridge University Press, 1996), 41–215.

6. Gordon E. Michalson Jr. and Michel Despland are but two of the Kant commentators who advance this position. See Michalson, *Fallen Freedom: Kant on Radical Evil and Moral Regeneration* (Cambridge: Cambridge University Press, 1990); Despland, *Kant on History* (Montréal and London: Queen's University Press, 1973).

7. Of course, it is possible to think, with Lyotard and others, that Kant very much anticipates Hegel in this respect, and that the *Critique of Judgment* not only demonstrates the power of thought to account for both our assumptions about and critical evaluation of fine art as well as our responses to the grandness of nature, but also requires a complexification of the model of knowing presented in the first *Critique.*

8. For a more extended reflection, see Paul Reading, *Hegel's Hermeneutic* (Ithaca: Cornell University Press, 1996), 35–49. See also Cyril O'Regan, "Hegel and the Folds of Discourse," in *International Philosophical Quarterly* 29, no. 2 (June 1999): 173–93. There I make the argument that Hegel very much extends the hermeneutic potency of Kant.

9. Of course, they mark Judaism even more. Kant begins a figuration that will be continued by Hegel, that is, that Catholicism is Judaism in Christian guise.

10. This point, however, is more explicit in *Conflict* than it is in *Religion.* See *Conflict,* 270.

11. The original German title was *Traüme eines Geistessehens, erläutert durch Traüme der Metaphysik.* For a convenient recent translation, see *Dreams of a Spirit Seer and Other Writings,* trans. Gregory R. Johnson and Glenn Alexander Magee (Philadelphia: Swendenborg Foundation, 2002), 1–63, notes pp. 156–82.

12. In *Spirit Seer* (SS) Kant is aware of the relation between Swendenborg and Friedrich Christoph Oetinger (1702–1782), who is a speculative Pietist with an enormous knowledge of the esoteric traditions, including Jacob Boehme (1575–1624) and various forms of the Kabbalah, which he puts in play to critique the rationalism of Spinoza and Leibniz. It was Oetinger who saw into publication a number of Swendenborg's works in the 1760s, which action incurred the wrath of some of the more conservative theological authorities. As with Swendenborg, Oetinger is known to favor and to practice an allegorical mode of biblical interpretation. Already in *Spirit Seer,* which predates

Religion and *Conflict* by about thirty years, Kant shows his disapproval of this hermeneutic style (53). By contrast, the hermeneutics of Johann Albrecht Bengel (1687–1752) shows a tendency towards a prophetic literalization in which the interest becomes the chiliastic one of predicting the end. Of course, Bengel's favorite text was Revelation, which traditionally had attracted just this kind of interpretation. In *Conflict* (282–83) it is perfectly clear that Kant is familiar with Bengel's view, and he paraphrases Bengel's *Ordine Temporum* (*The Order of Time*) (1741). Although Kant's famous essay "The End of All Things" (1794) represents a rebuttal of another enthusiast, that is, Lavater—also a target in *Spirit Seer*—it can be understood to be another shot at prophetic interpretation of Revelation, which not only illegitimately claims knowledge of the divine plan, but is divisive. On the most general level Kant tends to see the allegorical and the prophetic-literalistic interpretation as two sides of the same deficient coin.

13. The Kant text is *Von einem neuerdings erhobenen vornehmen Ton in der Philosophie.* For a convenient translation by John P. Leavey Jr. see *Raising the Tone of Philosophy: Late Essays by Immanuel Kant, Transformative Critique by Jacques Derrida,* ed. Peter Fenves (Baltimore: Johns Hopkins University Press, 1993), 51–72. Derrida's riff on this Kant text goes under the title of "On the Newly Arisen Apocalyptic Tone in Philosophy." This essay, translated by John P. Leavey Jr., can be found in *Raising the Tone of Philosophy,* 117–73.

14. See G. W. F. Hegel, *Faith and Knowledge,* trans. Walter Cerf and H. S. Harris (Albany: State University of New York Press, 1977). In this text Hegel criticizes Jacobi and Fichte as well as Kant. For his specific criticisms of Kant, see 67–96.

15. Kant also castigates them as "enthusiastic visionaries" (*schärmische Visionen*). See *Raising the Tone of Philosophy,* 117.

16. Di Giovanni, the new translator of *Die Religion innerhalb der Grenzen der blossen Vernunft,* makes it a point to translate *Grenzen* by "boundary" rather than "limit" in order to bring out the spatial or geographical root of the term as a border between two regions or states. See *Religion and Rational Theology,* 53.

17. Here I am thinking in particular of Derrida's powerful exposure of the "religious" thought of Hegel in *Glas* (1974). See the English translation by John P. Leavey Jr. and Richard Rand (Lincoln and London: University of Nebraska Press, 1990). In that text Derrida is exercised by the powerful logic of exclusion in Hegel's religious and political writings, beginning with the essay "The Spirit of Christianity and Its Fate" (1799), in G. W. F. Hegel, *Early Theological Writings,* trans. T. M. Knox (Philadelphia: University of Pennsylvania Press, 1971), 182–301. This logic engenders, or is constituted by, the binary oppositions of presence and absence, the ethical and the nonethical, the holy and the nonholy, man and woman, Christian and Jew.

18. It should be pointed out that one of these contexts is ethical or moral. *Adiaphoros* was a term used by Stoic philosophers to point to a phenomenon as being ethically or morally indifferent.

19. Marcion was a second-century Christian thinker who recommended that the Christian canon should not include any of the texts of Hebrew scripture on the theological ground that the actions of the God of Hebrew scripture indicate that this God more nearly corresponds to the "Prince of the World" than to the transcendent good God of Jesus Christ. Of course, the excision of Hebrew scriptures led to pruning of the New Testament texts as well, since the New Testament incessantly recalls the Hebrew Bible and recapitulates its themes, especially the theme of law. Obviously, compared with the historical Marcion's rejection of Judaism, Kant's is less biblically based and has more to do with what he takes to be the essential characteristics of Judaism and Christianity. Still, Kant's biblical hermeneutic at the very least tends to confirm his prejudices against the very notion of divine commands and the one who would so command. To think of Hegel's early "theological" writings as being essentially in line with the posture adopted by Kant is largely unproblematic, given the influence of *Religion* on Hegel early on. It is only after 1800 that Hegel familiarizes himself with the first two *Critiques.* This is not to say, however, that there is no movement between 1795 and 1799. Hegel does, indeed, begin to strike out in a more historical direction. Ironically, as he does so, he begins to take more seriously, as Kant did, the biblical narrative, thus making the later text, "The Spirit of Christianity and Its Fate," both more and less Kantian than the prior one, "The Positivity of the Christian Religion," in *Early Theological Writings,* ed. Knox, 67–181. Certainly, Judaism and its alienation-inducing deformation continues to be excoriated, and the God of command is replaced by the Johannine God of Love. When one reads in the *Phenomenology* (1807) the sections on "unhappy consciousness" in part 1 and the account of Judaism in part 2, as well as the way that the biblical narrative is a narrative of a divine who refuses to sanction heteronomy (sec. 7), then one is entitled to assume that Hegel's Marcionite commitment is chronic.

20. Goethe's recoil is evident in the following statement: "Kant, who spent a whole lifetime clearing his philosophical mantle from all kinds of prejudice which soiled it, has now ignominiously dirtied it again with the shameful spot of radical evil, so that Christians too can feel they ought to kiss the hem of it" (quoted in Despland, *Kant on History,* 169).

21. It is most especially the Augustinian traducianist view of original sin that Kant rejects, that is, that the original fault of Adam is communicated in the semen because of the concupiscence that is at the root of the sexual act in the fallen state. Paul Ricoeur especially hails Kant's move beyond Augustine in this respect. See Ricoeur's essay, "The Hermeneutics of Symbols and Philosophical Reflection: 1," in *The Conflict of Interpretations,* ed. Don Ihde (Evanston, IL:

Northwestern University Press, 1974), 287–314, esp. 304–9. There Ricoeur argues that in his expostulation on "radical evil" Kant completes Augustine's thought, but does so by correcting for Augustine's own relapse into Gnostic or Manichaean mythology by speaking of sin under the auspices of the biologism of transmission. See also Ricoeur's highly critical essay on Augustine, "'Original Sin': A Study in Meaning," in *Conflict of Interpretations,* 269–86.

22. For an English translation of *Die menschliche Freiheit,* see *On Human Freedom,* trans. James Gutman (Chicago: Open Court, 1936). For an accurate and comprehensive account of the relation of Schelling to Jacob Boehme, see Robert F. Brown, *The Later Schelling: The Influence of Boehme on the Work of 1809–1815* (Lewisburg, PA: Bucknell University Press, 1977). Although the language of the text has rightly been traced back to Boehme, this does not mean that it is entirely inappropriate to think of Schelling's emphasis on "primordial will" as radicalizing Kant's notion of *Willkür.*

23. Ernst Cassirer quite rightly emphasizes this relation in his *Kant's Life and Thought,* trans. James Haden with an introduction by Stephan Körner (New Haven: Yale University Press, 1981), 86–90, 235–36. This connection is highlighted even more in Cassirer's *Rousseau, Kant, and Goethe* (New York: Harper, 1962).

24. It is not only in bk. 4 of *Religion* that Kant's commitment to the history of salvation is in play, but also in his essays on eschatology, as well as his reflections on history. See "The End of All Things," in Wood and di Giovanni, *Religion and Rational Theology,* 221–31.

25. Hegel's move beyond the Kantian view of morality was fairly quick. By the time of his essay "The Spirit of Christianity and Its Fate" (1799), Hegel thought the subject of history and moral judgment to be corporate rather than individual. Thereafter *Sittlichkeit,* or community and that which holds it together, maintains critical leverage on *Moralität.* This is true of Hegel's 1802/1803 lectures on the subject, his discussion of *Sittlichkeit* in the section on reason in the *Phenomenology.* Neither the *Encyclopedia* nor *Philosophy of Right* rescinds this preference, which paradoxically is prepared for in *Religion,* which opens up not only a historical but a corporate vista.

26. Kant's embargo does include the primarily unphilosophical way of assuming the extra-mental existence of the world. Compared with Husserl, however, Kant more nearly targets the philosophical tradition, whereas Husserl is more concerned with the unphilosophical stance towards the world that he calls the "natural attitude."

27. See Despland, *Kant on History*; Martin Heidegger, *Kant and the Problem of Metaphysics,* trans. James S. Churchill (Bloomington: Indiana University Press, 1968).

28. That there is something of a circle here is undoubtedly true. However, since *Being and Time,* we have become accustomed to asking the question whether a circle is vicious or an illustration of a hermeneutic circle. This back-

and-forth of antecedent and consequent, and specifically between affirming that biblical symbols and narrative make knowledge possible and insisting that only reason makes biblical symbols and narrative intelligible, provides a classic instance of the hermeneutical circle. The modern religious thinker whose interpretive operation is closest to that of Kant is probably Ricoeur.

29. Kant makes a big distinction between origin "according to principle" and origin "according to time." As applied to the fall into sin, this distinction means that the biblical text, in representing the fall as the adoption of an evil maxim, cannot help but represent it also as a temporal event. Kant thinks that an adequate interpretation of the biblical text will tend to correct for the "temporal" or "historical" suggestion that the narrative genre cannot help making. The "temporal" and "historical" senses of Scripture are examples of adiaphora.

30. I do not mean to suggest that these two points are totally separate from each other. Kant's embeddedness in biblical culture is a function of his relation to Pietism, which was centrally concerned with moving beyond the dogma of justification of faith to consider the prospects of sanctification, the living of a holy life. Although not unanticipated, the generative figure was Philipp Jacob Spener (1635–1705). His major text was *Pia Desideria,* which was published in 1675. For particular passages on sanctification, which goes under the alias of "new birth," see *Pia Desideria,* trans. Theodore G. Tappert (Philadelphia: Fortress Press, 1964), 46–47, 50, 55, 64–65, 95, 104, 116–17. At the same time, the practical dimension of Pietism was to the fore, since the transformation issued in modes of behavior that signified regeneration. Technically speaking, this was called the *praxis pietatis.* Ironically, the most lucid discussion of this joining of elements in Pietism is to be found in a book on Hegel rather than Kant. See Laurence Dickey, *Hegel: Religion, Economics, and the Politics of Spirit, 1770–1807* (Cambridge: Cambridge University Press, 1987), 65–80.

31. This would have been popular in the illuminist and apocalyptic circles, the circles, respectively, of Oetinger and Bengel.

32. This figure is central in the *Phenomenology,* and one could argue that it guides all the "journey" and "narrative" motifs in Hegel's texts, which suggest a wandering that results in a coming home, an erring that finds a definitive correction. Much of Lévinas's critique of Hegel in *Totality and Infinity* is prosecuted in and through an analysis of the invidious implications of this particular figure.

33. See especially Derrida's discussion of *pharmakon* in *Dissemination,* in his interpretation of the word in Plato's *Phaedrus* (*Dissemination,* trans. Barbara Johnson [Chicago: University of Chicago Press, 1981], 96–97, 127).

34. Here I am thinking of *Nathan the Wise* (*Nathan der Weise*) (1779), in which Lessing essentially equalizes the three religions by reducing them to the ethical essence. Here Lessing remains faithful to the position that gets expressed in the Reimarus fragments (1774), which in turn is fairly continuous with the position of Spinoza as elaborated in the *Tractatus Theologico-Politicus.*

35. Kant was fully aware of Mendelssohn's project (classically expressed in *Jerusalem*) of squaring Torah with reason, but did not think either that Mendelssohn had succeeded in fact, or that he could ever succeed in such a venture.

36. Hegel makes the connection as early as the essay "The Positivity of the Christian Religion" (1795).

37. Schleiermacher's *On Religion,* which articulated a religion based on "feeling," was published in 1799, six years after the publication of Kant's *Religion.* Kant had before him Herder, Jacobi, and Hamann as very different kinds of examples.

38. Postcolonial theory in the wake of Edward Said has drawn attention to this feature of a hegemonic discourse.

39. This is a general feature of the *oecumene.* On a smaller scale we can think of the same phenomenon being in operation in the short-lived Greek empire.

40. Kant shows evidence of this knowledge throughout *Religion,* constantly calling attention to accounts of the behaviors of North American Indians and accounts of the behavior of groups on the Pacific islands. Of course, with Herder, Kant made a significant contribution to the emerging science of anthropology, and could be classed as a competitor. See John H. Zammito's substantial *Kant, Herder, and the Birth of Anthropology* (Chicago: University of Chicago Press, 2002), esp. ch. 7, pp. 258–307. It should be remembered that when Kant offered his definitive rendition of his anthropology in 1798, he had been studying and teaching this topic for over twenty-five years. See *Anthropology from a Pragmatic Point of View,* trans. Robert B. Louden, with an introduction by Manfred Kuehn (Cambridge: Cambridge University Press, 2006).

41. This is brought out gloriously by J. M. Coetzee's powerful novel, *Waiting for the Barbarians* (New York: Penguin, 1982).

42. My point here is not that Kant will argue that any particular group of people are, precisely as human, inferior to another. Kant is sufficiently a universalist not to give much comfort to the racist. Still, Kant has a strong view of what constitutes "civilized" human being, and this encourages hierarchies, which, though not ontological, are in any event extreme.

43. This, in any event, is the kind of question that Lévinas would address to Kant, this despite the close relation between their thought which prioritizes the ethical. This Lévinasian question is directed at *Religion* and *Conflict* by Hent de Vries in *Religion and Violence: Philosophical Perspectives from Kant to Derrida* (Baltimore: Johns Hopkins University Press, 2001).

44. Stoics, of course, did have cosmological, even metaphysical, commitments that centered on reason being a principle of the world (at once immanent in it and transcendent to it), yet these were subordinate to the ethical as a form of life.

45. Stoic philosophers such as Seneca and Cicero, who are cited by Kant, essentially hold this view. So also does Varro, with whom Augustine engages in dialogue in *The City of God.*

46. It is an important question whether what might be called Kant's "hermeneutic revolution" is in excess of his "Copernican Revolution" or simply one facet of it. This essay postpones discussion of this issue.

47. Karl Barth, *Protestant Thought from Rousseau to Ritschl* (New York: Clarion, 1969), 150–96.

48. See especially *Nine Talmudic Readings,* trans. and ed. Annette Aronowicz (Bloomington: Indiana University Press, 1994). See in particular Aronowicz's fine introduction, ix–xxxix.

49. See *Otherwise Than Being or Beyond Essence,* trans. Alphonso Lingis (The Hague: Martinus Nijhoff, 1981). "Substitution" is the subject of ch. 4 of the text. "Prophecy," "witness," "inspiration," and "glory" are fundamental categories of ch. 5.

50. Of course, Lévinas's idea of "first philosophy" as a phenomenology that necessarily gets ethically inflected puts him at odds with Kant's transcendental interpretation, as it does with Aristotle's more realist view, which prioritizes substance.

51. See "Sauf le nom" (Post-Scriptum) and "Khora" in Jacques Derrida, *On the Name,* ed. Thomas Dutoit, trans. John P. Leavey Jr. and Ian McLeod (Stanford: Stanford University Press, 1995), 35–85, 87–127. The gist of these two essays is that *khora,* which Derrida lifts from Plato's *Timaeus* only to remove from it metaphysical connotations, whether of matter, space, or even nonbeing, is other than the "beyond being" (*epekeina tēs ousias*) of negative theology, whether of the less ecclesial (e.g., Eckhart and Angelus Silesius) or the more ecclesial type. Because of the inlay of Heidegger in both essays, and especially in "Sauf le nom," the former are to the fore. Nonetheless, the latter are implied to the extent to which self-consciously Marion's *Dieu sans l'être* is a target (62–63). For a good discussion of the relation-difference between deconstruction in general and negative theology, see John D. Caputo, *The Prayers and Tears of Jacques Derrida: Religion without Religion* (Bloomington: Indiana University Press, 1997), 1–54.

52. See Derrida, "On the Newly Arisen Apocalyptic Tone in Philosophy." See also parts 2 and 3, on apocalyptic and messianism, respectively, in Caputo, *The Prayers and Tears of Jacques Derrida,* 69–159.

53. See Jacques Derrida, "Faith and Knowledge: The Two Sources of 'Religion' and the Limits of Reason Alone," trans. Samuel Weber, in Jacques Derrida, *Acts of Religion,* ed. Gil Anidjar (New York: Routledge, 2002), 42–101. Two other essays collected in this volume represent significant encounters with the thought of Kant. The first is "Interpretations of War: Kant, the Jew, and German" (135–88), which reflects on the thought of early twentieth-century Jewish philosopher Hermann Cohen, and how Kant is introjected yet modified.

The second, "Force of Law: The 'Mystical Foundation of Authority'" (189–227), while more nearly on Walter Benjamin, also reflects in a significant way on Kant.

54. In essence, in "Faith and Knowledge" Voltaire functions as a synecdoche. Derrida is fully aware that with respect to the conjugation of faith and reason there are differences between Voltaire and Rousseau, on the one hand, and between Voltaire and the encyclopedists, on the other. Moreover, with respect to Voltaire, Derrida does not put himself under obligation to rehearse the manifold positions of this most chameleon-like of thinkers, who shifted easily between agnosticism, deism, and theism.

55. For a good edition of this famous text, see John Locke, *Writings on Religion,* ed. Victor Nuovo (Oxford: Clarendon Press, 2001), 85–210.

56. By no means do I want to suggest that Derrida has a well-worked-out position on the complexity of the Enlightenment of the sort to which Charles Taylor treats us in such copious works as *Sources of the Self* (Cambridge, MA: Harvard University Press, 1989) and *The Secular Age* (Cambridge, MA: Harvard University Press, 2007). A better template for the level of differentiation operative in "Faith and Knowledge" is provided by a work such as Ernst Cassirer's *The Philosophy of the Enlightenment,* trans. Fritz C. A. Koelln and James P. Pettegrove (Princeton: Princeton University Press, 1951), in which Cassirer is able to cast light on the distinction between the main figures of the French Enlightenment from Voltaire to the materialists, and between them and their German and English counterparts such as Kant and Locke.

57. A considerable portion of Derrida's later work has concerned the eclipse of Judaism in modern Western intellectual thought. Derrida has an interest in the fate of Judaism in Hegel and Heidegger as well as in Kant. For Hegel, see Rand and Leavey's translation of *Glas.* For Heidegger, see Jacques Derrida, *Of Spirit: Heidegger and the Question,* trans. Rachel Bowlby (Chicago: University of Chicago Press, 1989). For a text persuasive of the living power of Islam, see Derrida's "Hospitality," in *Acts of Religion,* 356–420, in which the Christian Massignon showed another nonviolent and nonproselytizing way of being Christian. See esp. 372–73. See also Gil Anidjar's comprehensive introductory essay in *Acts of Religion* on the importance of Judaism and Islam both as a matter of autobiography and increasingly a matter of intellectual and spiritual substance.

58. Presumption here is not simply presupposition, which is defensible on a pragmatic view of society, since shorthands are required for a society to function at all. Derrida's view is that such a view is full-blown ideology in that the view is more conscious than unconscious, and thus involved in the sifting of evidence which by no means confirms the presumption. And, of course, presumption thus understood is ideological from a classical Marxist perspective as well, in that the suggestion of the universality of critical reason disguises the interest of a particular group.

5 | On Knowing God through Loving Him

Beyond "Faith and Reason"

JEAN-YVES LACOSTE

I

Our vocabulary offers us two words: "faith" and "reason." And we step quickly from the existence of words to the existence of things, with the accepted theory telling us on one hand that reason has been bestowed on us and on the other that faith can be awakened in us, and that it is a matter therefore of two distinct (but complementary) modes of understanding. Let us specify. The accepted theory (which like all accepted theories is a recent theory) takes as its basis an affirmation as old as philosophy itself, and which is a philosophical affirmation: human beings are defined specifically by *logos,* called *ratio* in Latin, and accordingly, by "reason" and "rationality." In its Greek origins and as soon as it becomes Roman, moreover, rationality is unlimited. All that is given is grasped through the *logos.*[1] What appears to us, whatever its mode of appearing may be, is given to thought and gives itself for us to think it; the idea of an irrational real can no more be formed than can that of a suprarational real.[2] To be sure, Greece knows opinion, or belief, *doxa.* It also knows, at the same time, that one can "believe in," that for example Achilles can believe in Patrocles. It has, moreover, a word to designate the ensemble of the knowable: *phusis,* in Latin *natura,* which must not be identified too quickly with what we call "nature." In this way, two important questions are never posed: that of an act of understanding in which we exceed our definition as "rational animal" and, as its corollary, that of an object of understanding that exceeds the field of *phusis.* However, these questions are posed when, in the Christian world, knowledge of God and knowledge of divine things present themselves as exceeding the limits of reason.

Precisely what can reason do? A leap of almost eighteen centuries, from the origins of Christianity to the *Religion within the Limits of Reason Alone,* shows us that according to the self-definition of reason, its access to God and to divine things is as narrow as possible: a "religion of pure reason" can at most postulate the existence of God and the immortality of the soul, and pose transcendentally the existence of the community of those who thus believe. And if we move then from Kant to the First Vatican Council, here again reason, enriched by its "natural light," can do no more than affirm the existence of God and the immortality of the human soul. In the meantime, certainly prepared for a long time, there appears in the work of Scheeben an entity such as the "supernature" (French *surnature,* German *Übernatur*).[3] For the unity of the Greek cosmos there will thus have been substituted a theory of two worlds—the world of reason and the world of faith—and a frontier will have been traced. On one hand, there is the "reason" by which we know that God exists, and on the other hand there is the "faith" by which we know God is Trinity; on one hand the "reason" by which we know God as accessible, and on the other the "faith" by which we know God as supremely accessible in Jesus of Nazareth; and so on. From the origin of the theory to its latest forms no one would ever say that faith is without reason. It exceeds reason, and in this excess it does not cease to possess the character of knowledge, of *gnōsis.* All the same, here and there and in a manner increasingly forceful as "faith" and "reason" are inclined toward strict opposition, the two words tend to designate two distinct faculties, until it is affirmed to us, at the end of a long history, that "Faith and reason are like two wings on which the human spirit rises to the contemplation of truth."[4]

The line that we have just cited from Pope John Paul II's encyclical *Fides et ratio* is ambiguous. On one hand, it affirms that one (faith) is not without the other (reason). But on the other hand, it also affirms that one is not the other, and that we are thus capable of both. Domain of the "rational," domain of the "believable": the two are found neatly delimited. And one will recall that throughout the nineteenth century the bishops of Rome did not cease to fight against theories that permit the domain of the solely believable to encroach upon that of the solely rational (fideism) and against those that permit the domain of the solely rational to encroach on that of the solely believable (rationalism). These polemics are not dead, as is born out by the clarifications that the editor of *Fides et ratio* has considered it his duty to repeat. From the fact that they are not dead, can one then conclude that they are more than a survivor? We may advance some doubts.

1. The first doubt bears on the linguistic destiny by which the Greek *phusis* becomes the Latin *natura* and which presides at the birth of the concept of "natural knowledge." The concept is at once positive and negative. It is positive, for instance, in the text of Vatican I, when it is a matter of saying that we *can* know God "by the light of natural reason."[5] However, it is also negative inasmuch as the God thus knowable is and is only that of theism. Two worlds are thus knowable: the "natural" world, over which reigns an absolute creator whose invisibility is revealed by the visible; and the "supernatural" world, to which only faith has access, and by a strict change of order. Now, is this "theory of two worlds" essential to theology? It has incontestably become essential to it. To be more precise, it has become essential when theological Aristotelianism, and with it an autonomization of the "natural," was able to produce a strict theory of natural knowledge—of a knowledge that is not theological and that is philosophical. There is place for a natural knowledge of God when there is place for natural knowledge *tout court,* and when all continuity is broken between *pistis* and *gnōsis,* or *gnōsis* and *pistis.*

2. There is a posterity of theological Aristotelianism, unrecognized by itself as such, to be found in "rationalism," exemplarily in that of the Enlightenment: from "natural knowledge" to "pure reason," the step is easily taken. For however little one refuses to step from "reason" to "faith," still, the idea of a strictly "reasonable" faith will soon appear. The idea is far from foolish. "Natural knowledge" and "pure reason": we are there in the domain of what wishes to be sure and certain for us, always

and everywhere, and which need not be willed in order to be known. Nature and knowledge fascinate because their truth is available to us. The "confession of the philosopher" such as Leibniz has penned[6] does not pretend to take the place of the confession of the theologian. But already in Kant and elsewhere before him, on the other hand, the pretense is indeed made, as if the appearance of the idea of the "supernatural"[7] was destined to end by annulling the existence of the supernatural.

3. It is not by chance that the most vigorous thinkers of the first half of the nineteenth century encroach without scruple on the frontier of "reason" and "faith," or simply ignore its presumed existence. There is certainly place in Hegel for a concept of faith,[8] but the intelligence of faith ceases to be theological work in order to become philosophical mission. What passes as the privilege of theology, apprehending God in his revelation, is in Schelling a philosophical task (and a task he achieves in such a way that philosophy never lets appear the necessity of a theology of the revealed God distinct from a philosophy of revelation). And in Kierkegaard, who assuredly refuses to call himself either philosopher or theologian, the distinction between the philosophical and the theological disappears purely and simply at the heart of a "thought" that thinks both faith and reason, and refuses to think either without the other. Thus nothing remains of the gap established between the rational and the believable, or between the solely rational and the solely believable. And if it is little certain that Hegel and Schelling, or even Kierkegaard, have fallen under the influence of Augustine, they are incontestably witnesses of a rationality that skirts the opposition of the natural and the supernatural in favor of a vision of humanity free from any "theory of two worlds." Benefiting from a sensible certainty and enjoying absolute knowledge, to adopt a Hegelian example, are not the same thing. But the dialectical discontinuities between them do not rest on any caesura.

II

The first truths in the history of philosophy seem to resolve one problem, but mask the permanence of another one. It is incontestable that the God of Hegel is imposed on reason as a Trinitarian God. It is incontestable that the Schellingian project of a "positive" philosophy signifies that everything that has come—and it is as having come that God is manifest as Trinity—gives itself to thought *ipso facto.* And it is incontestable, finally, that if Kierkegaard knows a properly dramatic passage (a "leap") between the kingdom of the nonreligious and the kingdom of the religious, he is capable of labeling "fragments" that speak only of Christology, salvation, and faith as "philosophical." Now is it certain that God is given to thought purely and simply in the measure in which he says, "I AM," rather than in the measure to which thought says who he is? If God appears, is this only for a consciousness in an act of intelligence? We are entitled to some doubt.

1. Here Kierkegaard furnishes us with the surest Ariadne's thread. The God who "appears" in the *Fragments*—one who is present to us without giving us more than an index or two of his identity[9]—does not appear in order to be thought or described. God does not appear in order to be described because there is nothing to be described other than a man like other men. And God does not appear in order to be thought because the sole aim of the appearing is to be loved by us. To appear in order to be loved and for this alone, however, requires that God be present in a kenotic mode: God must be loved but not dazzle. There is appearance, for there is presence in the flesh. Yet, and this is the important point, there is not appearance for thought or for belief. The God of the *Fragments* is not present for us to believe that he is present. God is also not present, *a fortiori,* in order for that presence to become the object of philosophical or theological thought. The sole *logos* to which Kierkegaard appeals is that of love.

2. The thesis of an appearing for love, appearing in order to arouse love, in the final account to be recognized by consciousness only in an act of love, thus leads us back to a major problem of phenomenology. The problem is that of the "lovable." That there are lovable realities, no one will doubt. That there are furthermore realities that appear as such only to those of us who love them, almost no one will doubt: a prelude by Bach or the charity of Vincent de Paul is perceptible as such only if it is an object of our love. We perceive things, and we also perceive "values." Intersubjective understanding occurs without difficulty when it is a matter of things that we see or perceive (the "we" is easily constituted),

but occurs with greater difficulty when it is a matter of what we feel. The architecture of a prelude by Bach can displease. Vincent de Paul's charity seems to elicit unanimity, yet nothing guarantees that we all belong necessarily to the community of those who recognize it. A conclusion is therefore inevitable: whether aesthetic or moral, or otherwise, value is proposed and not imposed. And if, by simple definition, what we love belongs to the domain of values, it is necessary to say that love comes to light in proposing itself and not in imposing itself (the entire problematic of Kierkegaard's kenotic Christology is that of a God who refuses to constrain us to love him).

3. Must we then say that only those who love truly know? The thesis has been defended by Scheler,[10] who on this point follows some impulses coming from Augustine and Pascal, and whom Heidegger cites without reservation.[11] It calls for some parsing. On one hand the thesis outlines a general logic of relations between loving and knowing, while on the other hand it speaks of a strongly specific relation between us and him who is proposed to our love. Let us take particular interest in this second point. Only love, if we follow Kierkegaard, breaks through the incognito of the God who is present as servant. Now if this is the case, love does not follow from faith—as if we first recognize the God who is present in the flesh and then find that God lovable—but is instead purely and simply simultaneous with faith. We do not possess immemorial knowledge of God. We seem to have forgotten the occasion on which we have understood God's name, and have pronounced it, for the first time. "One" has spoken to us of god as one transmits information, but without the words having permitted God to be revealed to us. But how, regardless of how God has been spoken of to us, and regardless of the texts thus coming into use, is it possible that God appears to us as such, in flesh and blood? It is clear what our response must be: it is on the condition of perceiving a lovability that we shall perceive accurately at all. This response needs to be further articulated.

Common sense tells us that we first perceive and then love. This is not completely wrong. Were there nothing to perceive, there could be nothing to love. What then is there to perceive? On this point, Kierkegaard is right, and Balthasar has borrowed from him more than he admits: there is nothing to perceive except love.[12] The thesis is not merely rhetorical. One must make the acquaintance of Peter in order to then love him, and it is in loving him that one comes to fully know him. However, what holds for Peter does not hold for God, and in the latter case the idea of a knowledge that precedes love would be quite strange. To be sure, Peter merits being loved, and on more than one account, but he is powerless to excite that love. In God, by contrast, we are powerless to discern anything but a pure act of love, more fundamental than any pure act of being. Love can assuredly be misunderstood (can go unperceived), just as we can fail to perceive a prelude of Bach or a painting by Malevich as such. We can also interest ourselves in God without a care in the world for loving God: this is the case, for example, with the god of onto-theology, a god that is not interesting in itself. But it is in a single and same act that divine love, if it is recognized as such, is recognized and loved. To admit it, if one is willing to admit it, carries us far: it is to avow that faith and love are co-originary, and that one cannot organize a theology of faith that is not also, in the double sense of the genitive, a theory of the love *of* God. The conceptuality is awkward because the debt of Aquinas to Aristotle is on this point awkward, but one will not be wrong to say that love is the "form" of faith. Not only is no faith worthy of the name somehow prior to love, but also no faith worthy of the name can content itself with being solely an act of faith. Catholic devotion has known and still knows an "act of faith" notable (among other sins) for being neither an act of love nor an act of hope, as if it could be either dissociated from them or independent of them.[13] At what price could we affirm that we know an Absolute who is not only content to reveal itself in love, but which has only love to reveal, since there is in it an identity of loving and being? The question dictates our response: if there is credibility, it must be under the form of lovability.

III

Phenomenological precision must be imposed. God appears diversely. God has appeared (*in illo tempore*) and speaks today in the Scriptures which have the value of Word, and if it is necessary to speak of lovability then it is also necessary to say that God appears in giving himself to feeling. It would be wise not to imagine the life of the believer as a perpetual act of love responding to a perpetual act of manifestation. "Loving" is here to be understood as a disposition more (frequently) than as an occurrence. From the fact that the Absolute is manifest (from the fact that it has manifested itself), we need not conclude that it remains in the act of manifestation: John of the Cross will always remind us, opportunely, that the final word of God has been pronounced, and that we should not expect any others.

Now the multiplicity of appearances does not forbid us from, but in fact requires us to, inquire after the phenomenality proper to what gives itself to love and faith. We have already made two statements concerning this. Things appear to us in imposing themselves on us: I cannot not see the ashtray sitting on my desk, and this "I" easily transforms into a "we," since the perception of the ashtray, provided I am seated at my desk, has the character of the inevitable, just as it would have for anyone else who might be seated in my place. However, it requires little description in order to assure ourselves that nothing is given to love and faith, together, without proposing itself rather than imposing itself. It is probably beliefs that are imposed on us (and this is in fact the case with the majority of our beliefs). I hear a ring at the door and believe that it is Peter, because I expect a visit from him. I believe that it is raining, having heard a sound like rainfall but without casting a glance out my window. I believe that a theory is correct because the scientific community supports it almost unanimously, though I do not have any other means to "justify" my belief. And to this list, we could now add an embarrassing case: I may believe that there is a God because I belong to a community that shares this belief. However, the "credible" does not always impose itself on us. I do not want to believe that it is raining, but a glance out my window constrains me to believe that it is indeed so. But if what is given to faith is intelligible only in giving itself to love, then the appearance takes the form of solicitation or invitation, and not at all that of constraint. Love has its reasons, whether it is a matter of the reasons of the love that God shows to us or of the reasons that bring us to respond to this love with our own love. In any case, love, when it makes its appearance, would contradict its own essence or theme if it exercised constraint. If God appeared in his glory, Kierkegaard thus teaches, he could not be loved authentically, for love wants equality. His incognito, to be sure, is not absolute—it is proposed to us to love "the thing unknown"[14]—but the extravagance of the expression cannot conceal from us that, even on Lutheran terrain, something like a minimal motif of credibility is necessarily maintained. It remains essential—and Kierkegaard is not the only one to have seen it—that it would be contrary to love for it to appear violently.

Phenomenality of the believable, phenomenality of love: the two are theologically one and one only. What is proposed for belief, we have already said, is nothing other than divine love. Because this proposal comes by way of mediations—mediation of Scripture, mediation of affective experience—it is possible for us to not perceive it as what it properly is. A theology that would forge the divine identity of love and being (or the divine subordination of being to love; it matters little which) would run the risk of repressing this proposal. Where human love is proposed, it is possible for us to be mistaken or, if one prefers, see nothing (the other person is simply present, leaving us free to feel his presence as that of someone worthy of being loved), or see something else (the other person is simply present, but we are not interested in him *as* a someone who invites us to love but instead, for example, as an intelligence that we admire or an elegance that we envy, etc.). And where it is a matter of the divine love that proposes itself to us, we can also be mistaken: we can "criticize" the Gospels, dissociating the incontestable love of a man, Jesus, who has disappeared leaving only traces, from the divine love of a God in whom we do not believe. It is, in other words, possible for us to not perceive the ample divine movement which, from alpha to omega, rules only by a logic of love; we can interest ourselves in the letter of the texts without knowing that "everything that does not lead to charity is figurative."[15] Because it is proposed without constraint, love perpetually courts the risk of failure (*de l'chec*).

IV

The failure is of a single piece with the failure of faith. What would it mean to believe without loving? The reduction of faith (faith-in) to a belief, itself diffracted from a series of beliefs in propositions, would certainly permit the advent of an "I believe" dissociable from every "I love." However, the propositional theory of revelation is dead, or should be. And if on one hand the act of faith does not open on statements but on things,[16] and if on the other hand those things reduce to a single one—the revelation of divine love—then the idea of a faith independent of all love and all hope is without any legitimacy. Well then, if the destiny of love and the destiny of faith are bound together, one must take another step and suggest that if the lovable proposes itself without imposing itself, it is equally proper of the believable that it appears with the same discretion.

Reason is exercised through concepts, and the work of concepts aims at constraint. Here the "I" is present only accidentally. If "I am right" in the strong sense of the term, then we must all agree with "my" reasoning. All must do so, we emphasize, for in this case we are not called upon to exercise the least act of freedom. We must certainly think freedom in order to understand for ourselves what it is to not exercise even the least act of freedom, and we cannot enter into agreement with what is supposed to impose itself in the name of reason. Yet if it is therefore to an ideal image of the work of the concept that we always appeal, and to an image that perpetually contradicts our philosophical disagreements, we do not for all of that have to renounce the idea of a real that imposes itself independently of any exercise of freedom or acquiescence. The pen lying on my desk imposes itself on my perception. The conclusion of a logical demonstration likewise imposes itself on us (however little we might accept the logic to which one has recourse in this case). And no work of pure rationality can tell us that it is forbidden to put pressure on us, and that we are free to give to it or withhold from it our assent. A single criterion imposes itself: self-evidence. This has been defined as "experience of the truth."[17] And the definition must be rendered with due precision: the truth is not experienced in freedom, but imposes itself on us. How is it then with the believable, which is to say the theologically believable? That it does not impose itself on us is too obvious for it to be necessary that we insist on it. Under certain conditions, I necessarily believe that it is raining: certain conditions put pressure on me, and my freedom and will are bracketed. When, however, I believe that in a man present in history God himself has been present, no constraining reason can govern that belief. The history of apologetics and of theology has surely been one of a surplus of reasons. Pre-understandings, expectations, indexes, and so forth have all made it such that Kierkegaard's "thing unknown" is well and truly knowable and that this knowableness is not irrational. Nonetheless, the reasons on which this knowableness rests properly solicit without obliging. To appear as believable, to appear for faith and faith alone (provisionally, we leave between parentheses the fact that just an appearing is for faith and love indissociably), is thus to appear for freedom, and to place what appears at the mercy of freedom.

In this way, a fundamental mode of phenomenality presents itself for elucidation. To accept belief is to experience a truth: it is thus necessary to speak of self-evidence. Now evidence is there only for those who give their assent to what is proposed as believable. The agreement therefore confers the evidence, and it is necessary to say that the latter was previously absent. There certainly was credibility, perceived intuitively or manifest by force of reason. But where there was credibility, the truth, once again, occurs only in proposing itself to us: it will be only obvious to us that we ought to ratify this proposition. Evidence is thus the daughter of such a ratification.

Phenomenality of the lovable, phenomenality of the believable: the two are but one, at least theologically, and without inflicting the least brutality on philosophical reason. We have already stated the reasons: the *credendum* is nothing other than divine love; the site of faith is the human love that responds to this divine love; credibility and lovability cannot put pressure on us as does the splendor of a work of art. It is possible—and more than that, certainly probable—that phenomenology has traditionally granted a position of force to phenomena whose appearing imposes itself on us, to the visible, to propositions rich with meaning, to everything the reality of which cannot pass unperceived. Now if there is a singular property of the believable and the lovable, it is that believability and lovability can pass unperceived. The incognito of God cannot be absolutely pierced, and the indexes of his identity cannot be deciphered. What we cannot recognize except according to an act of love can be treated in an "everyday" mode, whether in remaining at the surface of what we see or (according to an example from Kierkegaard[18]) in treating it as what it is not (strictly philological approach to the Scriptures). To the Kierkegaardian concept of the paradox, it can thus be useful to respond by proposing that of a "paradoxical phenomenality," of an appearing that undoes all the common laws of phenomenality. Such a phenomenality is paradoxical because we will be incapable of receiving it as what it is if we reserve for it the same reception that we give to every phenomenon that does not appeal to our freedom. It is paradoxical because it cannot be perceived if a decision to see does not preside at the perception. And it is paradoxical because everything that we cannot perceive independently of such a decision to see — to believe — conceals itself from us. There is no lack of reasons to believe. We can even form a concept of "believableness" or "credibility" in order to indicate the moment when the decision to believe is imposed on us as the only morally legitimate decision. At the beginning, however, is a real that proposes itself without imposing itself and which is experienced in the element of nonevidence.

What we have just asserted does not hold only for the theological. Of the other man, too, it would be legitimate to say that we do not know him if we do not love him. The work of art does not appear to us as such if we do not allow ourselves to be moved by it — and we are capable of seeing it as only an object among other objects. Understanding and affection are partly linked. There is no going back over what we cannot let pass unperceived (exemplarily, all that sensation presents to us). But would not the richest phenomena be those that do not impose themselves on us, and that, if they give themselves in order to affect us, do so from more than the simple fact that they are objects of perception? A work of art can seduce us in the moment in which we perceive it, and even if we are distracted then by a memory, we do not cease to know that it has moved us, thus that we have loved it, and that these past occurrences authorize a certain prediction: when the work reappears, it will be able to move us anew. And yet the present of appearing can be that of a perception devoid of emotion. The other person, rather than appearing as someone I truly encounter, can be someone I am content to pass by and who will remain for me faceless. We may add an example. A scientific theory — mathematical, physical — can serve me as only an instrument of calculation or prediction. It is possible for it to appear to me only in the mode of utility. And if this is the case, I perceive neither the elegance nor the simplicity of the equations, nor the intelligence that has presided over the choice of axioms; in short, I certainly can acquire an understanding of the theory, but only superficially, and it is clear that the theory, reduced to its instrumentality, cannot move me as does a work of art, which it, in its own right, also is.

This last example is important for us, for enabling us to see that not only does (aesthetical) feeling include an act of understanding, but the work of understanding may be necessary for the genesis of emotion. Only the good mathematician will perceive the elegance of the theory and treat it with the respect that one owes the work of art, and good mathematicians are rare. Rare too are those who emote the moment their eye falls on a pictorial style with which they are not familiar: those who do not know painting more recent than that of the Impressionists would have to be taught to see in order to perceive the beauty (we cannot speak of elegance . . .) of a canvas of Malevich or Mondrian. Here the distinction between feeling (French: *sentir*) and work of reason strikes against an obstacle. What is more rational—a successful formalization—gives itself completely to feeling. In order to feel such a work of art, one must first learn to see in order to then learn to feel, and the apprenticeship of the gaze must be as rational as possible and must therefore appeal to what imposes itself purely and simply to every gaze. Several points are thus brought to our problem.

1. The first is that it would be erroneous to think that "faith" breaks with the modes of being and understanding that precede it. The Catholic tradition affirms that God can "with certainty be known with the help of natural reason,"[19] and a hyperbolic text issuing from the same tradition goes so far as to use the language of demonstration.[20] These texts have the wisdom of taking up the language of the possible, and refuse recourse to any itemized account of knowledge or demonstration. They must still be taken seriously: God does not belong to theology. There is more. The name of God has a theological history, and one can never place it at the end of the history—there where God appears only as love and in order to be loved—without knowing that it is by this history, and this history alone, that he can be recognized as the Absolute present in the form of the servant. Kierkegaard, whose theology of the incarnation

makes no use of the ancient covenant, is thus constrained to speak of a god that we neither expect nor foresee. Now, human beings have well and truly spoken of God, and have done so with sufficient precision before he was manifest definitively. And it can be useful to recall that Clement of Alexandria, of all theologians the most attached to noting that there can be no final word without a first word and a penultimate word, admitted the existence of three testaments — the old, the philosophical, and the new — and placed almost on equal footing religious preparation and rational preparation for recognition of the God who is present in Jesus Christ.[21] A faith that precedes rationality, a rationality that precedes faith: in both cases, understanding arrives in the element of a continuity as strong as any discontinuity.

2. An idol is thus in need of destroying, namely the Pascalian opposition of the "God of Abraham, God of Isaac, God of Jacob" and the "God of the Philosophers and sages." It is indeed an idol, for the opposition is not content to be a venerable relic but finds itself so well venerated that it is canonical. But the opposition is false, and its cult harmful. It will be noted first of all that it is without object, if one is willing to interpret the texts of those — Hegel, Schelling, Kierkegaard — who ignore the existence of a frontier between philosophical reason and theological reason. There is more, and as excessive as it may seem, the position of Clement of Alexandria is perfectly rigorous on the matter. Clement does not say that philosophy "comprehends" God, but that it prepares us to comprehend him, or more precisely to understand him. In the same way, he says that the Jewish Bible genuinely teaches us to know God, but that this knowing is wracked by incompleteness, and that it is inseparably both knowing and nonknowing. And in contending that the same work of revelation began in the alliance with philosophy and in the alliance with Israel, he forces us to admit that the first word belongs neither to a faith preceding "the" faith nor to a pure reason that would precede pure faith: in order to believe in him who comes in the form of a servant, one must either have already believed, or have already proceeded to a rational affirmation of God. Both of these are in fact forms of expectation and precomprehension.

3. Preliminary work of reason, preliminary work of faith — we can co-enumerate them and assign them a same function only on one con-

dition: the rational/philosophical affirmation of God must be interpreted as a response to a manifestation that God no longer has the power to impose on us. The Vatican I text to which we have already referred states that God is always accessible, everywhere and to everyone: anyone engaged with visible things "can" acquire (a certain) knowledge of God.[22] All the same, this possibility—that of a "knowledge" and not a "demonstration"—is not tied in the text to any constraint, but rather takes on the appearance of a task, a task that is proposed explicitly only after the Absolute has revealed itself and pronounced its final word. Should we say that our commerce with the created imposes on us that we acquire knowledge of God, or that such knowledge is proposed to us? The second alternative is best. Not only are philosophers few in number, but there are still fewer among them who know with certainty the existence of God and can utilize "God" without using the word mistakenly. Yet the philosopher is only a philosopher, and if one can define the "sages," with Heidegger, as "die im Verstehen lebenden,"[23] the philosopher must therefore be defined as the one who wishes or would love to live in the act of knowing—and to whom it is not guaranteed that it will be possible to avoid misunderstanding. A mathematical demonstration imposes itself on us regardless of whether certain preliminary conditions (agreement about axioms, e.g.) are satisfied, a sensory presentation imposes itself on everyone regardless of whether a preliminary condition is satisfied (as a matter of our disposition to the requirements of our sensory apparatus), but the philosopher, in contrast, proposes to us more reasons than he imposes on us. Now if there is in this instance a proposition, one can only conclude that the God of the philosophers, or of the philosophies, is offered to us as a believable God. The principal task of philosophy is not to speak of God. It nonetheless comes to speaking about God. It does so in such a manner that its words wish to constrain: the Thomistic five ways, as a brief philosophical preamble to an ample summa theologica, wish to constrain us with concepts. It remains true that we can refuse our assent to a logical proof, and can refuse it to a philosophical "proof" of the existence of God. And this means that the "God of the Philosophers and the sages" is proposed to an assent just as is the "God of Abraham, Isaac, and Jacob."

V

There is no use in concealing the aim of the foregoing developments: to erase the boundary found classically between faith and reason, and to erase it because it has existed only in an arbitrary manner.
Let us rejoin Clement of Alexandria's provocative and fertile thesis
concerning the "testamentary" character of philosophy. According to
Clement, "to believe" in the God of Abraham and to prepare oneself
philosophically for the manifestation of the God of Jesus Christ take
part in a same logic. It matters little that there is in the one here a logic
of "faith" and in the other there a logic of "reason," and it matters little
that both ways attend to the God who is manifest in Jesus Christ. What
is important first and above all is that the first major decision taken by
Christianity—the refusal of Gnostic anti-Semitism and the establishment of a strict identity between the God of Israel and the God of Jesus
Christ—here accompanies an equally important decision: the refusal
of what would eventually be the Pascalian opposition.

What is important next is that regarding the God "of the Philosophers" we cannot truly say that we "know" that he exists unless this
knowing is accompanied by free assent. Earlier, we evoked the case of
the God of Hegel, Schelling, and Kierkegaard, and it is not useless to return to it now. In Hegel, faith is destined to be absorbed into a knowledge, but it is not enough to read the *Phenomenology of Spirit* beginning
from its final section; one must still observe that no one reaches absolute knowledge without having passed through faith. The Schellingian
philosophy of revelation assigns to itself the overly modest aim of only
thinking what has taken place, but the phenomena that preoccupy this
philosophy (the manifestation of the Absolute in history) are no mere
facts among all the other facts, and interest us only because the Absolute is revealed in them.[24] And when Kierkegaard, in the *Fragments*,
proposes a conceptual schema where Christology, soteriology, and so
forth do not pretend to have any coherence other than that of logic, he
applies himself to the work of what must finally be called by its proper
name: the intelligence of faith.

No faith without rationality, none that will contest it: the believer
is an animal who speaks and who reasons, and the "credita" are likewise

"intelligibilia." No rationality without faith, and in any case none without belief; it is on this that we must insist here. That there is a place for "pure reason," no one will doubt. However, what is more important lies elsewhere, in the figures of the rationality in which the true does not evoke adherence solely because it is said, and where faith preexists itself in multiple links with reason and with belief. Is the God of "the Philosophers and the sages" a God of pure reason, thus of a reason free and clear from faith? We have already responded in the negative. We concede that God is "always greater," and that the final words of God critique as much as they confirm what we have taken the initiative to say of God. But to the degree that Clement's thesis is correct, we must then also admit that what we have taken the initiative to say philosophically of God is said within an economy of revelation, and benefits from a divine caution. The classical (?) distinction between "natural" and "supernatural," of "natural knowledge" and "supernatural knowledge" of God, thus appears highly problematic. The God "of the Philosophers and the sages" seems to be at our disposal, to be knowable by anyone who has reason and agrees to put it to use. But exactly what do we mean here by "knowing"?

One distinction is required in order to bring all affairs to a halt: that of calculation and thought. Calculation requires adhesion; as the example of Leibniz (and his posterity) shows us, philosophical reason can always dream of taking the form of calculative reasoning. But thought, to which geometrical work does not properly belong, and which collapses whenever it mistakenly thinks that such work does belong to it, is "personal" work before it is "rational" work,[25] and we cannot describe this work without noticing that it rests on beliefs without exposing them to doubt,[26] and above all without noticing that it leads to certain decisions. The phenomena that are proposed to us may be more numerous than those that are imposed on us. And if to some degree thinking always is equivalent to binding descriptions together, then we cannot do it without apprehending the phenomena in the "how" of their appearance—and thus phenomena can appear to us as offered to a free adhesion. Thought is never devoid of all decision. When it is a matter of realities that are "created" (but that we do not yet know are created!) and that allude to a "creator," it is by us, in our integrality, rationality, affection, and decision, that this allusion would be accepted. The idea of pure reason is thus destined to collapse, or at least to close itself within the narrow confines of the strictly demonstrable. There is the real whose reality is imposed on us—and Husserlian phenomenology has come to tell us that appearing is being—and there is the real of the being of which we cannot deny that it is given to us in flesh and blood. Husserlian phenomenology nonetheless does have the means to exceed itself from within, and what appears to us in proposing itself to us is perfectly thinkable there. The humanity of the other person, for example, can pass unperceived, and the situation described by Lévinas is in fact ideal (and rare): the other person, he suggests, appears to us in a manner constraining us to recognize him as another myself, and perhaps more. It is likewise possible for the work of art to not appear to us as such. And one must have already seen armchairs in order to perceive an armchair. Such examples are as innumerable as they are varied.

In any case, one point is of greatest importance: a reason emptied of freedom—an act of reason that puts out of play every act of freedom—is a possible reason (calculative reason), but the reason that applies itself to the work of thinking is a reason that integrates freedom. Calculation does not know the logic of assent except under the form of constraint. But thought does know this logic: we never truly think without deciding to take part.[27] Nothing forbids us the dream of total transparency about everything, a dream unlimited by evidence, such that it would have only to "see" and would have nothing to decide. But here and now, in a world that is not governed by our dreams, perfect self-evidence is rare. It is perfectly evident that an ashtray sits on my desk and that $2 + 2 = 4$ (assuming that we know what it is we speak of, and what our words mean). However, it is not certain that the visible owes its being to a first and invisible cause. And even if we will have done our best to demonstrate it, the demonstration, as distinct from one that is logico-mathematical, will not impose itself on us. Perhaps it will offer us a way to see the universe otherwise than as before, but it will nonetheless do so in the form of a proposition. It will be up to us in our freedom, then, to take a step toward saying not only that the Absolute "can" certainly be known but also that it truly "is" known thanks to such a demonstration. It is significant that no "proof" has yet been able to elicit an intersubjective agreement as clear as that which is elicited by mathematical proof. When we apply ourselves to thinking, thinking appeals together and at once to both reason and freedom.

It is therefore only superficially troubling to say that faith ("supernatural") preexists in "natural" knowledge of God, and that we do not venture into the territory of the latter without being fitted with a freedom to accept it. "Natural reason," "supernatural reason": the continuity is more remarkable than any discontinuity (and we will always have the right to ask what justifies the discontinuity). To be sure, the latter does exist. The knowledge said to be "of faith" perceives the Absolute in the past of a history, and today in the sole measure where this history gives form to the present—whereas the knowledge called "natural" perceives the Absolute in a present that is sufficient unto itself (i.e., the present of causality, of finality, of the dialectics of action, and of still other presents). What is perceived now requires our assent: it is useless to come back on this point. But does it require assent more, adhering now to a phenomenological interpretation, than what appears to us from the past? It certainly requires it *differently.* On one hand is what appears in the element of presence, on the other hand is what appears in the element of memory. Their evident difference in manner of appearing cannot, however, obscure the fact that in both cases it is not to the "impartial spectator" of Husserl's middle works[28] that there is appearance—and that if we were to allow such an impartial spectator to occupy the terrain in question all credibility would necessarily escape that terrain. The phenomena that preoccupy us here cannot in fact be recognized as such by an "impartial" gaze. They appear without us, but they require our assent in order to reach intelligibility. Reason is "pure," or in any case works in the richest mode, only when allied with the freedom of assent. And it is of such a reason, and not of that which rests exclusively on a calculus of concepts, that one speaks when inquiring after "natural" knowledge of the Absolute. This is likewise the case when faith comes into play. The revealed Absolute gives itself to be known. And if what it gives—texts and other traces—differs from what is given to "natural" knowledge, still it gives them freely to the coupling of reason and free assent. There is no "faith" without "reason," and rare is the "reason" with which freedom does not collaborate.

Self-involvement, commitment: the locus of election for such acts is the experience called "religious," and not the "supernatural" act of faith. We have nonetheless said more about this than Ian Ramsey, when we extended the field of "religious" experience to that of the rational affirmation of God. This was not in order to deprive the latter of its rationality and to submit it to the arbitrariness of our decisions, but instead to circumscribe a phenomenal field in which rationality appeals to freedom. Rejoining an earlier example, let us recall that for those who are familiar only with figurative painting, an entire work of reason (an entire apprenticeship of perception) is necessary in order for an abstract painting to appear as such. But this apprenticeship cannot guarantee certain access. Perhaps we will never perceive a work by Malevich as what it is. Perhaps, likewise, the *causa sui* or "first cause," or the "absolute idea," will appear to us only as a thinkable entity but never as a believable entity. Nothing could be more common than perceiving or understanding without taking part: the perception of an ashtray on my desk does not require me to take part, nor does the conclusion of a logical argument (again, assuming that we grant—or "stick to"—the logic at the interior of which the argument itself unfolds). But when the Absolute intervenes, taking part is necessary. God does not appear to us as the Alps appear to us, like a great object the existence of which would impose itself on us. And God does not appear to us at the end of a constraining argument like the one that constrains us to admit that Socrates is mortal if he is a man and all men are mortal. God appears to us, on the contrary, as that in whose favors we can take part, or not.

VI

Thus is opened an entire region of experience in which perception, in the largest sense of the word, is insufficient to generate assent but only makes it possible. In this region of experience it is not certain that we must distinguish brutally (with the brutality that distinguishes "natural" and "supernatural") the assent that we grant to a first cause and that which we grant to the identity, in God, of being and love. Even the God of Aristotle moves in being the object of a desire in which one may see a modality of love[29] (though this desire—and the specification is not unimportant—is provoked *necessarily* by the desirable). And if we bear in mind that the God of the philosophers is the God if the *philo*sophers, then we also keep in view the bond between knowing and loving, and thus also knowing and taking part. When it is a matter of affirming the existence of God, it is inevitably a matter of affirming freely. Freedom certainly does not contradict rationality: we do not lack reasons for saying that "God" has a sense and a reference (though we do not agree on these reasons, and we content ourselves with affirming that access to them is not prohibited). But these reasons call upon more than "pure reason." We can imagine being endowed with reason but not with freedom (why not?). Yet we do not inhabit such a world in which reason would thus reign, but instead the real world in which rationality and freedom are at some times dissociable and at others not. We thus can never praise *possibility* enough. Everything is opposed to the reasoning that would render *necessary* the affirmation of God. Whether it is in the so-called natural order or the so-called supernatural order, God is given to be known and given to be loved, and we never respond to love with love *by necessity*. In order to *be able to* grant our assent to the existence of God, we *must* decide freely and take part.

Do we rest, "fundamentally," on our "reason" or on our "faith"? Is the assent that we offer to God the work of "reason" or of "faith"? At the end of the route that we have just covered it must become clear that we cannot have an answer. We perceive intuitively that a "demonstration" of the existence of God or an apologetic argument in favor of the truth of Christianity does not constrain us as does a mathematical demonstration. We can as well perceive that our assent to God is not a work of possible reason that is accompanied by interest and self-involvement—which is a cautious way of saying that we do not accomplish a work of reason without loving to do so. It does not belong strictly to theology to perceive in the how of its appearing a phenomenon that solicits faith and love; the problem is not exclusively theological, but embraces problems belonging to philosophy and to theology. There is an experience of truth ("evidence") outside of any solicitation addressed to our freedom. We can "feel" that this is true at the same time that we "see" that it is true, but without our freedom coming into play: it is enough that we accept what is such as it is. But things are wholly otherwise when we occupy the interval of reason and faith. Fideism has thus been partly justified: here no conceptual constraint will suffice. But rationalism has also been partly justified: there is no clear boundary between the reasons that we invoke in favor of a First Cause and the reasons that we invoke in favor of an Absolute that is the "play of love with itself."[30] To theological reflection, nothing prevents us from saying that the God of the philosophers is not an available God but a God who is given to knowledge, and in a manner quite different than the God of Abraham is given to knowledge, but who is nonetheless given in both instances at the heart of a single and comprehensive economy of disclosure. And to philosophical reflection, nothing prevents us from saying that a divine manifestation which enters into history does not call for assent any more than does a manifestation that is given always, everywhere, and to everyone (even if the logic of its assent is different). Paradoxically, the God of the "Philosophers and sages" requires belief and even love. Rational affirmation of God's existence includes an act of faith and an act of love.

By way of conclusion, we call attention to a recent text already invoked here, and to the translation in which it is inscribed. The papal encyclical *Fides et ratio,* bearing the signature of John Paul II, is a vigorous plea in favor of truth in a double sense: God as supreme truth, and truth as the milieu in which reason moves. At the same time, the text also invests its own title with the incipit that we have already cited: "Faith and reason are like two wings on which the human spirit rises to the contemplation of truth." From a text that opens in this manner, one will not expect to have one's suspicion aroused as to its problematic. Here is *fides,* there is *ratio,* the two are two, both are indispensable, and with the author we may turn to Aquinas for clarification of their relation: according to Aquinas, "faith supposes and perfects reason,"[31] which the author considers to parallel the classical affirmation by which "grace supposes nature and bears it towards its fulfillment."[32] There is nothing new in this. And if one next inquires about the possible copresence of an act of love and an act of faith, or of an essential relation between credibility and lovability, one finds oneself again in familiar territory: love of God (subjective genitive) is evidently there,[33] the human love of truth and wisdom is also evidently there,[34] and human love of God—how could it be otherwise?—is equally a part of it.[35] Now, all of that said, it remains the case that the relation of knowledge and love is scarcely present in the text,[36] and even then only in a rather ornamental manner. Can one address the relation of faith and reason without saying that God is present indissociably in *ratio* and in *caritas?* Whoever expresses love of the truth also certainly expresses implicit love of God. When, however, it comes to God, this implicit presence carries no weight in the text. And we must recognize that in the encyclical God is given to understanding without being given indissociably to love. The reason for this is probably found in the definition of God as first truth, and first truth which is not the other side of first love. The text, in short, does not fail to appear unsatisfying. And in these pages we have done nothing other than propose a redistribution of roles and a redefinition of boundaries that might prevent a slip back into a pattern whose sole advantage consists in being classical.

Notes

1. It is only later, and under Eastern influences, that Neoplatonism loses its Greek confidence in reason and in speech, and remains in silence before the scene. See R. Mortley, *From Word to Silence,* 2 vols. (Bonn: P. Hanstein Verlag, 1986).

2. It is nonetheless necessary to cite a classical text, E. R. Dodds, *The Greek and the Irrational* (Berkeley: University of California Press, 1951).

3. M. J. Scheeben, *Natur und Gnade* (Mainz: Kirchheim, 1861). A man of only twenty-six may be excused for having promoted a reification as monstrous as this.

4. John Paul II, *Fides et ratio* (Vatican City, 1998), incipit.

5. *Enchiridion symbolorum et definitionum, quae de rebus fidei et morum a Conciliis oecumenicis et summis pontificibus emanarunt* (hereafter DS), ed. H. Denzinger (Freiburg: Herder, 1955), 3026.

6. Leibniz, *Confessio Philosophi* (New Haven: Yale University Press, 2004).

7. The word appears in Latin in the translation of the letters of Isidore de Peluse (d. 431) and in the Latin text of Pseudo-Dionysius. It receives its classical conceptual weight in Thomas Aquinas. See *De veritate,* q. 12, a. 7; *Summa theologiae* 2-1, qq. 109–14.

8. See A. Léonard, *La foi chez Hegel* (Paris: Desclée de Brouwer, 1970).

9. Translator's note: Tisseau's French translation employs "indice," which I retain here. The English term chosen by Hong and Hong is "hint." Kierkegaard's Danish invokes a God who "lets something of himself be known" (*Philosophical Fragments,* in *Søren Kierkegaards Skrifter* [hereafter SKS] [Copenhagen: Gads Forlag, 1997], 4:258).

10. See M. Scheler, "Liebe und Erkenntnis," in *Gesammelte Schriften,* vol. 6 (Bonn: Bouvier Verlag, 1986), 77–98; idem, "Ordo amoris," in *Schriften aus dem Nachlass,* vol. 1, *Zur Ethik und Erkenntnistheorie* (Berne: Francke Verlag, 1971), 345–76.

11. M. Heidegger, *Sein und Zeit,* sec. 29, p. 139, n. 3.

12. H. U. von Balthasar, *Glaubhaft ist nur Liebe* (Einsiedeln: Johannes Verlag, 1963).

13. Let us recall the embarrassing formulations of the "act of faith": "My God, I firmly believe all the truths that have been revealed and that teach us through your holy Church, for you could neither fail nor cause us to fail."

14. Kierkegaard, *Philosophical Fragments,* SKS 4:244.

15. Pascal, *Pensées,* ed. J. Chevalier (Paris: Gallimard/Bibliothèque de la Pléiade, 1939), no. 583.

16. Thomas Aquinas, *Summa theologiae* 2-1, q. 1, a. 2 ad 2.

17. E. Husserl, *Logische Untersuchungen* (The Hague: Martinus Nijhoff, 1975), 1:190; 3:122.

18. See, e.g., Kierkegaard, *Concluding Unscientific Postscript,* SKS 7:31–40.

19. Vatican I, DS 3026. We specify that "cognocere" does not mean "to know x" in the existential sense, but only "to know that x exists."

20. Cf. Oath against Modernism, DS 3538 ("certo cognosci, adeoque demonstrari etiam posse . . .").

21. See Clement of Alexandria *Stromates* 6.8, 6.67.

22. Vatican I, DS 3026.

23. M. Heidegger, *Gesamtausgabe* (Frankfurt: Vittorio Klostermann, 2005), 62:32 (translating *hoi sophoi*).

24. To this could be added the theory of revelation developed by W. Pannenberg (in Pannenberg et al., *Offenbarung als Geschichte* [Göttingen: Vandenhoeck & Ruprecht, 1961], 91–114), according to which divine revelation consists in historical events that are visible to "those who have eyes to see." All faith would thus appear evacuated in favor of immediate access to knowledge. But this rings false. The eyes that can see are, according to Pannenberg, eyes able to see what happens in a certain world—that of later Judaism. He who sees thus sees with eyes that have been prepared to see. There is no "New" Testament without an "Old" Testament. "Seeing" is thus included within a "believing."

25. See M. Polanyi, *Personal Knowledge* (Chicago: University of Chicago Press, 1958). On the interest of Polanyi's work for the entire theory of the relation between "faith" and "reason," see T. F. Torrance, ed., *Belief in Science and*

in Christian Life: The Relevance of Michael Polanyi's Thought for Christian Faith and Life (Edinburgh: Handsel Press, 1980).

26. Hence is the "life-world" in some of Husserl's texts a belief world (i.e., from a "basis in originary belief"). And likewise, when the concept of the reduction makes its appearance, the world of the "natural attitude" is the object of believing. See E. Husserl, *Ideas,* bk. 1, *Husserliana* 3, 1, secs. 27–30.

27. The argument proposed by I. Ramsey in *Religious Language: An Empirical Placing of Religious Sentences* (London: SCM Press, 1957) makes this point perfectly: the logic of religious language (but of other languages as well), and in fact the logic of religious *experience,* is that of situations in which an act of "discernment" is indissociable from an act of "commitment."

28. See, e.g., the 1922–1923 course *Einleitung in die Philosophie,* in *Husserliana* 35, sec. 16.

29. Aristotle *Metaphysics* 1172b—not to forget, however, that Aristotle's God is perhaps "loved," yet does not itself love anything but itself (nor to forget, for that matter, that "self-thinking thought" is living and pleasurable, and enjoys itself but without explicitly loving itself).

30. G. W. F. Hegel, *Phänomenologie des Geistes,* ed. J. Hoffmeister (Hamburg: Felix Meiner, 1952), 20.

31. John Paul II, *Fides et ratio,* sec. 43.

32. Aquinas, *Summa theologiae* 1, q. 1, a. 8 ad 2.

33. John Paul II, *Fides et ratio,* incipit; secs. 7, 10, 13, 15, 18, 23, 93, 107.

34. Ibid., sec. 2, note 1; secs. 3, 6, 16, 38, 44.

35. Ibid., sec. 32, concerning the love of God that is manifest in the martyr.

36. See ibid., incipit: "in order to know and to love"; sec. 42, paraphrasing Anselm: "The intellect must seek that which it loves: the more it loves, the more it desires to know. Whoever lives for the truth is reaching for a form of knowledge which is fired more and more with love for what it knows. . . ."; sec. 107: "call to know and love God." Most noteworthy in all of this: that "knowing" and "loving" appear here as two distinct operations concerning which nothing guarantees that they are indissociable—and that the text itself in fact treats them as dissociable.

6 | Phenomenality and Christianity

KEVIN HART

I begin by considering three propositions, each of which sum-
marizes a complex position: (1) there cannot be a phenomenology of
Christianity; (2) there can be a phenomenology of Christianity; and
(3) Christianity is already a phenomenology. I shall discuss them one at
a time in the order given.

The first proposition makes a significant concession to objections
leveled against the phenomenology of religion as developed in the first
half of the twentieth century. For it speaks of Christianity, not religion,
thereby admitting that religion is too diverse a field to have an *eidos* that
can be discerned and varied imaginatively. An entire literature by and
centered on Mircea Eliade is therefore put to one side. Even so, the proposition remains combative. We might wonder about the status of Martin
Heidegger's course "Augustine and Neo-Platonism" (1921), his notes for
"The Philosophical Foundations of Medieval Mysticism" (1918–1919),
and his lectures "The Problem of Sin in Luther" (1924) and "Phenomenology and Theology" (1927), the last of which argues that theology's
proper object is faith, not God.[1] These, surely, are evidence of very early
interest in the phenomenology of Christianity and, more obliquely, evidence of the relations between phenomenology and theology, and they
can be bolstered by pointing to Max Scheler's *On the Eternal in Man*

(1921), Otto Gründler's *Elemente zu einer Religionsphilosophie auf phä-nomenologischer Grundlage* (1922), Kurt Stavenhagen's *Absolute Stellung-nahme* (1925), and Jean Hering's *Phénoménologie et philosophie religieuse* (1926).[2] Other works that do not circle around Edmund Husserl, even at a distance, could readily be cited, for the phenomenology of religion precedes phenomenology as classically proposed in the *Logical Inves-tigations* (1900–1901), *The Idea of Phenomenology* (1907), and *Ideas* 1 (1913).[3] Works of concrete or reconstructive phenomenology are not of immediate interest here, my concern being with essential phenome-nology in its various forms, extensions, and revisions.[4]

Against proposition (1) one might say that there is nothing in the philosophy of disclosure, as conceived and endlessly refined by Hus-serl, to prevent core Christian practices and experiences from being re-duced to pure phenomena. Robert Sokolowski considers the modes of disclosure in the Eucharist, for example, without any special pleading as to procedure or vocabulary; and, from another perspective, Jean-Yves Lacoste does the same, although for him liturgical life, life before God, is essentially marked by nonexperience rather than experience.[5] Our life with God is not characterized by presence but by absence, by our openness to God rather than by any feeling of His closeness, he thinks. Yet absence has its own modes of phenomenality, that is, the manners of self-showing, the angles of coming forward, of the structure of ap-pearance; and these modes are recognized and registered and may be analyzed.[6] How someone or something is absent is not always the same. Not all phenomenologists have placed their emphases as Lacoste has done, however. Paul Ricoeur offers a phenomenology of confession, and then—braiding hermeneutics and phenomenology—attends to the sacred and scriptural testimony.[7] And in a still more mediated manner, sometimes at the very edge of phenomenology, Jean-Louis Chrétien de-scribes prayer and the dynamic of divine call and human response.[8] Yet when one attempts to bring God directly into the field of study, a diffi-culty arises, one seen less as a problem than as a stark impossibility. Husserl identifies it in paragraph 58 of *Ideas* 1 with the pithy heading "The Transcendency, God, Excluded."[9] Only those transcendent entities that can be led back to pure consciousness can be objects of study, and God's self-revelation, it is said, "in its very essence is, and remains, concealed."[10] For Husserl, even if God is immanent in consciousness, he is there in a manner other than as a mental process, and so cannot be a part of phenomenological investigation. To seek the "absolute monad" requires us to go along other paths to which phenomenology can perhaps lead us but which Husserl did not finally discern.[11] If Christianity is figured by way of faith, ritual, and encounters with the holy, then it can be submitted to intentional analysis. But if it requires a necessary reference to the God of Jesus of Nazareth, and therefore involves an appeal to religious transcendence, there can be no phenomenology of Christianity, for the Christian God is irreducible.

The second proposition contests the conclusion drawn by advocates of the first. There can be a phenomenology of Christianity, despite its commitment to the irreducibility of God, if one speaks of the self-revelation of God. This would require one not to limit the scope of phenomena to those appearances that are poor in intuition (numbers but not, presumably, theorems of any richness) or that are common objects of science. The plausibility of (1) fades when one discharges the Leibnizian and Kantian metaphysics on which Husserl relies in assigning a deficit or adequacy of intuition to phenomena.[12] If all phenomena are construed as fully able to give themselves, the gauge for phenomenality will no longer be set exclusively in terms of the objectness of objects. The realm of phenomena is broader than the realm of objects, even ideal objects: values and numbers are phenomena, for example, and anticipation and memory have distinct modes of phenomenality. Often enough, meaning consumes phenomenality (as in numbers, shopping lists, and short memos, and as in encounters with simple objects); the structure of appearance is exclusively epistemic. It need not be so: sometimes phenomenality is the stark absence of meaning (as in "the dark night of the soul"), while sometimes it is the sharpness of feeling (with or without meaning), and sometimes again it is a gap between experience and meaning, which, when other human beings are involved, might be anguished or might be merely puzzling. The phenomenality of touching a person is not the same as the phenomenality of remembering that touch (which in turn is not the same when one sees a photograph of the person and when one recalls an image of her), and is not the same as the phenomenality of anticipating touching her again. God, being infinite, is not a phenomenon, although Scripture refers to phenomenalizations of Him, such as the burning bush. The phenomenality of God when one reads St. Thomas's "five ways" is not the same light as shines when one prays to God in the silence of one's room, and prayer is not always practiced in the same mode: most often it is an opening, an exposure, to phenomenality of one sort (infinite love) and a being pierced by phenomenality of another sort (disappointment, boredom, remorse). When one looks at the ragged beauty of a waterfall in a wilderness and allows God to come to mind, the phenomenality at issue then is not the same as when one reads the parable of the prodigal son; much less is it the same as "seeing" Christ before you, as St. Teresa of Ávila testifies once happened to her.[13]

Heidegger was aware of the range of phenomenality, which I have barely begun to indicate, when he observed, with Aristotle's *Physics* in mind, that modernity was a style of thinking that reduces beings to objects and then allows "the being of beings to be exhausted in the objectivity of the object."[14] Husserl's late essay "The Origin of Geometry" (1936) would be a good example.[15] Heidegger was aware of the general point also in his 1921 classes on the first letter to the Thessalonians when he read St. Paul as being concerned not with the "what" of faith but with its "how." How do the new converts relate to Paul? That is one of the apostle's concerns (1 Thess. 2:8). Another, more fundamental apprehension is how one is to live. "Before God" is the answer. But *how?* Only in factical life experience, in the body, here and now, Heidegger says with and for Paul, "in much affliction, with joy of the Holy Ghost" (1 Thess. 1:6 KJV). It is the phenomenality of the joy of new life in Christ that is important to the converts, and also (though Heidegger does not dwell on this) the anticipation of their possible martyrdom: they live with a double phenomenality of joy and affliction. The New Testament, as the young Heidegger saw, can be read phenomenologically because it is already posing the phenomenological question, "How?" and is doing so without being exclusively oriented to the objectness of objects.

Jean-Luc Marion seeks to go further than Heidegger in freeing phenomenality from both objectness and being. Or, rather, Marion seeks to retrace Heidegger's initial interest in givenness, appearing as early as the War Emergency Seminar of 1919 and being strongly evident in *Being and Time* (1927), and to bring out its significance as a mode of phenomenality.[16] A third reduction, precipitated by the *Stimmung* of deep boredom and set in motion by the pure call, leads us beyond objects and being, he argues, to sheer givenness, and can be captured in the maxim "So much reduction, so much givenness."[17] If it is reduction that yields givenness, it is givenness that determines phenomenality, here glossed as the right and power of the phenomenon (or, better, a profile of the phenomenon) "to show *itself* on its own terms" to someone.[18] Like Hegel, Husserl must be made to stand on his feet rather than his head: the primacy of intuition with respect to intentionality must be affirmed. One part of this reorientation is acknowledging the importance of reverse intentionality, pioneered by Lévinas, and another part is a rethinking of the "subject," perhaps along the lines drawn by Marion, so that the "I" is now the one called, the witness, the receiver, the clerk, *l'adonné*, the passive screen on which phenomena crash.[19] Phenomena give themselves to *l'adonné* before they show themselves, exceeding both intention and concept. Some we cannot foresee, others dazzle us, do not depend on a horizon, or cannot be looked at. Revelation is a saturated phenomenon to the second degree: in Christ we find all four types of saturation.[20]

Notwithstanding charges to the contrary, most notably as voiced by Jacques Derrida and Dominique Janicaud, Marion does not contend that givenness is to be figured as a divine gift.[21] His argument turns on the evident phenomenality of Christianity, the fact that it has shown itself in the world, that a call has been phenomenalized in the responses of believers, although of course not everything a believer takes to be central to the faith can be shown.[22] "God," as Marion uses the word in *Étant donné*, even in contexts that seem profoundly Christian, remains chiefly a philosophical term. There can be no disclosure of the Trinitarian life of the Deity, for example.[23] So Marion respects the borderline that runs between philosophy and theology, however disjointed it may sometimes be, and regards phenomenology as the philosophy that survives the end of metaphysics. Accordingly, he rebuts Janicaud's charge that he has illegitimately introduced theological assumptions into his analyses. "*Here,* I am not broaching Revelation in its theological pretension to the truth," he says, for that is "something faith alone can dare to do. I am outlining it as a possibility—in fact the ultimate possibility, the paradox of paradoxes—of phenomenality, such that it is carried out in a possible saturated phenomenon."[24]

Christian revelation, for Marion, can be described, even though it might not belong to positive history or might have slipped beneath it.[25] Transcendent with respect to experience, revelation nevertheless manifests itself in experience but beyond or before any transcendental conditions that might be adduced for it.[26] The formulation is made precise only years later. Revelation is not to be accommodated by experience, either *Erlebnis* or *Erfahrung,* since our intentions are overwhelmed by what is given to us or disappointed when they cannot find correlates. We must speak, rather, of counterexperience, "the experience of what irreducibly contradicts the conditions for the experience of objects."[27] To speak of counterexperience, then, is to countenance an extension of what is taken to be the usual range of phenomenality. Accordingly, theological modernism with its reliance on experience is to be set aside, although we need not thereby find ourselves pushed into the company of antimodernists. Revelation is a possibility, Marion urges, not a factual or a logical possibility but a being-possible, *Möglichsein,* and indeed he holds with Heidegger (and against Aristotle) that possibility in this sense is higher than actuality.[28] The claim is better understood when we see revelation in Meinongian terms: its *Sosein* (the properties something has) is independent of its *Sein* (its existential status). The very possibility that God is revealed in Jesus is meaningful in and of itself; it has an *eidos,* and is therefore open to analysis. For the theologian, though not for the philosopher, phenomenology becomes a new *preambula fidei.*

The third proposition is the least familiar, and will require more explication. It is associated with Michel Henry's later work, and it too is combative in its own way. Like Marion, Henry is pledged to describe givenness, manifestation, or revelation without any limits being placed on what counts as being given, made manifest, or revealed. Once again, givenness is taken to precede both appearing and being.[29] Unlike Marion, though, Henry finds a phenomenology already in the New Testament, one that is apparent in Christ's words about himself.[30] This is not to say, as Rudolph Bultmann once did, that the content of the New Testament

can be adequately stated without recourse to myth in the language of
Being and Time. Not at all: the gospel *itself* is an exercise in phenomenology, as are Acts, the Pauline Epistles, the Catholic Epistles, and the
Revelation to John. Does this mean that the New Testament is concerned
to study God as a phenomenon and thereby to reduce revelation to
human experience? By no means: the New Testament is not a phenomenology because it examines a particular content but because it attends
to manifestation as such (as indicated in 1 John 1:1–2, for example). To
read the New Testament well, for Henry, would mean that we attend to
the double nature of Christ's words, as human language (teaching ethics) and as the self-revelation of revelation (the farewell discourse in
John). It is only by resisting the uncritical equation of human and
worldly words that we can properly understand claims that Jesus is the
Son of God.[31] But we cannot consider the proposition that he is the
Second Person of the Trinity or that he was conscious of being so.[32]
Those claims belong to a higher level of theological speculation and ecclesial judgment. They may be true, but their truth has little or no phenomenological justification in the New Testament. What is at issue for
Henry is not a claim about Jesus that can be verified or falsified by the
historical-critical method, or any other means, but the inner truth of
the statement that Jesus is the Christ. He is close in some ways to the
Kierkegaard of "He Was Believed in the World."[33]

Henry will tell us that we have no right to distribute words such as
"appearance," "disclosure," "givenness," "manifestation," and "revelation" by way of a modern division between philosophy and theology.[34]
Phenomenology is prior to the division. Heidegger had already pointed
us in the correct direction when he redefined "phenomenology" in paragraph seven of *Being and Time*: "Thus 'phenomenology' means . . . to
let that which shows itself be seen from itself in the very way in which it
shows itself from itself" [*Phänomenologie sagt denn . . . Das was sich zeigt,
so wie es sich von ihm selbst her zeigt, von ihm selbst her sehen lassen*].[35] At
risk, then, is not a method but patience, a way of letting something—
in principle, anything that discloses itself—be seen. We become phenomenologists in order to nudge phenomena into the light, which we
do by training ourselves to see well. Yet Henry distances himself from
this definition in two ways, first by granting priority to phenomenality

over phenomenon, the "how" of self-showing over the "what," and second by indicating incommensurable ways in which phenomenality can be construed. The upshot will be something that Heidegger mused on only late in life, a phenomenology of the inapparent or, as Henry prefers, the invisible.[36] We can best see what is at issue by returning to the moment when the complexity of the relation between phenomenon and phenomenality was first acknowledged, in Husserl's remarks on the topic in his Amsterdam lectures of 1928.

"Whenever we speak of appearing," Husserl says, "we are led back to subjects to whom something appears; at the same time, however, we are also led to moments of their mental life in which an appearance takes place as the appearing of something, of that which is appearing in it."[37] He goes on to suggest, admitting that he is perhaps stretching a point in doing so, that there is an ambiguity in the very idea of phenomenality. On the one hand, it is "a characteristic that specifically belongs to appearing and to the thing that appears," while, on the other hand, "if understood in this broadened sense of the term [it would be] the fundamental characteristic of the mental" (218). Henry challenges Husserl's conception of phenomenality as a characteristic of intentional consciousness. Were Husserl correct, it would be obscure how consciousness reveals itself to itself. Either one must appeal to a higher level of consciousness than is provided by intentionality, or one must affirm another mode of revelation. The former leads to an infinite regress; the latter severs the connection between phenomenon and consciousness; and neither is defensible on Husserlian grounds.[38] Husserl's mistake, Henry maintains, is to specify all phenomenality by way of the world, itself understood as the horizon of light and time. (All the examples I have given of phenomenality would fall within the scope of Henry's criticism.) On Husserl's conception we have no choice but to begin with the phenomenon, and to elaborate an ontology of representation. Only that which can be projected from consciousness into the world can be part of this ontology, and consequently if anything other than a common object is rendered manifest, it will also withdraw into itself. My grief will be apparent in my tears, if I shed any, but my grieving as such will be invisible. Dismissing the ontological monism upon which classical phenomenology rests, Henry seeks to reconceive the discipline by taking account of the most original form of phenomenality there is, which he takes to be self-affect. On this conception, phenomenality does not externalize and dissimulate itself; its truth is not that of the world, the revelation of something to someone, but that of Life itself, the revelation of revelation.[39]

From this perspective, the New Testament becomes legible as an exercise in phenomenology, though of an unusual sort. For there is no phenomenality, no essence of truth, that discloses itself in the world, and so revelation is a massive re-veiling as well as a revealing. Instead of being subject to validation in the terms of the world—history and language—Christianity abides in another truth, one that is not grounded in a relation of adequacy with the world or its phenomena, but is a truth that reveals itself in and through itself.[40] Put philosophically, the New Testament would testify to the self-phenomenalizing of an unconditioned phenomenality. Put theologically, it would teach that there is no distance between God and what God reveals in Jesus Christ. Jesus's words, especially those about himself, would be the revelation of revelation, and to accept them would be not to flee from the world but to recognize that their message is prior to "world" as a category. God would be "without being," since "being" is co-ordinate with "world," and the invitation would be to figure God as Life. I become Christian, Henry thinks, when I accept Christ as the Word of Life, when I abandon all grounds other than that of Life, which is not a ground, and accept the life that is given to me to live in a singular manner.[41] And so a thread is pulled in the complex weave of Christianity, and several authors are suddenly bunched together: St. John the Evangelist, especially his farewell discourse; the Meister Eckhart who preaches the eternal birth of the Word in the soul; the Fichte of the *Religionslehre* (1806); and of course Henry himself.[42] We might also add Pseudo-Dionysius the Areopagite, who affirms "Life" as one of the divine names, although we would do so without verbal support from Henry.[43]

Let us return to the start and make some clarifications. "Christianity" does not mean the same thing in the three propositions with which I started. The Christianity that cannot be rendered immanent in

(1) is restricted to what is irreducible in God—his aseity and triune nature, for instance—and the same is true of (2), although there is room here for the possibility of the revelation of God in Jesus. Proposition (3) is concerned with a Christianity restricted to the New Testament, preeminently Jesus's words about himself, although a loop via the Valentinian *The Gospel of Truth* must be noted.

In the same spirit, "phenomenology" does not mean the same thing in the three propositions. If (1) is the classical understanding of the discipline, (2) and (3) inflect it in new ways. We can consider (2) and (3) as stretched phenomenologies, in the sense that a limousine can be stretched—stripped, cut in two, put back together with additional material in the middle, and then refitted for greater comfort. For Marion, the extension is done by way of broadening intuition; for Lacoste and Marion, by way of expanding the range of phenomenality; and for Henry, by extending (and restricting) what *counts* as phenomenality. Heidegger was the first to perform this operation by returning to the sixth of the *Logical Investigations* as the means by which the being of the a priori can be ascertained and phenomenology can become a fundamental ontology.

Yet Emmanuel Lévinas was the first to stretch phenomenology with religion in view, even if he uses "religion" in a Pickwickian sense, to denote a peculiar relation with the other person, a "relation without relation," which brings God to mind, and which is anterior to a system of beliefs or a life of faith.[44] Although our theme is phenomenality and Christianity, we need to pass by way of Lévinas, partly because he is the one who stretches phenomenology by the discovery of reverse intentionality and partly because he shows us what happens when we detach phenomenality from God and let it appear (if it does appear) only in the sphere of justice. This initial detour has the benefit of making us negotiate an understanding of Judaism before we encounter Christianity, for no phenomenology of Christianity can be adequate if it does not find at least some of its meanings in the horizons of Judaism. Lévinas's stretching of phenomenology begins by contesting the intellectualism of Husserl's doctrine of intentionality along Heideggerian lines and then continues by distancing itself from fundamental ontology. Our conscious life is not fully determined by mental acts that presume moments of presence or representation, as Brentano taught and Husserl continued to teach. Rather, representation finds itself positioned in horizons that have not been willed by an intentional consciousness but that have been maintaining consciousness in its naïve state.[45] Once the right of epistemology to determine the scope of all bestowals of meaning has been contested, an ethical *Sinngebung* emerges as a genuine possibility.

This immanent critique of theoretical intentionality shows that the self is already in relation with the things of the world, including other human beings. It does not specify that relation in terms of responsibility, however, or grant any priority to human beings. Lévinas wishes to do both things. If we examine his thought in its most considered form, and from a fair distance, three main, interlocking features can be seen. First, he follows Descartes in the "Third Meditation" in arguing, like others before him, that what the idea of the infinite aims at, its *ideatum,* exceeds the idea, so that the idea of infinity contains more than can be thought.[46] For Lévinas, taking a hint from Nikolai Berdyaev, the infinity at issue here is philosophical rather than religious; it is not the infinite substance that, for Descartes, defines God—"in me the notion of the infinite ... the notion of God" [*in me esse perceptionem infiniti ... hoc est Dei*], he says—but an existential structure of transcendence that can be detached from the nature of God.[47] The *ideatum* is exteriority as such, which he assimilates without argument to the human other. In *Totality and Infinity* (1961) the *ideatum* is desire for the other person, a desire without concupiscence and that can never be satisfied. Irreducible to the order of knowledge, this desire is therefore not subject to any theoretical judgment. It cannot be arrested in a relation of fusion or dialectical overcoming, but becomes the "relation without relation." In *Otherwise Than Being* (1974) the infinite abides in my preoriginal passivity; I am always and already a hostage of the other person. This leads us to the second of the three points, in which the influence of Henri Bergson can be felt.

Just as Bergson finds *la durée* to be anterior to objective time, so Lévinas determines that there is a deformalized temporality that is prior to our consciousness of time.[48] Yet where *la durée* is required for me to be free, the temporality of interest to Lévinas, that of a "deep past," ordains me to be responsible before I am admitted to a limited freedom. The subject is created by having been punctured by infinity, as we have seen, so that there arises in the subject an unlimited desire for the other person. Lévinas now construes this subjectivity of the subject by way of an original and concrete temporality. My being-for-the-other abides *en deçà,* behind intentional consciousness; it awakens that consciousness, but can never coincide with it. Lévinas calls its mode of priority the immemorial past. It is important that it is a deep past, and not a past that has been present or a moment that is or will be present. There is no time I am not already responsible for the other and no future time when I will have acquitted myself of my debt. The face of the other—Lévinas is thinking of vulnerability, not specific features—signifies the infinite that has always and already overflowed the borders of its concept, and has done so without depending on any context. I have an immediate ethical intuition of the other because the other is already in me.

Relying on Husserl's understanding of phenomenality as objectness, Lévinas will maintain that the face of the other person is "the very collapse of phenomenality";[49] and he will say this because the face is no phenomenon but is consumed in the declaration "Thou shalt not kill," which is to be pronounced in every register (do not murder me, sustain me, respect my way of being, allow me my dignity, and so on). In responding to this command, I pass from my own being to the other person who transcends me, a movement that Lévinas figures as an ascent to the good beyond being. Plato's metaphysical notion of the good—simple, nonnatural, and indefinable—is reset in the register of ethics. In being recast, the good is rendered more modest. Vasily Grossman anticipates Lévinas's sense of the good exactly in his novel *Life and Fate* (1960). There Ikonnokov, a former Tolstoyan and "holy fool," writes, "As well as this terrible Good with a capital 'G,' there is everyday human kindness. The kindness of an old woman carrying a piece of bread to a prisoner, the kindness of a soldier allowing a wounded enemy to drink from his water-flask, the kindness of youth towards age, the kindness of a peasant hiding an old Jew in his loft."[50] Here then is a good that abides in the cracks of the Good. And the third and final feature of Lévinas's thought concerns the placing of his deformalized account of temporality. It is embedded in a rich phenomenological description of my dealings with the other person. It is this description, and not any argument, that restricts Lévinas's ethics to human beings and that *de facto* excludes animals, the environment, and other candidates for moral concern.

Taking the three features together, Lévinas furnishes an "Ethics of Ethics," as Derrida puts it, an account of "the essence of the ethical relation in general."[51] So *Totality and Infinity* would judge the ethics of holding or practicing deontologism, eudaimonism, utilitarianism, virtue ethics, and all the rest. On Derrida's reading, there is no first-order moral theory that directly follows from Lévinas's reflections on being, totality, and infinity. All the same, it would seem that the proper thinking of the essence of the ethical relation disables some moral theories (eudaimonism, for example) while lending general support to others (deontologism, for instance). How we might pass from the essence of ethics to first-order moral positions is never made clear. That it is a movement from ethics to justice is plain from his granting of the claim of the third person with respect to the dyad of self and other, and it is only at this stage that phenomenality becomes an issue.[52] No theory of justice is given, however, and were one attempted, it would surely not look like John Rawls's; one does not turn to Lévinas for a defense of liberalism.[53] On the occasions when Lévinas seems, perhaps despite himself, to be offering an ethics rather than an ethics of ethics, he urges a nonformal ethics of values, not one committed to "goods and purposes" but only to the good, not one valid only a posteriori but determined by an immemorial past, and at the antipodes of hedonism. Whether Lévinas's nonformal ethics always finds justice (and not law), however, is far from certain, and it lacks any sense of proper esteem for the self, even if "self" is not taken to be primary.[54] I put the matter aside. For I wish to consider a related issue, that in securing the *eidos* of ethics Lévinas also introduces an intriguing way of doing philosophical theology.

Of course, this philosophical theology puts down roots in earlier thought. Lévinas is Cartesian with respect to the priority of the infinite over the finite, as we have seen. He is not Kantian in any of the usual ways, not being a supporter of human autonomy, the a priori, or the categorical imperative (except in his admiration for its second formulation).[55] Yet his philosophy of revelation is a relict of Kant's. Or, rather, it would be if he did not quietly use Hermann Cohen to reanimate, reset, and redirect the program of *Religion within the Limits of Reason Alone* (1793).[56] Judaism, not Christianity, becomes the exemplary moral religion, at the cost of most reasons for retaining Jewish particularity; and the generality of the moral law is rejected in favor of the subject's responsibility, each time singular, for the other person. As subject, I have meaning, before any act of the will or any claim of society at large, by being "persecuted" by the other person, or—put less dramatically— because the *ideatum* of infinity awakens me, prevents my consciousness from closing in upon itself, before I can have any rapport with another person. In the other person I do not find a truth that I can think but a trans-ascendance that never terminates, a kind of philosophical equivalent to *epektasis* as St. Gregory of Nyssa uses the word. Thus God "comes to mind" [*vient à l'idée*] in a twofold sense. I am reminded of the deity when I turn towards another person, and also, before any empirical event, God comes to mind when the *ideatum* of infinity descends into the idea of infinity.[57] This God cannot be figured as the highest being, pure subsistent being, or the being of being because he precedes all presence. Nor is this God a being in whom I can believe in the sense of assenting to various metaphysical claims about him or finding myself in a singular relationship with him outside all history and tradition. Rather, in a far more reserved way, characteristic of Jewish discretion with respect to the name of God, I am called to witness the trace of his passing by, and to find myself in that trace as moving "to-God" [*à-Dieu*] when aiding the other person instead of persisting in my own being.[58]

Such is the biblical Lord of Hosts, it will be said by some Jews, though certainly not by all. At any rate, there is reason to say that a phenomenology of the Hebrew Bible precedes a similar engagement with the New Testament. The claim would be based on a few verses— Exodus 33:19–23, Deuteronomy 10:19, 1 Samuel 3:1–10, and Isaiah 57:19, among others—to which Lévinas appeals at important moments, as well as on a wealth of Talmudic commentary. All this exegesis is grounded in the assertion that the word *God* is significant regardless of whether or not it denotes a reality; it is meaningful "even if it cuts across all phenomenality" [*même si elle tranche sur toute phénomé-*

nalité].[59] To distinguish phenomenological concreteness in religious practice from the phenomenality of revelation is a thoroughly Kantian gesture, all the more so when the religious practice goes exclusively by way of ethical action. Yet even here Lévinas is not simply Kantian, for he insists that phenomenological concreteness is subject to diachrony. We pass from the saying to the said, but the said can be unsaid. The secularism of the Kantian reformulation of religion is disturbed by the difference between testimony and manifestation at issue here.[60] We can glimpse a long history of devout study in which Torah, oral as well as written, is kept alive in an unceasing unsaying of what has been said. Thanks to diachrony, God is not subject to proof or disproof; yet the accent is placed on being a witness to God rather than believing in him in the sense of affirming various creedal statements.

Lévinas retains from Enlightenment philosophy of revelation, Fichte's as well as Kant's, the priority of possibility with respect to actuality.[61] And, following Franz Rosenzweig, he upsets the unity of being (and, with it, the unities of reason and truth). We read in Rosenzweig's *The Star of Redemption* (1920), "He who questions the totality of being, as is the case here, refutes the unity of thinking. He who does this throws the gauntlet to the whole venerable brotherhood of philosophers from Ionia to Jena."[62] The questioning of the totality of being continues in Lévinas's *Totality and Infinity* (1961) and *Otherwise Than Being* (1974). The unity of truth is not compromised in the name of actual revelation that interrupts the world, as it is for Rosenzweig, but in the testimony that is prompted by an immemorial past that precedes the idea of world. There is no "double truth" at issue in the conjunction of philosophy and theology, if there ever was (even in the twelfth century), since for Lévinas the passage from saying to the said stymies any synchronization of philosophical and theological truths.[63] But there is a doubling of truth caused by interruptions of discourse rather than of immanent causal sequences, one that is resolved in the name of manifestation by attempts to knot the broken threads of discourse together.

Revelation for Lévinas will be the nonintentional waking of the self by the *ideatum* of infinity, or, seen from another angle, revelation will be the interruption of discourse by acts of saying and unsaying. The little dogma there is in Judaism (some orthodox Jews would dispute the qualification) would be the settling down of the saying in the said, and it would be interpreted by the ethics that follows from the preoriginal disturbance of revelation. From the perspective of philosophy, there is no overturning of the Kantian model of religion, even as reworked by Cohen. Nor is a clear understanding given of what it means for God to speak from a past that was never present. This could mean that although God is eternally present ontologically, the human being is structured so that we cannot have epistemological access to him in the present. Or it could mean that we should act as though we do not have direct relations with God. Or, again, it could mean that insofar as we can reason in this area, God is no more than a limit-concept, despite vivid stories in the Bible that suggest otherwise. Any way one looks at the matter, the world for Lévinas remains insulated against divine revelation happening or even occurring in history partly because the divine is sequestered to a past that cannot be represented and partly because the divine is drained of all phenomenality.[64] And although he speaks of prayer, his general philosophical position renders it deeply problematic.[65] That prayer is a *mitzvah* does not need to be underlined; it is amply discussed in the Talmud (*Ta'anit* 2a). The command to pray could be regarded as coming from an immemorial past, yet without a realist notion of God it may be doubted whether such prayer can be connected to worship. Perhaps Lévinas has such a notion of God—the possibility that God is eternally present but by design inaccessible to us—yet it is not marked in his philosophical architectonic. And what is important in his thought, the biblical injunction against representing the Lord recast as the deep past, makes it difficult for him to articulate a realist notion of God.

One can complain that Lévinas turns his criticisms of themes into a theme, though only if one overlooks the role of diachrony. Even so, there is cause for concern. Lévinas's use of deformalized temporality makes Torah subject to the one exegetical grid when at least several are needed, including that of history. No convincing account can be given of the irreducibly strange writing gathered under the nineteenth-century hypothesis of the Jahwist, for example, if one is constrained to think of God by way of illeity.[66] And little positive sense can be made of the Lord acting in strength, as when he manifests himself in a burning bush, delivers his people from bondage in Egypt, appears in a vision before Ezekiel, and rescues Daniel's companions from the fiery furnace. And the same is true of moments when the Lord reveals himself in gentleness and silence, as in the "still small voice" that speaks to Elijah (1 Kings 19:12 KJV). Lévinas asks us to read Scripture while suspending the phenomenality of God, that is, to consider Torah as a privileged document of ethics and justice. Yet does not Scripture depend on that phenomenality in order to claim special attention, in order to distinguish itself from *Gilgamesh* or the *Theogony*? Is Scripture not *norma normans non normata,* a norm that norms but is not normed? Lévinas will cite Rabbi Ishmael, who says, "The Torah speaks the language of men," and, in general, will use Talmudic commentary as a way of demythologizing—or, better, deontologizing—Scripture.[67] And yet something is needed in the first place to identify Torah as "the Word of God." Lévinas will appeal to "the Infinite in the Finite, as in keeping with Descartes's 'idea of God,'" but that is precisely what he has denied himself in following Berdyaev and electing existential over religious transcendence.[68]

If the mighty and gentle deeds of the Lord are what often strike us when reading the Bible, the absolute singularity of God is what presses on us when thinking philosophically or theologically about what we are told there. Lévinas sees divine revelation deriving from the disturbance of the infinite in my encounter with the other person. For the sake of argument, we might grant that existential transcendence is anterior to God; even so, we are obliged to separate the properties attached to God (as Descartes conceives him) from those that are predicated of transcendence. Simple natures are comprehensible for Descartes, but not so God, who cannot be grasped at all: "This very incomprehensibility is comprised within the formal concept of the infinite" [*incomprehensibilitas in ratione formali infinit continetur*], we are told in the replies to the fifth set of objections.[69] God is singular, even with respect to beings with simple nature. Lévinas implicitly asks two things of us: that we put aside the singularity of God and figure exteriority as an infinite term of a relation, and that we allow talk of relation with the other person, trans-ascendance, to supervene with respect to a personal relationship with God. It will be objected that Lévinas erases the difference between the absolute singularity of God and the relative singularity of the other person. Is the objection valid? In moving towards the other person, Lévinas says, I find myself in the trace of God. This trace would be, precisely, the withdrawal of the absolute character of God's singularity in the moment of my engagement with the other person. The *imago dei* is to be discerned only in retreat and only in a relation with the other person. And so Lévinas can preserve a distinction between the absolute singularity of God and the relative singularity of the other person. The distinction opens a space between worship and ethics, but in such a way that Lévinas is unable to give sufficient weight to worship. And to speak of God without it following ineluctably that He is to be worshiped for His own sake is to miss the meaning of "God."

The attention paid to Lévinas prepares us to think harder not only about a phenomenology of the New Testament, in both senses of the genitive, but also about the status of revelation as possibility and as nonintentional manifestation. It is not simply a matter of passing from Lévinas to Henry, since a reading of Henry is already implicit in Lévinas's most considered thought in *Otherwise Than Being* and later essays. I say "reading of," not "agreement with." If Lévinas bequeaths reverse intentionality to Marion, for whom it opens the problematic of the saturated phenomenon, he gladly accepts in his final version of human subjectivity Henry's notion of a nonintentional psyche, which Lévinas situates at the back of intentional consciousness. For his part, when Henry proposes that the New Testament is a phenomenology, he affirms, as he always does, that the essence of revelation is nonintentional. There is no inevitable interpolation of a "you" between the divine and me, however, no other who is always and already within my psyche. For Henry, the divine is not weak in phenomenality, or subject to a philosophical suspension of it, but is the singular instance of phenomenality at its most radical and most pure. The claim comes by way of a sharp distinction between two modes of truth, not the beginning of a theory of "double truth" but a theory of truth that is Christic in shape, being both human and divine. New Testament Christianity presumes a God who is otherwise than the world and seeks a truth that is irreducible to the world's truth.

Having made that point, Henry then insists that this divine phenomenality is Life, and that Life phenomenalizes itself as life. In terms of reading the gospel, this relation of phenomenality and phenomenon yields a very high Christology in which what the Father reveals in the Son is God and only God. Yet the height of the Christology is perhaps delusive, for this Christ is no more than an archetype needed in order for gospels to be written. Certainly not an ascending Christology—for the Synoptics are regulated by John—Henry's phenomenology of the Arch-Son is also not a descending Christology, or, rather, the descent is arrested before the Jewish horizons of Jesus's acts and words start to impinge on us. Although Henry distinguishes absolute and relative sonship, the difference between Christ and me is not marked by the decisive act of Christ's passion. To be sure, "Life" is one of the divine names, although its semantic base predominates in the fourth gospel, and cannot be used to give a sufficiently thick description of the relations between the Father and the Son in any part of the New Testament.[70] Those relations are worked out in terms of Love, seen as an intentional structure, and while Henry talks of the love of life, it remains part of a nonintentional essence. It might also be pointed out that Henry has no place for the *Frühkatholizismus* in the New Testament. He has nothing to say about hierarchy or sacramentalism, nothing about parenesis or the parousia (as second coming); and, aside from proto-Catholicism, he can offer no convincing account of the triune nature of God in terms of the binary of Life and life. That he reduces Christianity to the New Testament is clear, but so too is what falls outside his reduction, the Semitic horizons of the gospel. No theology of religions could be grounded in this phenomenology, no more so than an understanding of God as Creator.[71]

Given that Henry does not have a concept of God as free Creator, it is hardly surprising that he does not have a robust sense of the deity as radically independent of creation. Yet if there is no revelation other than revelation itself, it must be said that this revelation is nonetheless real. It is not confined to the realm of possibility in either the Kantian or the Husserlian senses of the word. Revelation occurs as self-affection or, if the expression be strictly monitored, as "inner experience" in Avery Dulles's sense of the words rather than Georges Bataille's. Henry's God is "without being" and is certainly "God without being God," but in a quite different sense of the expressions than is at work in Marion's *Dieu sans l'être* (1982). God can properly be said to be "without being" for

Marion only in the strict sense that the divine name "Love" is prior to "Being." Yet Marion cannot say that Love phenomenalizes itself as love because for him the proposition belongs to faith, and therefore falls outside the scope of phenomenology as he conceives it. Besides, we know—or think we know—what love is in the world, but we have hardly any idea what Love is. Is the image of a man who has been tortured and hanged upon a tree anything like how we usually imagine Love?

Taking another path than the one explored by Henry, the Marion of *Étant donné* insists on the evident phenomenality of Christianity, the fact of its self-showing in the New Testament and thereafter, but will examine it only as an eidetic possibility, one among others in the world religions. The inspection examines the concatenation of the four sorts of saturation. We may not be referred to the Kantian model of religion, but we remain in a world that is restricted to the scope of the Kantian table of categories—four sorts of saturation and no more—and is redescribed by means of an inversion and overflowing of those categories. There may well be contents of revelation that are possible, not actual, but the vehicle of revelation always requires a reference to an act, however it is conceived. Joseph Maréchal, for instance, will argue that God is possible only if he is real, but Marion will not take that route, preferring to trust in a distinction between Revelation and revelation, his version of the theological duality of *Offenbarung* and *Offenbarkeit*.[72] For Marion, the self-manifestation of phenomena provides the reference in question: Revelation differs from it only to the extent that it is regarded as raised to the second degree and that it is possible, not necessarily actual.[73] Yet one might wonder about the efficacy of the distinction. Phenomenology trades in the possible, needless to say, but does it reach a limit when considering the self-revelation of the God who cannot be possible because his essence and his being are one? At this juncture we need to disentangle two questions. First, whether *Offenbarung* is independent of all conditions, and, second, whether *l'adonné* receives this revelation independently of all conditions.

For Marion, as much as for Barth, *Offenbarung* does not require conditions of reception, natural or transcendental, in human being. God reveals himself by himself in his own way. Revelation manifests itself in the sphere of experience and gives rise to the experience of nonexperience. We can distinguish what limits God (nothing at all) and what limits us in hearing God (a great deal: our finitude, our sinfulness). When revelation imposes itself on the screen of *l'adonné,* as Marion would phrase it, does this happen or occur in terms of a prior hermeneutical structure of reception? There is reason to think that it should. "A thing is received according to the mode of the receiver" [*unumquodque recipitur in aliquo secundum mensuram recipientis*], says St. Thomas in a fundamental canon of all hermeneutics.[74] And a caution of Husserl's also comes to mind, that is, the need for "*zigzag* judging . . . first making straight for the givenness of something itself, but then going back *critically* to the provisional results already obtained—whereupon [the scientist's] criticism must also be subject to criticism."[75] Marion will speak of *l'adonné*'s resistance to givenness, though what enables this resistance or sponsors degrees of it is not made clear.[76] In general, he affirms that phenomena and hermeneutics arrive together: *l'adonné* may have a filter, but not before "the phenomenalized given gives itself."[77] Revelation is given absolutely, without a horizon of manifestation, and it is in infinite interpretation that its unlimited character is experienced. Still, we can distinguish between the *call* to interpret, which is given by revelation and which is made manifest in interpretation, and the *power* to interpret, which precedes the divine call. Without some minimal structure of interpretation, prior to revelation, experience could not be experienced differently.[78]

Theologians will have further concerns, not least of all that Marion's conception of revelation limits the revelation to which the New Testament is a complex testimony. It is not that quantity, quality, relation, and modality do not sufficiently encompass the play of sameness and otherness in the world of phenomena, but that we have no reason to think that, even when they overflow, they can indicate the divinity that is other than the duality of same and other. Christ is the saturation of saturation, yet this singular status is gained only in terms of exceeding mundane categories. If God reveals himself in Christ, there must be a radical otherness in him that neither Kant nor Marion is able to acknowledge. One cannot recognize what cannot be cognized in the first place. What phenomenological justification is there for a radical otherness? The question must be answered before we can know what to make of a phenomenology of Christianity, and whether we should read that expression with an objective or a subjective genitive.

A Christian theology would have the form of a circle whose center is God and whose circumference traces the extent of his self-revelation in Jesus. A phenomenology of Christianity would have the form of an ellipse, with one focus being eidetic variation of "God" and the other being description of revelation. One might say that so far all we have done is trace the drawing of three secants: a denial of divine phenomenality, an affirmation of the same, and a registration of the phenomenality of revelation. In the first case, the concept of God loses intelligibility to the extent that ethics opens a space between moral action and worship but cannot give any content to the latter. If the first case draws from the profundity of the senior religion of the Judeo-Christian revelation, it remains, from the viewpoint of the history of Christianity, remarkably modern: St. Gregory of Nyssa would not have seen why a line should be drawn between adoration and moral action, or why the ethical should be the sole horizon of responsibility. In the second case, the liberation of phenomenality has allowed us to see God revealing himself by right and in power, although that unlimited phenomenality is quickly restricted to the one divine name, Life, and we might wonder if the New Testament teaches no more than the immanence of revelation. And in the third case, the phenomenality of revelation is secured as possibility, if at the risk of restricting revelation to the overflowing of mundane categories. Can a fourth case be developed? It would have to begin with an eidetic variation of "God."

Nowhere is this variation done better than by St. Thomas Aquinas. In the *Summa theologiae, De veritate,* and *De potentia dei,* he performs an imaginative variation by way of considering human-divine relations.[79] Our relations with God are real (*relatio realis*), but God's relations with us are not (*relatio rationis tantum*). The relation between God and us is radically asymmetrical, and this discloses something about God as he is in himself and God as Creator. God does not rely existentially on the world, because he already enjoys all possible perfections, yet the existence of the world depends unreservedly on the will of God. Such is what Sokolowski (a phenomenologist, remember), faithful here to St. Anselm as well as St. Thomas, calls "the Christian distinction."[80] Two important things follow from this simple clarification. First, the whole of creation is a free gift of God, and consequently our being is to be grasped only in terms of a relation with him, whether acknowledged or left unacknowledged. It does not follow that God does not love his creation, only that he does not need it in order to achieve the full potential of his being. The inner life of the immanent Trinity is already a Love than which none greater can be conceived. Second, the duality between myself and the other person is qualitatively distinct from the radical otherness of the Creator. When we talk of God as "other" or as being "otherwise," the adjective or adverb is also a catachresis. We cannot turn God into a theme. Why? Not because he has always and already passed by but because the self-other relation occurs only in the sphere of themes.[81] To conceive God beyond that sphere, as the idea of Creation requires, is to admit that we rely on revelation to apprehend anything of God. When we say, "God is Love," we are confessing, first and foremost, that we do not know what this Love is. We cannot coax "Love" from the depths of our word "love"; we can approach it only through what Jesus tells us and shows us.

Eidetic variation of "God" reveals a free Creator who is other in a sense other than in any distinction we might make in the world between self and other. This variation does not disclose particular understandings of how this God reveals himself, not even in creation as revelation. All that can be said is that if God reveals himself, it is because he has the right and the power to do so: his phenomenality would be unlimited. There is no continuous passage from saying "if God reveals himself" to a study of what is revealed; there is only the grammar of "God"— as shown in *Summa contra gentiles* 1.42, for instance—and the texts that testify to the revelation of God. We can grasp revelation, if at all, only by inquiring into its sites, which by its own witness are multiple, from creation to covenant, from the "Christ event" (both his words and his acts) to the hope of redemption based on the testimony that Jesus is the firstborn of the resurrected. Those texts are incapable of limiting the revelation to which they bear witness; they can point to it, not encase it. They generate a tradition, more like an expanding circle of waves than a letter sent from a distant country that is always received and read in the same way.

If phenomenology is the study of how things disclose themselves to us from different regions of being or even beyond being, in the sense of being as *ens creatum,* there is no reason in principle why we cannot follow the ways in which the Christian God is said to reveal himself. That would happen only if a prior decision had been made to restrict phenomenality, so that philosophy might limit theology or, equally, so that theology might guard a body of dogma. To grant God unlimited phenomenality in his relations with us would be to respect and repeat all the divine names, not just Life; to examine all the possible sites of self-revelation, including those that fall within our anticipation and memory; and to take stock of the different modes of revelation appropriate to the regional ontologies and any meontologies through which revelation passes in order to encounter us. A phenomenology of Christianity must be more than a doctrine of God and Creation; it will involve the study of where God reveals himself in Jesus. That there are theophanies and miracles to be considered goes without saying, yet anterior to these are the acts and sayings of Jesus. If the theophanies and miracles require readjusting a relation between phenomenality and consciousness, the same is surely true of what Jesus says and does. Henry points us to those statements when Jesus speaks of himself, and accords them a special privilege because they indicate what for him is a pure phenomenological truth. He also speaks of parables, though in a peculiar sense (he finds them in John). Yet is it not in the actual preaching of the parables that we find Jesus revealing the proper relation with the Father? And is it not in parable itself that we find consciousness challenged to the limit by the phenomenality of revelation?

I will conclude in the space opened by those two questions but without being able to venture beyond its borderland in this paper. Even the most minimal phenomenology of Christianity would have to make decent sense of the parables of Jesus, for the horizons they make visible—revelation and the kingdom of the Father, ethics and judgment—are those of Christianity itself, a Christianity that emerges from Judaism and remains in continuous conversation with it. A Christian theology that grounds itself in the parables of Jesus is one that knows its soil to

be Jewish even if many its building blocks are quarried in Greece.[82]
Read properly, the parables of Jesus are a phenomenology of the kingdom, since they are narrative studies of the ways in which the *basileia*
has appeared, is appearing, or will appear. This manifestation is, to be
sure, mysterious: we approach the phenomenon by way of phenomenality. In the preaching of Jesus, parables present being without being,
for they are metaphors and narratives, and that is the nature of their
ontology. This might serve to remind us that Christian theology, whatever else it is, must also be a practice of literary criticism. That said, the
phenomenality of this particular being without being is powerful beyond literariness. How a parable allows the kingdom to become present, namely speech (and for us, born long after the death of Jesus, written speech), does not bespeak all the modes of that presence.

The parables of Jesus tell us more than the immanence of divine
life in our lives; they indicate that divine love has an intentional structure, one that we can and should imitate at the risk of exceeding our
natural abilities. When we read or hear the parables, we find ourselves
faced with a form of counterintentionality, one that the faithful take as
a figure of revelation. Certainly the appearing of the kingdom is not restricted to any regional ontology: it comes to us by way of promise and
anticipation, not as a present phenomenon. It comes to us here and now,
as revealed in a smile, in hard and often frustrating work for a measure
of justice to be achieved in the world, in generosity, and in love; and,
even so, its phenomenality is largely given in anticipation, not in the
presence of good things that come to us, even though all too rarely. What
a parable reveals is characteristically not a revelation of a certain content that supplies its own mode of self-evidence but a double revelation
of otherness and radical otherness, what the kingdom is like and what it
is unlike, what the Father is like and—even more—what he is unlike,
what divine Love is like and—even more—how very far it is from any
human idea we have of love. We have to hold those things in tandem
with little or no idea of how to do so. Such is Christian "experience."

We are told that the kingdom is like a grain of mustard seed, and in
truth something great comes from something tiny in Christian faith.
Yet the kingdom is unlike any mustard seed we have ever known, for it
grows so vast, like a cedar of Lebanon, that all the birds of the air nest

in it. The kingdom is common; it is extraordinary. We have had experience of it; we have never seen such a thing. What manifests the kingdom the more, our common experience of it or what abides at the edges of our experience? If the kingdom comes to us in ordinary acts of kindness, it also does so in anticipation of a dazzling presence that we cannot anticipate in any clear way, the full life of being with Christ our light, phenomenality in the extreme. Parables open a space at once simple and bizarre in which we can have not a new set of experiences but a new allegiance, a new experience of experience, one that turns on the phenomenality of God, not the experience of God. The structure of the kingdom comes momentarily to light, in Eucharist, and in other forms of communion. Before any of this, however, the believer will tell us that the parables of the kingdom are revelation itself, preached at a high cost—torture and execution—and then gloriously affirmed and confirmed by the resurrection of Jesus. The phenomenologist might understand the claim, but only the Christian will live within it, knowing its phenomenalities day by day and night by night.

Notes

I would like to thank Jean-Yves Lacoste and Michael A. Signer for comments on an earlier version of this essay.

   1. See Martin Heidegger, *The Phenomenology of Religious Life,* trans. Matthias Fritsch and Jennifer Anna Gosetti-Ferencei (Bloomington: Indiana University Press, 2004). Also see idem, "Phenomenology and Theology," in *Pathmarks,* ed. William McNeill (Cambridge: Cambridge University Press, 1998). In "The Problem of Sin in Luther" Heidegger maintains, "The object of theology is God," a view he changed three years later. See idem, "The Problem of Sin in Luther," *Supplements: From the Earliest Essays to "Being and Time" and Beyond,* ed. John van Buren (Albany: State University of New York Press, 2002), 105.
   2. See Max Scheler, *On the Eternal in Man,* trans. Bernard Noble (Hamden, CT: Archon Books, 1972); Otto Gründler, *Elemente zu einer Religionsphilosophie auf phänomenologischer Grundlage* (Munich: J. Kösel and F. Pustet, 1922); Kurt Stavenhagen, *Absolute Stellungnahme: Eine ontologische Untersuchung über das Wesen der Religion* (Erlangen: Verlag der Philosophischen Akadamie, 1925); Jean Hering, *Phénoménologie et philosophie religieuse: Étude sur la théorie de la connaissance religieuse* (Paris: Felix Alcan, 1926). Also see Max Scheler, *Formalism in Ethics and Non-Formal Ethics of Values,* trans. Man-

fred S. Frings and Roger L. Funk (Evanston, IL: Northwestern University Press, 1973), 292–95.

3. The earliest use of "phenomenology" in the context of religion occurs in Pierre Daniël Chantepie de la Saussaye's "Phänomenologischer Theil," which appeared in his *Sammlung Theologischer Lehrbücher: Religionsgeschichte* (Freiburg im Breisgau: J. C. B. Mohr [Siebeck], 1887–1889), Erster Band, secs. 9–27. Other exponents of the phenomenology of religion, as developed before or irrespective of Husserl, include W. Brede Kristensen and Gerardus van der Leeuw. One important study written after Husserl, although without mentioning him, is Rudolph Otto's *The Idea of the Holy: An Inquiry into the Non-Rational Factor in the Idea of the Divine and Its Relation to the Rational,* trans. John W. Harvey (London: Oxford University Press, 1958). Otto's book was originally published in German in 1917.

4. The distinction between reconstructive and essential phenomenology is Scheler's. See his *On the Eternal in Man,* 18, 161.

5. See Robert Sokolowski, *Eucharistic Presence: A Study in the Theology of Disclosure* (Washington, DC: Catholic University of America Press, 1994); Jean-Yves Lacoste, *Experience and the Absolute: Disputed Questions on the Humanity of Man,* trans. Mark Raftery-Skeban (New York: Fordham University Press, 2004).

6. Also see Lacoste, *La phénoménalité de Dieu: Neuf études* (Paris: Éditions du Cerf, 2008). For a longer consideration of Lacoste, see Kevin Hart, "The Liturgical Reduction," *Josephinum Journal of Theology* 15, no. 1 (2008): 41–66.

7. See Paul Ricoeur, *The Symbolism of Evil,* trans. Emerson Buchanan (Boston: Beacon Press, 1969), and, among many other later works, idem, *Figuring the Sacred: Religion, Narrative and Imagination,* ed. Mark I. Wallace and trans. David Pellauer (Minneapolis: Fortress Press, 1995).

8. See Jean-Louis Chrétien, "Wounded Speech," in *The Ark of Speech,* trans. Andrew Brown (London: Routledge, 2004); idem, *The Call and the Response,* trans. Anne A. Davenport (New York: Fordham University Press, 2004).

9. Edmund Husserl, *Ideas Pertaining to a Pure Phenomenology and to a Phenomenological Philosophy, First Book: General Introduction to a Pure Phenomenology,* trans. F. Kersten (Boston: Kluwer Academic Publishers, 1983), sec. 58.

10. Gerardus van der Leeuw, *Religion in Essence and Manifestation,* 2 vols. (Gloucester, MA: Peter Smith, 1967), 2:683.

11. See Husserl, *Ideas* 1, sec. 51 note. Yet Husserl plainly had a phenomenology of God on his agenda. See, for example, "Empathy of the Other-Consciousness and Divine All-Consciousness (1908)," in *The Basic Problems of Phenomenology: From the Lectures, Winter Semester, 1910–1911,* trans. Ingo Farin and James G. Hart (Dordrecht: Springer, 2006), 177–78. More generally, see Angela Ales Bello, *The Divine in Husserl and Other Explorations,* Analecta Husserliana 98 (Dordrecht: Springer, 2009).

12. See Jean-Luc Marion, "The Breakthrough and the Broadening," in *Reduction and Givenness: Investigations of Husserl, Heidegger, and Phenomenology,* trans. Thomas A. Carlson (Evanston, IL: Northwestern University Press, 1998). I leave aside Marion's earlier work, partly phenomenological and partly theological, in which he seeks to approach God without using the language of being. See idem, *God without Being: Hors-Texte,* trans. Thomas A. Carlson, foreword by David Tracy (Chicago: University of Chicago Press, 1991); idem, *The Idol and Distance: Five Studies,* trans. Thomas A. Carlson (New York: Fordham University Press, 2001).

13. Teresa of Ávila, *The Life of Saint Teresa of Ávila by Herself,* trans. J. M. Cohen (London: Penguin Books, 1957), 188.

14. Martin Heidegger, "On the Essence and Concept of 'Phusis' in Aristotle's *Physics* B," trans. Thomas Sheehan, in McNeil, *Pathmarks,* 192.

15. Indeed, Jacques Derrida points out that for Husserl the geometrical object is the model of all objects. See Jacques Derrida, *Edmund Husserl's "The Origin of Geometry": An Introduction,* ed. David B. Allison, trans. and with a preface by John P. Leavey Jr. (Stony Brook, NY: Nicolas Hays, 1978), 66.

16. See, in particular, Jean-Luc Marion, "The Phenomenological Origin of the Concept of Givenness," in *The Reason for the Gift,* trans. and with an introduction by Stephen E. Lewis (Charlottesville: University of Virginia Press, 2010).

17. See Marion, *Reduction and Givenness,* 192–98.

18. Jean-Luc Marion, *Being Given: Towards a Phenomenology of Givenness,* trans. Jeffrey L. Kosky (Stanford: Stanford University Press, 2002), 19. On the importance of giving *itself,* see *Being Given,* 131.

19. See Jean-Luc Marion, *In Excess: Studies of Saturated Phenomena,* trans. Robyn Horner and Vincent Berraud (New York: Fordham University Press, 2002), 26, 50.

20. See Marion, *Being Given,* sec. 24.

21. See Jacques Derrida's remarks in "On the Gift: A Discussion between Jacques Derrida and Jean-Luc Marion," in *God, the Gift, and Postmodernism,* ed. John D. Caputo and Michael J. Scanlon (Bloomington: Indiana University Press, 1999), 60–61, 66–67. Also see Dominique Janicaud, "The Theological Turn of French Phenomenology," in *Phenomenology and the "Theological Turn": The French Debate,* trans. Bernard G. Prusak et al. (New York: Fordham University Press, 2000), 50–69; idem, *Phenomenology "Wide Open": After the French Debate,* trans. Charles N. Cabral (New York: Fordham University Press, 2005), 5–10. Hering anticipated Janicaud's concerns when he noted that phenomenology might well be abused for religious reasons. See Jean Hering, *Phénoménologie et philosophie religieuse,* 73–74. Marion rejects the criticism in *Being Given,* 5, 234. The source of the initial claim would seem to be Marion's talk of God coming to us as a divine gift. See Marion, *God without Being,* 3.

22. Marion, *Being Given,* 5.

23. Ibid., 115.

24. Ibid., 5, trans. slightly altered. In the second edition of *Étant donné* (1998), Marion writes "Révélation" in both sentences and not "révélation" in the second.

25. Avery Dulles proposes several senses of "revelation": as doctrine, as history, as inner experience, as dialectical presence, and as new awareness. Revelation as inner experience and as new awareness might not have any significant public dimension until proclaimed. See Avery Dulles, *Models of Revelation* (New York: Doubleday and Co., 1983), part 1.

26. See Jean-Luc Marion, "Le possible et la révélation," in *Le visible et le révélé* (Paris: Éditions du Cerf, 2005), 14. The essay first appeared in 1992, and it is here that the notion of the saturated phenomenon is announced.

27. Marion, *Being Given,* 215. Counterexperience is not restricted to divine revelation, however; it occurs whenever there is a saturated phenomenon. See Marion's essay "The Banality of Saturation," in Kevin Hart, ed., *Counter-Experiences: Reading Jean-Luc Marion* (Notre Dame, IN: University of Notre Dame Press, 2006). For Blanchot's sense of experience, see Kevin Hart, *The Dark Gaze: Maurice Blanchot and the Sacred* (Chicago: University of Chicago Press, 2004), ch. 5.

28. See Marion, *Being Given,* 235; Aristotle *Metaphysics* 9, 1049b; Heidegger, *Being and Time,* trans. John Macquarrie and Edward Robinson (Oxford: Basil Blackwell, 1973), § 7, 63 (38), § 31, 183 (144).

29. See Michel Henry, "Quatre principes de la phénoménologie," in *Phénoménologie de la vie,* vol. 1, *De la phénoménologie* (Paris: Presses Universitaires de France, 2003); Marion, *Being Given.*

30. See, in particular, Michel Henry, *I Am the Truth: Toward a Philosophy of Christianity,* trans. Susan Emmanuel (Stanford: Stanford University Press, 2003); idem, *Incarnation: Une philosophie de la chair* (Paris: Seuil, 2000); idem, *Paroles du Christ* (Paris: Seuil, 2002). The heavy emphasis on the Johannine Christ in the first of the trilogy is relaxed somewhat by the third.

31. See Henry, *Paroles du Christ,* 8, 127. Also see idem, "Material Phenomenology and Language (or, Pathos and Language)," trans. Leonard Lawlor, *Continental Philosophy Review* 32 (1999): 343–65.

32. For a quite extreme example, see John C. O'Neil, *Who Did Jesus Think He Was?* (Leiden: Brill, 1995). It should be noted that Henry does not hesitate to talk in phenomenological terms of the binatarian life of the Father and the Son. See Henry, *I Am the Truth,* 92.

33. See Søren Kierkegaard, "He Was Believed in the World," in *Christian Discourses: "The Crisis" and "A Crisis in the Life of an Actress,"* ed. and trans. Howard V. Hong and Edna H. Hong, Kierkegaard's Writings 17 (Princeton: Princeton University Press, 1997), esp. 245–46.

34. See Henry, *Incarnation,* 37; idem, *I Am the Truth,* 23.

35. Heidegger, *Being and Time,* 58.

36. See Martin Heidegger, *Four Seminars*, trans. Andrew Mitchell and François Raffoul (Bloomington: Indiana University Press, 2003), 80. Henry tends to overstate the newness of nonintentional phenomenology. While Henry's originality is not to be doubted, one can see the beginnings of nonintentional phenomenology in Husserl. See, in particular, Edmund Husserl, *On the Phenomenology of the Consciousness of Internal Time (1893–1917)*, vol. 4 of *Edmund Husserl Collected Works*, trans. John Barnett Brough (Boston: Kluwer Academic Publishers, 1991), sec. 39; idem, *Analyses concerning Passive and Active Syntheses: Lectures on Transcendental Logic*, vol. 9 of *Edmund Husserl Collected Works*, trans. Anthony J. Steinbock (Boston: Kluwer Academic Publishers, 2001), sec. 23.

37. Edmund Husserl, *Psychological and Transcendental Phenomenology and the Confrontation with Heidegger (1927–1931)*, vol. 6 of *Edmund Husserl Collected Works*, ed. and trans. Thomas Sheehan and Richard E. Palmer (Boston: Kluwer Academic Publishers, 1997), 218. Also see *Otherwise Than Being or Beyond Essence*, trans. Alphonso Lingis (The Hague: Martinus Nijhoff, 1981), 131.

38. See Henry, *De la phénoménologie*, 61.

39. Yet unless Henry can demonstrate that ecstatic phenomenology arises from, or depends on, enstatic phenomenology while remaining distinct from it, he reinstates an ontological monism in another place. See Kevin Hart, " 'Without World': Eschatology in Michel Henry," in *Phenomenology and Eschatology: Not Yet in the Now*, ed. Neal DeRoo and John Panteleimon Manoussakis (Farnham, UK: Ashgate, 2009), 167–92.

40. See Henry, *I Am the Truth*, 10.

41. Henry originally argued that religion is concerned with "the immediate consciousness of Being." His later reflections on Christianity do not use the language of Being at all. See Michel Henry, *The Essence of Manifestation*, trans. Girard Etzkorn (The Hague: Martinus Nijhoff, 1973), 405.

42. Consider the following passage, for example, taken from Fichte's fifth lecture of his *The Doctrine of Religion*: "God enters into us in his actual, true, and immediate LIFE; or, to express it more strictly, we ourselves are this his immediate Life. But we are not conscious of this immediate Divine Life . . ." (*The Popular Works of Johann Gottlieb Fichte*, trans. William Smith [London: Trübner, 1873], 2:459).

43. Pseudo-Dionysius the Areopagite states, "The divine life beyond every life gives life and subsistence to life itself" (*The Divine Names and Mystical Theology*, trans. John D. Jones [Milwaukee: Marquette University Press, 1980], 173).

44. See Emmanuel Lévinas, *Totality and Infinity: An Essay on Exteriority*, trans. Alphonso Lingis (The Hague: Martinus Nijhoff, 1979), 40. At his first meeting of Le Colloque des intellectuels juifs de langue française, Lévinas ventured to say in the discussion following Edmond Fleg's paper that Judaism is not a religion. See Emmanuel Lévinas, "Sens de l'histoire juive," in *La conscience*

juive (Paris: Presses Universitaires de France, 1962), 1:15–16. When Lévinas decides to use the word "religion," as he does in a study of Rosenzweig read at the second meeting of the Colloque in 1959, he uses it in the prescriptive sense of devotion to the other person. Religion, for Rosenzweig and as accepted by Lévinas, "is totally different from [the view of religion] that secularism combats" (Emmanuel Lévinas, " 'Between Two Words,' " in *Difficult Freedom: Essays on Judaism,* trans. Seán Hand [Baltimore: Johns Hopkins University Press, 1990], 187). See in particular the discussion following this paper in *La conscience juive,* 1:148.

45. See Lévinas, "The Ruin of Representation," in *Discovering Existence with Husserl,* trans. Richard A. Cohen and Michael B. Smith (Evanston, IL: Northwestern University Press, 1998), 121. Also see Franz Brentano, *Psychology from an Empirical Standpoint,* trans. A. C. Rancurello, D. B. Terrell, and L. L. McAlister, 2nd ed., introduction by Peter Simons (London: Routledge, 1995), 198.

46. See Descartes's "Meditations on First Philosophy," in *The Philosophical Works of Descartes,* trans. Elizabeth Haldane and G. R. T. Ross (Cambridge: Cambridge University Press, 1972), 1:166. Also see Lévinas, "Philosophy and the Idea of Infinity," in *Collected Philosophical Papers,* trans. Alphonso Lingis (The Hague: Martinus Nijhoff, 1987), 54.

47. See Berdyaev's comments in Jean Wahl, *Existence humaine et transcendance* (Neuchâtel: Éditions de la Baconnière, 1944), 129. See Lévinas, *Totality and Infinity,* 48. See Descartes, "Meditations on First Philosophy," 1:166.

48. See Henri Bergson, *Time and Free Will,* trans. F. L. Pogson (London: Macmillan, 1950).

49. Lévinas, *Otherwise Than Being,* 88.

50. Vasily Grossman, *Life and Fate,* trans. and with an introduction by Robert Chandler (New York: New York Review Books, 2006), 407–8.

51. See Jacques Derrida, "Violence and Metaphysics," in *Writing and Difference,* trans. Alan Bass (London: Routledge & Kegan Paul, 1978), 111.

52. See Lévinas, *Otherwise Than Being,* 160, 163.

53. For Lévinas, liberalism would require an a priori commitment to the equality of all persons, and would therefore be inconsistent with a primary affirmation of the transcendence of the other person. This is not to say, of course, that Lévinas does not recognize the value of liberalism in Western societies.

54. As Derrida remarks in a parenthetical comment, Lévinas's ethics are "nothing less than Schelerian." See his "Violence and Metaphysics," 98. Does this mean that, for Derrida, Scheler also concerns himself with an "Ethics of Ethics," or that Lévinas adopts a first-order moral position from time to time? Derrida does not say. Lévinas talks of giving the other priority over the self as the sole "absolute value" in "Philosophy, Justice, and Love," trans. Michael B. Smith, in *Is It Righteous to Be? Interviews with Emmanuel Lévinas,* ed. Jill Robbins (Stanford:

Stanford University Press, 2001), 170. I allude in the passage in the body of the text to Max Scheler's introductory remarks on nonformal ethics of values in his *Formalism in Ethics and Non-Formal Ethics of Values,* 6–7.

55. See Lévinas, "Reality Has Weight," trans. Alin Cristian and Bettina Bergo, in *Is it Righteous to Be?*, 163. Also see Immanuel Kant, *Groundwork of the Metaphysic of Morals,* trans. H. J. Paton (New York: Harper & Row, 1964), 96.

56. See Hermann Cohen, *Religion of Reason: Out of the Sources of Judaism,* trans. and with an introduction by Simon Kaplan (Atlanta: Scholars Press, 1995). A covert influence of Moses Mendelssohn, especially his *Jerusalem, oder über religiöse Macht und Judentum* (1783), is also possible.

57. See Lévinas, *Of God Who Comes to Mind,* trans. Bettina Bergo (Stanford: Stanford University Press, 1998).

58. See Lévinas, *Otherwise Than Being,* 149.

59. Lévinas, *Of God Who Comes to Mind,* xi.

60. See Lévinas, *Otherwise Than Being,* ch. 5, sections 1 and 2; idem, "Truth of Disclosure and Truth of Testimony," in *Basic Philosophical Writings,* ed. Adriaan T. Peperzak, Simon Critchley, and Robert Bernasconi (Bloomington: Indiana University Press, 1996).

61. See Johann Gottlieb Fichte, *Attempt at a Critique of All Revelation,* trans. and with an introduction by Garrett Green (Cambridge: Cambridge University Press, 1978), sec. 13. In one respect Lévinas is closer to Fichte than to Kant. Unlike Kant, Fichte offers no redescription of Christianity by way of practice, belief, and church, and one finds no similar attempt to redescribe the whole of Judaism on the basis of Lévinas's model of revelation.

62. Franz Rosenzweig, *The Star of Redemption,* trans. Barbara E. Galli (Madison: University of Wisconsin Press, 2005), 18. See Lévinas's comments in "Philosophy, Justice, and Love," 173.

63. See Lévinas, "Revelation in the Jewish Tradition," in *Beyond the Verse: Talmudic Readings and Lectures,* trans. Gary D. Mole (Bloomington: Indiana University Press, 1994), 149–50.

64. On the distinction between happening and occurring, see Jacques Derrida, "A Witness Forever," in *Nowhere without No: In Memory of Maurice Blanchot,* ed. Kevin Hart (Sydney: Vagabond Press, 2003), 48.

65. See Lévinas, "Prayer without Demand," in *The Levinas Reader,* ed. Seán Hand (Oxford: Basil Blackwell, 1989), 227–34.

66. Harold Bloom has performed the great service of making the writings of the Jahwist strange for us once again. See his *The Book of J* (New York: Grove Weidenfeld, 1990), which contains a retranslation of the Jahwist texts by David Rosenberg.

67. See Lévinas, foreword to *Beyond the Verse,* x. Deontologizing, as I am using the word here, differs from demythologizing to the extent that, on Lévinas's understanding, the saying inexorably leads to the said, the realm of ontology, even though the said can be unsaid.

68. In the foreword to *Beyond the Verse* Lévinas identifies Descartes's infinite with God. Elsewhere, though, he distinguishes the structure of transcendence it bespeaks from God.

69. René Descartes, "Reply to Objections, 5," in *Philosophical Works of Descartes,* 2:218.

70. Henry could cite, however, Matt. 10:39, Mark 9:43, and Luke 12:23; 14:26.

71. On the relations between Henry and Gnosticism, see Jad Hatem, *Le savoir et les viscères de l'être: Sur le gnosticisme et Michel Henry* (Paris: L'Hamattan, 2004).

72. See Joseph Donceel, ed., *A Maréchal Reader* (New York: Herder & Herder, 1970), 156.

73. See Jean-Luc Marion, *In Excess,* 52.

74. Thomas Aquinas, *In duodecim libros Metaphysicorum Aristotelis Expositio,* ed. M. R. Cathala and R. M. Spiazzi (Turin: Marietti, 1964), cap. 1, lect. 10 [167], 48.

75. Edmund Husserl, *Formal and Transcendental Logic,* trans. Dorion Cairns (The Hague: Martinus Nijhoff, 1978), 125.

76. See Marion, *In Excess,* 52.

77. Marion, *Being Given,* 265. Marlène Zarader is mistaken to suggest that Marion contradicts himself in his account of the filter. See her "Phenomenality and Transcendence," in *Transcendence in Philosophy and Religion,* ed. James E. Faulconer (Bloomington: Indiana University Press, 2003), 114.

78. It would of course be quite possible to imagine *l'advenant* as a Christian, even though the project is not one that interests Claude Romano. See Romano's discussion of events that open new possibilities for *l'advenant* and reset the world for him or her in his *L'événement et le monde,* 2nd ed. (Paris: Presses Universitaires de France, 1999), 45, 55.

79. See Thomas Aquinas *Summa theologiae* 1, q. 13, art. 7, c; 1, q. 28, art. 1, ad 3; 1, q. 45, art. 3; idem, *On the Power of God,* trans. Lawrence Shapcote (1932; repr., Eugene, OR: Wipf & Stock, 2004), bk. 1, q. 3, art. 3. Also see *De veritate,* q. 4, art. 5, c.

80. See Robert Sokolowski, *The God of Faith and Reason: Foundations of Christian Theology* (Washington, DC: Catholic University of America Press, 1982), chs. 2 and 3. Also see David Burrell, *Faith and Freedom: An Interfaith Perspective* (Oxford: Basil Blackwell, 2004), chs. 1 and 14.

81. Lévinas also points out that God is other than the other person. See "God and Philosophy," in *Of God Who Comes to Mind,* 69.

82. See Harvey K. McArthur and Robert M. Johnson, eds., *They Also Taught in Parables: Rabbinic Parables from the First Centuries of the Christian Era* (Grand Rapids: Zondervan, 1990).

Making the Resurrection Reasonable— or Reason "Resurrectional"?

ANTHONY J. KELLY

Christ's rising from the dead is an irreplaceable "given" in the consciousness of Christian faith:[1] "No Christianity without the resurrection of Jesus. As Jesus is the single great 'presupposition' of Christianity, so also is the resurrection of Jesus."[2] In the same vein, Pheme Perkins considered that the resurrection is "the condition for the emergence of Christian speech itself."[3] Without this event there would be no New Testament. Only the light of the resurrection can prevent the life, teaching, and death of Jesus from being lost in the largely irrecoverable particularities of the past. Because the resurrection is central to faith's perception of the saving action of God, it inspires the experience of its universal significance and continuing effect in every age. But theological reflection on this topic is not without its problems. Let me indicate some of them.

THEOLOGY'S PROBLEMS IN "PLACING" THE RESURRECTION

As a foundational event, the resurrection is so embedded in Christian tradition that it has never required "definition" in the way that the

187

mysteries of the incarnation and the Trinity eventually demanded doctrinal clarification. Though doctrinally undefined, the resurrection of the crucified Jesus is the indefinable factor in every aspect of Christological, Trinitarian, ecclesial, sacramental, and eschatological theology. Still, there is also a certain sense of defeat. The resurrection, however focal, however pervasive its effect on the whole of Christian life and experience, however much it animates an eschatological hope, often in fact leaves theology tongue-tied. The singular event of Christ's rising from the dead provokes a certain embarrassment and diffidence compared to the assurance with which the supposedly meatier themes of Christian life and practice are treated. Perhaps it is inevitable that the resurrection must represent for theology not only a peculiar difficulty but also something of a frustration or even failure. It is true that the dominant focus of theology from the third century has been on the incarnation. But unless Christ had been raised, there would be no theology of the incarnation—and no "merry Christmas" in popular greeting. However much one may subscribe to a thoroughly incarnational theology in the tradition of Chalcedon, one cannot but notice that this classic Christological definition does not so much as mention the resurrection in its lapidary phrasing. It may well have established the basic grammar for all subsequent Christology, but it would have provided no answer and provoked no questions if Jesus had not risen from the tomb.

F.-X. Durrwell's *The Resurrection* appeared fifty years ago in its original French edition.[4] It stands out as a brave attempt to recall theology to its focal point. Yet it came, and went, possibly because it was lost in the no-man's land of "biblical theology"—too biblical for theology, and too theological for the exegetical styles that were then developing. It lacked the critical hermeneutical categories it would have needed to have a lasting effect. To a lesser extent, this is the case with N. T. Wright's monumental study.[5] He embarks on what is termed a "ground clearing task," with the aim of directing his readers back to "a phenomenon so striking and remarkable that it demands a serious and well-grounded historical explanation."[6] Yet note how Wright quickly moves from this "striking and remarkable phenomenon" to offering a "serious and well-grounded historical explanation," with an explicit apologetic intent. We may ask whether more attention should be given to the phenomenon itself. A renewed attention to what is most obvious, most taken for granted, is surely a humble but often overlooked function of a theology. Yet the taken-for-granted "obviousness" of faith in the resurrection is also what has made it most vulnerable to a strange neglect. Karl Rahner lamented, decades ago, the dwindling theology of the resurrection.[7] Before him, Durrwell expressed a similar concern: "Not so long ago theologians used to study the Redemption without mentioning the Resurrection at all."[8] Theology seems to observe a strange silence here. It is not only the women in Mark's Gospel who "said nothing to anyone, for they were afraid" (Mark 16:8) when it comes to speaking of what made all the difference.[9] We can sympathize with the quandary of the Roman governor Porcius Festus concerning "a certain Jesus, who had died, but whom Paul asserted to be alive." Festus was "at a loss how to investigate these questions," and so he "asked whether [Paul] wished to go to Jerusalem and be tried there on these charges" (Acts 25:19). Festus is not the only voice of common sense finding itself "at a loss" when it comes to the resurrection, and therefore willing to refer it to the adjudication of higher authorities.[10]

However many centuries have passed since then, the puzzlement continues, and the stakes are still as high. Festus found that Paul was asserting the crucified Jesus "to be alive." How this is so continues to provoke many a question for pagan governor and Christian believer alike. Still, Paul was intimately convinced of the reality that had been revealed to him, understanding it to be central to the tradition he knew and handed on. In addressing a situation of confusion in the Christian community of Corinth, he expressed a vigorous logic: "If Christ has not been raised, your faith is futile and you are still in your sins" (1 Cor. 15:17). Paul presumes a knowledge of the life, death, and words of Jesus, and even includes a saying of Jesus not recorded in the Gospels (Acts 20:35). It remains, however, that the resurrection of the crucified One is for him the decisive event. Later theology inherits Paul's conviction, but also the apostle's frustration in trying to communicate it. After all, if theology is to speak of the resurrection to its contemporaries in any age, it must face the problem of appearing oddly mythological in a world where the dead do not rise. Paul knew this back then, and theology knows it now. The apostle earned the mockery of the Areopagus after his attempt to tell his learned audience of "the good news about Jesus and the resurrection" (Acts 17:18). If the cross is a stumbling block to the Jews and foolishness to the Gentiles (1 Cor. 1:23)—to say nothing of its subversive impact on Roman imperial claims—the resurrection makes it more so.

The church is inevitably preoccupied with defending its freedom to exist and conduct its mission, especially today in non-Christian or post-Christian societies. More positively, it rightly assumes the role of guardian of ethical values and the promoter of human dignity. However urgent such concerns, the true assurance of ecclesial identity is to be found only in the resurrection effect pervading every aspect of its communal life and mission.

Then, in terms of Christian ethics, the situation is somewhat alarming.[11] Paul's speaks of the new creation and conformity to Christ crucified and risen, and John elaborates on "this life . . . that . . . was revealed" (1 John 1:2). In contrast, moral theology is most occupied with speaking of the "natural law" of a shared world in which the resurrection has made little difference. Likewise, in treatises on the sacraments, though sophisticated and helpful connections are made with the anthropology of ritual, symbols, and signs, the resurrection effect can be muted. Here, I have in mind two recent works of sacramentality in which the resurrection is barely mentioned![12] I would not for a moment indulge in an arrogant dismissal of such excellent works— especially since one of these authors has written a book on the resurrection[13]—but they do illustrate the problem: the resurrection is simply taken for granted, and not *as* granted, the culmination and the focus of a gift given from beyond this world but having its transformative effect within it.

Furthermore, it must be recognized that there is always the temptation to reduce the resurrection to the faith's experience of the Spirit. The crucified Jesus does not rise, but faith is empowered to leap into a new spiritual assurance. Though all agree that a refreshed theology of Spirit is long overdue, it can never be a substitute for the resurrection event. The givenness of this event and the gift of the Spirit are interrelated distinct events in the economy of salvation. In the resurrection of the crucified One, the transforming power of the Spirit is climactically manifested, overflowing from him into the lives of all believers.

And so the situation is something like this: If theology concentrates on the incarnation, the defining character of the resurrection is too easily presumed. If it highlights the postresurrectional life in the Spirit unfolding in history, the resurrection of Jesus is easily relegated to a mythological past. If theology addresses the responsibilities inherent in a compassionate involvement in the liberation of communities and peoples from dehumanizing political and economic oppression, the resurrection of Jesus appears as a distraction from the future that is still to be realized. Even von Balthasar's dramatic treatment of the paschal mystery seems to have exhausted its creativity in a rather operatic treatment of Holy Saturday.[14] Then, in the sphere of interfaith dialogue, when theology searches for points of contact with the great spiritualities of the world, the resurrection so intensifies the particularity of Christ that it might be best left unmentioned. Perhaps it might be given the status of an addendum to be considered later, but in the business of dialogue it has no productive significance in its own right. It is certainly not to be used as the knockdown argument justifying Christian imperialism, so to render genuine dialogue impossible. On the other hand, when Christians engage in reverent dialogue with people of other faiths or spiritualities, the transparency of such engagements is rather compromised if the resurrection of the crucified victim remains hidden in the realm of what cannot be mentioned—deemed by implication to be irrelevant to the sharing of hope. How, then, does theology keep its resurrectional focus?

A MORE PHENOMENOLOGICAL APPROACH

The challenge remains of pointing the way forward. With a more phenomenological awareness, theology can recover its original freshness and overcome the threat of boredom and stagnation. It will mean not taking the resurrection event *for* granted, but *as* granted, as originally given into consciousness. The phenomenon must be appreciated first of all on its own terms.[15] The resurrection is not first of all a theoretical problem but a gift to be lived. Newman catches the point: "Instead of looking out of ourselves . . . throwing ourselves forward upon Him and waiting for Him, we sit at home bringing everything to ourselves. . . .

Nothing is considered to have an existence so far forth as our minds discern it. . . . In a word, the idea of Mystery is discarded."[16]

The current philosophical preference for phenomenological methods over metaphysical systems[17] presents a fresh opportunity for theology to revaluate the place of the resurrection in Christian theological reflection. If the phenomenality of the experience of faith is lacking, the metaphysical categories and systems supporting doctrinal positions cannot but appear as ice sculptures needing the controlled atmosphere of a protective philosophical system, now threatened by the hot winds and the changing seasons of historical experience. Without phenomenological perception and vigilance, theology will be confined in the locked room of its own making: its floors and ceilings allow for a certain number of doors and windows—but all along, letting in the light and atmosphere of an eschatological event is at stake. Just as the risen Jesus entered the locked rooms to the surprise of his fearful disciples, a more phenomenological approach might make any theological space more hospitable to light of Christ and the fresh air of his Spirit. The conclusion of John's Gospel remains a healthy reminder: the risen Jesus is not contained within the linear print of any book—or of all the books of the world (John 21:25). The phenomenon precedes and exceeds all efforts to express it. In a more contemporary vein, theology is not engaged in a video replay of the highlights of the game, passively assured of the outcome, once one's team has won. For beyond the play of images, there is the risk of openness to the "given." It is not a matter of reproducing impressions or trying to capture a dwindling aftereffect, but of becoming involved with what causes everything to be seen anew.

Aquinas understands that the radical darkness inherent in our knowledge of God remains, but that the dark knowledge of faith is illumined by "many and more excellent effects" disclosed in the history of salvation: "Although through the revelation of grace in this life we may not know the essence of God (*quid est*), and so are united to him as to one unknown, nonetheless we know God more fully in as much as many and more excellent effects disclose him to us; and, in so far as we attribute to him from divine revelation things that natural reason cannot attain, as that God is both one and three."[18] We can specify the direction of his thinking here in regard to the "more excellent effect" of the resurrection itself. The God who acts in the resurrection remains unknown, and, in a sense, more "unknown" to the natural scope of reason limited to a world of death in which the resurrection is not a possibility. On the other hand, Aquinas is pointing to a more and more intimate participation in the life of God through the personal and cosmic effects of Christ's rising from the tomb. Moreover, he is offering possibilities of a further graced mode of knowing through the light that emanates from that resurrection. Amongst "the more excellent effects," the resurrection has a focal status in that it illuminates the whole climactic movement of divine self-disclosure. Implicit in this outstanding effect is that of the witness of the tradition to which the events of revelation give rise, above all the testimony of the chosen witnesses to whom the risen Christ has disclosed himself, as divine revelation is unfolded in history.

Attentiveness to the focal phenomenon of the resurrection will have a purgative effect on theology, expelling the waste material of misplaced rationalism that has long accumulated. This will be no unhealthy outcome if the resurrection is allowed to shock theology to its foundations with the immeasurable, original "excess" embodied in the risen Jesus. Thus, the silvering which backs the mirrors of theological perception is stripped away, so as to let the light of the "given" shine through.

What is required is a continuing conversion to the data. Again, Aquinas is instructive. We catch him reacting to the objection that his employment of the psychological analogy amounts to an attempt to prove the mystery of the Trinity. He defends his procedure: *posita trinitate, congruunt huiusmodi rationes*[19]—translatable as, "once given the Trinity, an analogical manner of elucidating it is appropriate." This, of course, raises the question of how the mystery of the Trinity is first "given" or assumed or "posited," and the question of the sense of congruence or "fittingness" in theological manners of thinking about it. But while Thomas certainly takes as given the scriptural and doctrinal tradition, he also speaks of the quasiexperimental knowledge of the Trinity through the missions of the divine persons in the gift of grace.[20] There is a gift experienced before it is objectified in propositional form, an instance of his realist sense of faith: "The act of the believer does not reach its end in the proposition, but in the revealed reality itself."[21] The sense of "fittingness" and analogical congruence in theological reasoning derives from a primary contact with the revealed realities.

Though St. Thomas is no phenomenologist in the contemporary sense, he provides clues to a less propositional and more experiential approach to the data of revelation. Here, we limit our reflections to the primary datum, to what originally collapsed all categories and left tongue-tied the original disciples who witnessed to it. Christ's rising interrupts the linear format of our books and enters the locked doors of all previous positions. Something else is at work, involving believers in a way that no video replay of highlights can satisfy. How might this decisive event be best approached?

A "TURBULENCE" IN THE HISTORY OF REASON

To heighten a sense of the phenomenality of the resurrection, we refer now to Eric Voegelin's treatment of Paul's experience of the risen Christ, as it is set out in his great unfinished *Order and History.*[22] He locates this experience within the context of a profound contemplation of the direction of human existence and the meaning of history itself. For him, history is the realm of existence in which the directional movement of the cosmic order becomes luminous in human consciousness.[23] It is imperative never to foreclose the openness of "being," nor lose its "in-between" character—the *metaxy* in Voegelin's terms. Metaxic consciousness finds expression in the key "symbolic" experiences keeping history open to a transcendent, ever-indefinable order of being and life. As affected by the resurrection, Paul experiences a "theophanic" event— in contrast to a purely human "egophanic" projection. Here, Voegelin is concerned to reject any doctrinally rigid or superficial objectification of what occurs in the depths of existence. That would result in congealing the open-endedness of the quest and reducing it to subjective or "egophanic" limits of the self-projective ego. In contrast, participation in the transcendent order is a depth experience, never to be fully objectified in mundane and established categories. Yet, as a movement "in between," such an experience is, of its nature, proleptic and provisional. In the in-betweenness of this enlargement of consciousness, categories such as subject and object, even human and divine, prove too dogmatically rigid and exclusive. What counts is the occurrence of the irreducible experience. It can be expressed only in the compact "symbolic" terms determined by the experience itself, mediating the inspiration that moves the historical passage through time and history.[24] From a luminous center, Paul looks outward to the whole of reality transfigured by what has taken place.[25] His vision evidences a sense of passing from decay to transformation. It occurs beyond any mundane conception or calculation: "If for this life only we have hoped in Christ, we are of all people most to be pitied" (1 Cor. 15:19).

Paul's experience is profoundly vertiginous. It leaves the apostle pushed to the limits of language and expression. Voegelin describes the giddying character of this experience in a key passage:

> In its experiential depth, a theophanic event is a turbulence in reality. The thinker who is engulfed by it must try to rise . . . from the depth to the surface of exegesis. When he comes up he wonders whether the tale he tells is indeed the story of the turbulence or whether he has not slanted his account to one or other aspect of the complex event; and he will wonder rightly, because the outcome depends on the interaction of the divine presence and the human response in the depth, as well as the cultural context on the surface that will bias his exegesis toward what appears at the time the most important part of the truth newly discovered.[26]

The impact of revelation occasions a "turbulence" in Paul's way of seeing the world, even if revelation remains always vulnerable to a pragmatic or ideological reduction. Though the experience occurs as event in the depths of reality, "engulfing" its addressee, its wording and communication are inevitably conditioned by the surface needs of social and cultural concerns and structures. The temptation is so to shape the event that it will lead eventually to conceptual abstraction or pragmatic usefulness, thus to be assimilated by routine patterns of thought and expectation. On the other hand, if the irruptive and turbulent excess of the event is respected in its givenness, if its witnesses and participants communicate its novelty, its effect continues, moving history forward by enlarging the sense of transcendent order of existence.[27] Attempts to define precisely what has taken place float on the surface of the experiential turbulence from which it has emerged, ever in danger of being lost in superficial concerns. The eventful "mutation"—to borrow a term from evolutionary science—can be missed. A theophanic experience can be reduced to "egophanic" projections of either a dogmatic or pragmatic type. The egologically or self-referentially structured consciousness becomes closed in on itself and loses the "metaxy" of its depth experience. The theophanic character of the Pauline vision of the risen Christ is no longer permitted to affect the constitutive meaning in history. The advance of insight is frustrated.[28] As a result, the egophanic revolt of modernity disallows the breakthrough that has taken place, and floods consciousness with new forms of ideology and Gnostic totalitarianism.[29] Voegelin sees that a symptom of this is the modern concentration on the "historicity of Christ," which reduces the "symbolic" character of the event to the world of abstraction and pragmatic control. This mind-set of historical analysis has been irremediably infected by centuries of separating symbols from experience. As a result, the experience is missed, and new mystical possibilities are not pursued.[30] Under the dead hand of analysis, abstraction, and control, existence atrophies, and the vacuum of forgetfulness is filled by egophanic ideologies of power. The radically world-forming event is interpreted on the surface level of rational analysis in terms of cause and effect. The revelatory "given" thus loses its originating uniqueness. The glory on the face of Christ is only a mirror image of ourselves.

There is no need to pretend that Voegelin's account of the revelatory impact of the risen Christ on Paul comprehends the full scope of Christian experience—in all its historical, liturgical, mystical, doctrinal, moral, and theological dimensions. Voegelin is more inclined to consider the Christ symbol than the historical person of Jesus—which is, in fact, far removed from Paul's approach. Moreover, key Christian doctrines are interpreted as dogmatic distortions. Here, Voegelin falls short of an adequate appreciation of the historic objectivity of revelatory events. For instance, the incarnation of the Word, and the realism of faith in its differentiated sacramental and doctrinal expressions, are not his concern.[31]

Nonetheless, Voegelin's analysis is immediately relevant to our investigation in five ways. These can be summarized as follows: (1) the Pauline vision of the risen Christ constitutes a decisive event in the openness of history towards its consummation; (2) it communicates a quality of self-transcending consciousness, opening its horizons to the radically new; (3) it eludes all articulation, so that any social or cultural effort to put a meaning on it can easily end in forgetting the experience; (4) the turbulent fertility of Paul's visionary experience, though never objectifiable, comes to expression in different contexts; (5) the egological character of modernity, because of both its ideology and its pragmatism, works against an appreciation of the singular originality of the phenomenon. Each of these five points underscores the need of a refreshed phenomenological approach to what Paul witnesses to in such a personal manner.[32] How, then, can Voegelin's approach be made more specific?

ASPECTS OF A THEOLOGICAL PHENOMENOLOGY OF THE RESURRECTION

Theology can begin to develop a more adequate sense of the resurrection by calling on the resources of phenomenology. Here, we are limiting ourselves mainly to the writings of Marion.[33] He makes his point in reference to five especially saturated phenomena: an event, a painting, the flesh, the face, and, in a way that tends to combine all four, revelation.[34] All five saturated instances of phenomenona have in common a primordial self-giving.[35] None of them is constituted by the subject; each appears in its originality and self-imposing power. Thus, the subject comes to itself in a new consciousness only through self-giving otherness of the phenomena concerned.

Dominique Janicaud has objected to an unwarranted intrusion of theological perspectives into phenomenological methods.[36] But that is not our problem. In fact, Marion conveniently poses a question: "Could not theology, in virtue of its own demands, and solely in view of formulating them, suggest certain modifications of method and operations to phenomenology? . . . Could not theology's demands allow phenomenology to transgress its own limits, so as finally to attain the free

possibility at which, from its origin, it claims to aim?"[37] I think so. Theology can be only enriched by a more phenomenological method. And,
in its turn, it can enrich that method with possibilities deriving from
attentiveness to the singularity of positive revelation.[38] Still, the general
phenomenological principle stands. The saturated phenomenon shows
itself by giving itself, and in a more intense and saturated manner in the
case of theology.[39] Let us then apply some instances of Marion's (mainly)
saturated phenomena to the resurrection.

The Resurrection as Revelation

For our theological purposes, it is best to start with the phenomenon of revelation,[40] and then offer a brief exposition of the phenomena
of event, art, flesh, and face. Philosophy's difficulties in dealing with
religion, let alone divine revelation in history and the singularities it
contains, are well known and understandable. Though metaphysical
perspectives can accommodate mythic and symbolic expressions, the
historic particular is off the page. The speculative impossibility of anything being God-given is often entrenched in philosophical systems
and the ideologies they support.[41] An idealist or empiricist system must
have difficulty with the singular phenomenon of any self-revelation of
a transcendent Other.[42] With some theological abandon, Marion focuses
on Christ as the phenomenon saturating the whole of the New Testament and Christian life.[43] For Christ is given in a way that exceeds all
expectations. He gives himself by way of an excess. The density and expansiveness of the resurrection of the crucified One outstrips quantitative assessment of any kind. Moreover, there is a qualitative intensity
inherent in the Christ event that makes it "unbearable" (John 16:12).
The resurrection appearances are a troubling irruption.[44] The whole
frame of previous relationships is radically rearranged: the Word becomes flesh, and in that flesh he is crucified and raised from the dead.[45]
A plurality of horizons converge and collide in the inexhaustible excess
confronting any human expression of the event (cf. John 21:25). The
singularity of Christ's appearances overflows the expressive range of all
the terms, genres, symbols, concepts, testimonies, and descriptions related to time and place and form.[46]

The self-revealing phenomenon is presented to faith, not to theoretic understanding. What is perceived in the excess of the given phenomenon leaves the believer tongue-tied. Because intelligence is at a loss to frame what has been received in faith into any conceptual system, it is in a sense dazzled and rendered sightless:

> Standing before Christ in glory, in agony or resurrected, it is always words (and therefore concepts) that we lack in order to say what we see, in short to see that with which intuition floods our eyes. . . . God does not measure out his intuitive manifestation stingily, as though he wanted to mask himself at the moment of showing himself. But we, we do not offer concepts capable of handling a gift without measure and, overwhelmed, dazzled and submerged by his glory, we no longer see anything.[47]

Marion is making an important point. Still, the event of revelation, with its form revealed on the face and in the flesh of the risen One, does not so stun and overwhelm contemplative intelligence that understanding necessarily atrophies. Insights, judgments, artistic expression, and verbal forms, however limping in their respective contexts, can positively nourish and direct the contemplation of faith. An appropriately critical realism is governed by the imperative to allow the Christian phenomenon to give itself in its own evidence and on its own terms. For Christ is encountered as the revelation of a love and the source of life, at once within the world and beyond it. The excess of light transgresses the capacities of meaning.[48] There is a play of appearance and disappearance, of presence and absence, of self-revelation and withdrawal.

Yet this saturated phenomenon *par excellence* continues to give itself through its manifold effect in the life and mission of the church.[49] The self-disclosure of Christ once enabled a privileged seeing on the part of chosen witnesses, but the record of that sight has passed into the tradition. Compared to their "seeing," faith is the experience of "not seeing," but believing—to that degree, an experience of nonexperience. But faith is not a form of blindness, nor a surrender to nothing or no one. The self-giving of the risen One saturates faith's other senses. Faith hearkens to the Word.[50] It breathes the Holy Spirit. It is strengthened by the testimony of privileged "eyewitnesses" and cumulative evidence of transformed lives. It sacramentally eats and drinks the "real presence" of the One who gives himself. It tastes through the savor of mystical wisdom. It enjoys the flickering illuminations of theology itself. Though all this, the self-giving phenomenon of Christ draws believers into its field, in the summoning to a conversion that is never fully attained. This drawing-in amounts to a rebirth in a new world of praise, thanksgiving, communion, compassionate intercession, and confident prayer.

With the resurrection in mind, we now turn to other kinds of saturated phenomena,[51] namely, the event, the aesthetic form, the flesh, and the face.

The Resurrection as Event

In its singular and expanding impact, the phenomenon of an event is not circumscribed by any concept of reality or being in general. Needless to say, it bears little resemblance to the mass production of events for any limited purpose, for example, entertainment, religious gatherings, or political rallies. For an event in the saturated sense is inexpressible in its scope and implications. It occurs outside any calculus of cause and effect. The origins and effect of such events can never be fully grasped, despite their expanding impact.[52] In its "excess" and unrepeatable particularity, the event disrupts any metaphysical theory.[53] The tragedy of the First World War is still largely inexplicable in destructiveness. It overflowed the bounds of any horizon of rationality.[54] More positively, the historical emergence of Christianity, and, indeed, the emergences of other world religions, are events of world-shaping proportions. Attempts to reduce such events to a circumscribable object serve only to blind rationality to the overwhelming character of what has taken place. Claude Romano helpfully distinguishes a mere event from a far more significant happening.[55] A factually recorded event is impersonal in its objectivity. It has no existential import. It is datable as a *fait accompli*—an innerworldly empirical fact. In contrast, there is an event of another kind. This happens beyond all previous calculations and intimately involves those caught up in it. Its impact leads to world-changing decisions.

For the world of one's previous life is reconfigured and made newly meaningful and significant, outside the logic of cause and effect. Obvious examples would be, say, religious or moral conversion, a devastating grief or failure, or falling in love, or even a deeply significant friendship. Events in this sense give rise to a certain "anarchy," as the fixed points of previous horizons are dramatically shifted. As a result, the full significance of the event in question can only emerge, as it awaits a future to unfold.[56] The self is caught up in an incalculable existential venture, not as a passive recipient, but as an active participant, and as inspired to a new level of action. In this respect, it is not a matter of projecting new possibilities on an already established world, but of being involved in a new register of existence—within a world newly understood. Something has occurred from outside any previous individual horizon. A convenient example is one's own birth—or that of others. For each birth is an event that occurs as given from beyond, yet at the same time it opens possibilities that are not predetermined against any settled horizon.[57]

The resurrection of the crucified is preeminently such an event. By any showing, it is a world-changing occurrence. It radically shifts the death-bound horizon of existence to open it to the promise of eternal life already anticipated in the act of God's raising Jesus from the tomb. The origin and outcome of the resurrection transcend the world of previous calculations. Yet the resurrection "saturates" with Easter significance the lives of Christian believers to affect their sense of the universe itself: "If anyone is in Christ, there is a new creation: everything old has passed away; see, everything has become new" (2 Cor. 5:17). This "new creation" is presented in various ways as a new spiritual birth, the beginning of a life that looks to an eschatological fulfillment (1 John 3:2). The Christian—to accommodate Romano's usage—is an *adventant,* one caught up and carried forward in an adventure of life, to a degree unimaginable within the horizon of previous existence.

The Resurrection as Aesthetic Form

The phenomenon of art adds a further dimension. A great painting saturates our perceptions in an especially intense fashion. It cannot be merely a tasteful adornment to the décor of a room or a dwelling. Its aesthetic impact causes everything to be rearranged in the living space of our mundane experience. If the artwork is regarded as an item of decoration, something owned and cataloged as property, it simply mirrors back one's own criteria of taste or status. A great work of art overflows any individual mode of appreciation because of its universal appeal. The painting dazzles the viewers' limited perceptions with a peculiar and inexhaustible excess, and so invites an endless contemplation that exceeds any flat manner of looking at an object.[58] Viewers, with their varying sensitivities and appreciative capacities, are drawn to behold what it frames to see the world anew. In this regard, a great painting possesses an iconic quality. It does not so much present itself as an arresting object within the routine scope of our vision, but is luminous with a light beyond the familiar.[59]

Theology is indebted to Hans Urs von Balthasar for attempting to restore an aesthetic dimension into the heart of faith. The first of his three volumes of *Herrlichkeit* (*The Glory of the Lord*), *Seeing the Form,* appeals to the aesthetic form of divine revelation itself. Before God's self-revelation is taken into various systematic expositions, it is first of all a glory, a beauty, and with its own attractive force. It comes as a *Gestalt,* an irreducibly concrete, whole, and complete form. Beholding this form does not stop short at the limits of vision. The work invites participation. Its radiance sweeps up the beholder into an *eros* and rapture, under the attraction of what is revealed in Christ.[60] Von Balthasar writes,

> The Gospel presents Christ's form in such a way that "flesh" and "spirit," incarnation to the point of suffering and death, and resurrected life, are all interrelated down to the smallest details. If the Resurrection is excised, then not only certain things but simply everything about Jesus' earthly life becomes incomprehensible. . . . [His] death and resurrection . . . are comprehensible only if they are understood as the transformation of this earthly form by God's power, and not as the form's spiritualisation or apotheosis.[61]

David Bentley Hart's theological aesthetics[62] is closely related to von Balthasar's approach.[63] The self-revealing phenomenon of beauty comes on its own terms and transfigures the world of our experience. It makes its own space and keeps its own distance, for it eludes any fixed structure of apprehension or control.[64] The beautiful form gives itself, not as a pleasurable satisfaction, but as summoning to a self-transcendence in the light of the truth and value it represents. The beautiful crosses all boundaries, all types of being. It permeates creation in such a way as to subvert totalizing ideologies, be they in mythic, conceptual, or pragmatic form.

Hart's theological aesthetics is focused in the resurrection. The rhetoric celebrating the form of the risen One possesses "an infinite power of expression" eluding all efforts to silence it.[65] In reference to Luke 24:13–35, Hart remarks: "As the disciples who encounter the risen Christ on the road to Emmaus discover, Christ can now no longer be recognized merely as an available and objective datum, a simple given, but must be received entirely as a *donum*, as gift, in the breaking of the bread, in the offer of fellowship given anew even when the hope of all fellowship seems to have been extinguished."[66] For Hart as for von Balthasar, the resurrection does not figure simply as an aesthetic principle. It radically subverts all totalitarian pretensions, be they political, cultural, or intellectual. The dehumanizing forces of culture appear triumphant in the crucifixion. The cross is their final word in their effort to determine the form of the world.[67] Yet at that very point, the Word of God is definitively and inexhaustibly pronounced: Christ is risen.

The Resurrection as "Flesh"

The phenomenon of "my body" or "flesh" is saturated with a special sense of immediacy and unobjectifiable intimacy. While it is "mine," it is the field of communication with the other. The body or "flesh," so intimately constituting the subject, gives the possibilities of intimate self-giving and self-disclosure, as in the case of erotic or maternal love. In this sense, the flesh is a field of mutual indwelling, a being with and for the other. In the eros and generativity of love, my bodily being is re-experienced in the flesh of the other.[68] Embodied existence transcends the status of being simply a physical body in a material world. The human body is the zone of incarnated relationships.[69] The body is my conscious being, affected by and affecting the larger phenomenon of the world. This body is at once my "natal bond" with the world, an immediate exposure to it, an immediate participation in it, and a primal communication within it.[70]

In this respect, the phenomenon of the resurrection is a communication of the "body" of Christ in the Pauline sense, or "flesh" of the Risen One in a more Johannine expression. In the Pauline vocabulary, of course, the "flesh" has negative connotations. Nonetheless, Paul envisages a transformed physicality in a bodily sense: "For just as the body is one and has many members, and all the members of the body, though many, are one body, so it is with Christ" (1 Cor. 12:12). With the diversity of the many spiritual gifts, "you are the body of Christ and individually members of it" (1 Cor. 12:27). The shared breath or living atmosphere of the body is the Holy Spirit: this one Spirit is manifested in the diversity of gifts. In this one Spirit, "we were all baptized into one body . . . and . . . made to drink of the one Spirit" (1 Cor. 12:13). To change the metaphor, with some reliance on Merleau-Ponty, the Spirit of Christ is the "inspiration" and "expiration" of the risen One invigorating the whole body of Christ.

The body or flesh of the risen Lord, transformed itself, is also transformative in its effect. The Word became flesh; and in that flesh he is crucified and raised from the dead.[71] The flesh, with all the organic and social limitations that it implies, is still, after the resurrection, God's chosen field of communication. For the Christian phenomenon is not accessible to the order of thought alone. It is disclosed only in the phenomenality of body, flesh, and "incarnation." Pseudo-Dionysius speaks of *pati divina,* "to experience the things of God," as transcending all thought and imagination. This venerable phrase has a strongly mystical overtone, and figures as such in the elaboration of negative theology. Nonetheless, the tradition it represents must never be separated from the bodily event of the resurrection of crucified One. Experiencing "the things of God" revealed in the death and resurrection of the incarnate Word presupposes the mediation of Jesus's flesh and of his risen bodily form. The primary Christian import of the mystical phrase *pati divina* suggests the possibility of interpreting it also as *pati humana et carnalia*—the experience of God in the flesh and body of Jesus Christ. In Tertullian's cryptic wordplay, *caro est salutis cardo:* the flesh (*caro*) of

Christ is the turning point (*cardo*) of the salvation of our embodied existence—as Michel Henry so vividly appreciated. The risen Lord is not the source of a new theology. Christians are not involved in any ongoing theological seminar. Christ is the form and source of incarnate, bodily communication. God made him "the head over all things for the church, which is his body, the fullness of him who fills all in all" (Eph. 1:22–23).

The phenomenology of the body inevitably strains against excessively spiritual interpretations. Yet the church is the body of Christ. He is the head, and we the members. In Johannine idiom, he is the vine and we the branches (John 15:5), as his flesh is given "for the life of the world" (John 6:51). Christ's flesh/body is the field of his relationship to the world, as both affected by and affecting the manifold phenomenon of our incarnate coexistence. Though now transformed, his risen body continues to be his "natal bond" with the world. It expresses the immediacy of his exposure to the world in the process of its transformation in him. Through the body, he, the Word incarnate, is constituted in a primal communication with all incarnate beings and continues to affect the material universe. In that transformed bodily being, he breathes his Spirit into all his members, so that there is one Spirit-vitalized body— even if he is risen and his members are on the way to being transformed as he is.

Through incorporation into that subjective body of Christ, his living flesh, his members find the world discosed to them in its original and eschatological significance. Consciousness is illumined with the "light of life" (John 8:12). Though he has come and remains in the flesh, his vitality emanates from the very life of God: "What has come into being in him was life, and the life was the light of all people" (John 1:3–4). The primordial generative mystery of the Father is thus revealed in the flesh: "Just as the Father has life in himself, so he has granted the Son also to have life in himself" (John 5:26). In answer to Philip's request, "Lord, show us the Father, and we will be satisfied" (John 14:8), Jesus replies, "Whoever has seen me has seen the Father. . . . Do you not believe that I am in the Father and Father is in me?" (John 14:9–10). Life flows from a source beyond time and space into the living flesh of Christ and those united to him. It constitutes the phenomenological condition of Christian corporate existence. In this regard, there results an extraordinary sense of intersubjectivity and mutual indwelling within the incarnational field of communication. Jesus prays, "I ask . . . that they may all be one. As you, Father, are in me and I am in you, may they also be in us" (John 17:21). The incarnate "word of life" (1 John 1:1) takes the form of a communal existence: "This life was revealed, and we have seen it and testify to it, and declare to you the eternal life that was with the Father and was revealed to us . . . so that you also may have fellowship with us; and truly our fellowship is with the Father and with his Son Jesus Christ" (1 John 1:2–3).

The life of the vine flows into the branches (John 15:5), just as the head of the body governs the activity of each of its members (Eph. 1:22–23). The incarnation, already reaching its fulfillment in him, is extended into a living, corporate form of the church. It determines a form of self-giving love for those who are "members of one another" (Eph. 4:25), "for no one ever hates his own body, but he nourishes and tenderly cares for it, just as Christ does for the church, because we are members of his body" (Eph. 5:29–30). The Letter to the Ephesians does not hesitate to appeal to the most intimate, ecstatic, and generative human experience of the body in spousal love to express Christ's relationship to the ecclesial body of believers. Just as man and woman become "one flesh" (Gen. 2:24), the risen One is one flesh with the communion of believers. As Wittgenstein remarked, "It is *love* that believes the resurrection."[72]

Though Jesus is glorified in the flesh, it is still marked by the wounds of the cross, thus representing his compassionate involvement with humanity in its sufferings and with the whole groaning reality of creation (cf. Rom. 8). The power of his resurrection reaches into the alienated and mortal sphere of our corporate existence, for "even when we were dead through our trespasses, [God] made us alive together with Christ . . . and raised us up with him" (Eph. 2:5–6). A new field of incarnate relationship is disclosed in the phenomenon of the resurrection. Christ's rising from the dead does not mean disincarnation, but a new form of incarnation. The former sphere of fleshly divisions is now relocated, as it were, in a new form of incarnate existence (Eph. 2:14–22). Its vitality derives from Christ's self-giving love, in order that we may "grow up in every way into him who is the head, into Christ, from whom the whole body, joined and knit together by every ligament with which it is equipped, as each part is working properly, promotes the body's growth in building itself up in love" (Eph. 4:15–16). Physical existence is transformed—a bodily "mutation" has occurred whose lifeblood is the love that possessed the Head and conforms his members to him. His giving is embodied: "The bread that I will give for the life of the world is my flesh" (John 6:51). By sacramentally assimilating his flesh and blood, given and outpoured for the life of the world, believers are conformed to his risen life: "Those who eat my flesh and drink my blood have eternal life, and I will raise them up on the last day; for my flesh is true food and my blood is true drink" (John 6:55).

In the risen Christ, communication in the flesh does not cease, but opens out to an unimaginable fulfillment. The mutual indwelling and openness to the other characterizing the earthly experience of the flesh is now actualized in a new mode of mutual co-inherence: "Those who eat my flesh and drink my blood abide in me, and I in them" (John 6:56; cf. 15:4, 6). In this paschal realm, believers "abide in the Son and in the Father" (1 John 2:24; cf. 3:24), and so inhabit a field of love in which earthly *eros* is subsumed into the *agape* of the divine self-giving: "God is love, and those who abide in love abide in God, and God abides in them" (1 John 4:16). To the degree that faith assimilates his flesh and blood and Spirit, there is new sight, hearing, touching, tasting, eating and drinking, feeling and indwelling—the new senses of faith, as Origen recognized so clearly.[73] Because of its unobjectifiable immediacy, the phenomenon of the flesh earths and embodies faith in the risen One with fresh directness. There is less risk of rising to a level of abstraction, either in thought or in symbol, that ill serves what has been uniquely given.

The Resurrection and the Face of Christ

The phenomenon of the face is saturated with significance, in a more distanced manner than the intimacy of the flesh. George Orwell saw something of this experience in his verse tribute to the "crystal spirit" on the faces of the young Italian militiamen with whom he served in Spain—and also in the terrifying emptiness written on the face of "Big Brother."[74] Whenever he read a moving piece of writing, Orwell found himself conscious of "the face somewhere behind the page, which is not necessarily the actual face of the writer," but, as he put it, "the face that the writer *ought* to have."[75] Here he had Charles Dickens especially in mind. This reference conveniently leads into the elusive but ever arresting phenomenon we here consider.

When "faced" with the other, I am not looking at something amongst other objects in the world, or at a "somebody" in the crowd. When someone looks at me, I meet with a striking otherness. It lays claim to my attention and concern. Here Marion is influenced by Lévinas's widely influential account of the other, especially in his/her suffering. To be faced with this other is to feel the force of the question, where were you, given what you now see?[76] The face paradoxically makes visible the invisible totality of the other. It resists objectification. At the same time, this "you" calls for a respect and regard, in such a way as to render inhuman any gaze that is just a mere "looking at," as in the inspection of objects. The center of gravity is shifted; not *here,* in the perception of the self-contained ego, but *there,* in the other, whose look stops us in our tracks. In this sense, the face of the other is a commanding presence.[77] The face of the other does not reflect back to me what I desire to possess or dominate. It takes me out of myself, into the disturbing world of responsibility, respect, and love. The face is not a mirror in which I see myself, but more a window through which the light of arresting otherness breaks through. It calls forth a self-transcendence that goes beyond any symmetries of an "I and Thou" relationship. For this other who confronts me, face-to-face, breaks into my awareness as inviolable uniqueness—"Thou shalt not kill"—despite the disruption of the secure world of the ego.

As regards the face of Christ, we have to admit that the New Testament, when speaking of the risen Jesus, as well as at every stage in his earthly life, shows no interest to describe a face in any conventional terms. Icons, of course, and the long tradition of Christian art already referred to, have sought to serve revelation and faith by expressing, in Orwell's terms, the face somewhere behind the biblical accounts of Jesus's deeds and words. But at its best, faith seeking to find its best artistic expression is intent on the phenomenon of the face of Christ, the icon of the self-revealing God. Paul speaks expansively of Christ, "the image of the invisible God" (Col. 1:15). But the otherness of the transcendent must be allowed to come on its own terms—looking us in the face, rather than being a projection of our look.[78] The only appropriate attitude for one who is faced by the icon is prayer, adoration, and self-surrender. The unenvisageable is rendered visible only to faith, hope, and love. Surrender to this kind of evidence exceeds a full cognitive or conceptual comprehension. It enjoins a waiting and longing for its final appearance, typified in the earliest recorded Christian prayer, *Maranatha,* "Come, Lord!" (1 Cor. 16:22; Rev. 22:20).[79] The face of Christ as the one who is to come allows for a deferral and delay, filled with an endless diversity of significations through the course of history.

The face of Christ is not the face of any other that would call forth the biblical prohibition against killing, and so too demand reverence and care for anyone bearing the image of God. For Christian faith looks upon the Jesus who has in fact been killed by human agencies. He has been raised up, as the embodiment of God's self-giving love: "They will look on the one whom they have pierced" (John 19:37). In this kind of gaze, faith lives in the world of dim reflections of the future "face to face" vision (1 Cor. 13:12). Yet, in the bold Pauline idiom, there is already a kind of experience of the face of Christ, who is turned toward us in a light from beyond this world: "For it is the God who said, 'Let light shine out of darkness,' who has shone in our hearts to give the light of the knowledge of the glory of God in the face of Jesus Christ" (2 Cor. 4:6). The most striking aspect of the face of Christ is not so much our seeing, but that of "being seen through." In its apocalyptic rhetoric, the book of Revelation gives a visionary description of the face of Jesus with "eyes . . . like a flame of fire" (Rev. 1:14; 2:18), and he declares, "I know your works," "your affliction and your poverty," and "where you are living" (Rev 2:2, 9, 13, 19; 3:1, 8, 15). He identifies himself as "the living one" and declares, "I was dead, and see, I am alive forever and ever" (Rev 1:18). The transparency of all who encounter him pervades the Gospel accounts (e.g., Luke 9:47; 11:17; John 1:48). Before there are any "resurrection appearances," before the chosen witnesses see him, he sees them (e.g., John 20:27–29). They experience themselves as being "seen through," and so faced with him as the truth of who they are and what they are now called to be.

FROM PHENOMENON TO MEANING

After we have made these initial correlations of the resurrection to Marion's list of saturated phenomena, his question lingers: "Could not theology's demands allow phenomenology to transgress its own limits, so as finally to attain the free possibility at which, from its origin, it claims to aim?"[80] This theological essay is not concerned to teach anything to phenomenology, but to learn a fresh orientation from it. Theology must go on, patiently making correlations and picking its way beyond univocity and equivocity in order to say what it has to say. But, on the other hand, resurrection faith displays its own rationality. It must take account of a singular datum: God is not giving us a saturated phenomenon, nor a suggestive analogy, but revealing Christ, and in him the whole of creation newly sensed in its original and final coherence (Col. 1:15–18). Christ is not a transcendental signifier external to the world of faith's rationality. He does not rise from the tomb to go to another place. There is a counterintuitive moment. Our reason and our perceiving also rise from the tomb. They begin to occupy their proper place in a world made new, at least new-in-the-making. Christian phenomenality must learn to account for the God-given perceptions of faith, hope, and love.

The phenomenon is productive of various dimensions of meaning. The rhetoric of the New Testament unfolds in three great arcs.[81] First, Christ is presented as the fulfillment of all the promises of God—for he is the "yes" to all God's promises, and the "amen" to all our prayers (2 Cor. 1:20). Second, to live, now and forever, is to participate in what he is, be it in a Johannine mutual indwelling and communion (John 17:20–21; 1 John 1:1–3) or in the Pauline idiom of being baptized into his death and resurrection (Rom. 6:3–11). Third, in the resurrection the cosmic expansiveness of God's design in Christ comes to light, with everything created in him, through him, for him, so that in him "all things hold together" (Col. 1:15–18). Christ is, as it were, the divine "univocity," even if the human mind, impatient to capture it, would veer toward a Gnostic ideology. Theology must be content with a nexus of analogies and fragmented perceptions, ever ready to defer to what can be revealed only in the end. In short, the phenomena we have correlated to the resurrection are "saturated" only because that is the way creation-in-Christ actually is. At the risk of putting it all too crudely and forcing terms beyond any reasonable extension, phenomena are saturated because the risen Christ saturates all phenomena. There is a giving and a givenness beyond anything the phenomenal world can give.

Working within this supersaturated Christic world, the mind can be productive of meaning.[82] This meaning is *effective;* it shapes the world in different ways: if Christ is risen, then there is work to be done. The violence of oppressors must not go unchallenged, neither must the suffering be left without hope, nor the guilty without forgiveness. The meaning of Christ, crucified and risen, is also *communicative.* It forms a historical community, living from and mediating "the resurrection and the life" (John 11:25). Further, such meaning is *constitutive:* it informs human consciousness to affect one's sense of self and one's experience of subjectivity: "If Christ has not been raised, your faith is futile and you are still in your sins" (1 Cor. 15:17). More ontologically, the meaning of the resurrection is *cognitive.* Theology affirms something, not nothing. It knows the difference between plenitude and emptiness, life and death, truth and illusion, divine action and human response, seeing and believing, and all the rest. N. T. Wright and J. D. Crossan would seem to agree in every domain of meaning except the cognitive.[83] Yet without it, the salvific realism of faith is lacking.

Paradoxically perhaps, the salvific realism inherent in the cognitive dimension of faith's meaning will be most served by a disciplined return to the phenomenality of the resurrection. The adjective "salvific" is used to highlight the precise kind of realism involved. It is not contrary to the respective realisms of phenomenological, historical, metaphysical, scientific, and anthropological methods. Each has its own limitations, particular concerns, traditions of interpretation, criteria of evidence. Salvific realism is focused on a unique event. It is, first of all, intent on being receptive to the phenomenality of the event which is the focal point of faith and a shock at the foundations of every theology.[84] If the methods of other forms of phenomenological disclosure and patterns of knowing end by declaring the resurrection to be a nonreality, a nonevent, the problem could be one of unexamined prejudice against the effects of historical phenomena. If this is the case, it is not helped by a theological method either unaware of what is at stake, or simply taking for granted what should be taken *as* granted, and respected in the

singular conditions of its "givenness." It is of greatest theological importance not to be distracted into apologetics before discerning the unique
form of what has been given. Apologetics is at its most persuasive when
Christian faith risks being rejected for the right reasons. Only in this
way can the resurrection be perceived as reasonable, and reason be receptive to the "resurrectional." The phenomenology of resurrection faith
has reasons that Enlightenment reason has yet to discover.

Notes

1. For a fuller treatment of this topic, see Anthony J. Kelly, *The Resurrection Effect: Transforming Christian Life and Thought* (Maryknoll, NY:
Orbis, 2008).

2. James D. G. Dunn, *Christianity in the Making,* vol. 1, *Jesus Remembered* (Grand Rapids: Eerdmans, 2003), 826.

3. Pheme Perkins, *Resurrection: New Testament Witness and Contemporary Reflection* (Garden City, NY: Doubleday, 1984), 18.

4. F.-X. Durrwell, *The Resurrection* (London: Sheed & Ward, 1960).

5. N. T. Wright, *The Resurrection of the Son of God* (Minneapolis: Fortress Press, 2003).

6. Robert B. Stewart, ed., *The Resurrection of Jesus: John Dominic Crossan
and N. T. Wright in Dialogue* (Minneapolis: Fortress Press, 2006), 18.

7. Karl Rahner, "Dogmatic Questions on Easter," in *Theological Investigations,* trans. Kevin Smyth (Baltimore: Helicon Press, 1966), 4:121–33.

8. Durrwell, *Resurrection,* xxiii.

9. All quotations from the Bible, unless otherwise specified, are from
the New Revised Standard Version (NRSV).

10. For a fuller treatment of these points, see Kelly, *The Resurrection Effect,*
1–23.

11. Brian V. Johnstone, CSsR, "Transformation Ethics: The Moral Implications of the Resurrection," in *The Resurrection: An Interdisciplinary Sympo-
sium on the Resurrection of Jesus,* ed. Stephen T. Davis, Daniel Kendall, SJ, and
Gerald O'Collins, SJ, 339–60 (New York: Oxford University Press, 1997).

12. Kenan Osborne, OFM, *Christian Sacraments in a Postmodern World: A
Theology for the Third Millennium* (Mahwah, NJ: Paulist Press, 1999); David N.
Power, *Sacrament: The Language of God's Giving* (New York: Crossroad, 1999).

13. Kenan Osborne, OFM, *The Resurrection of Jesus: New Considerations
for Its Theological Interpretation* (New York: Paulist Press, 1997).

14. As will be clear, I depend on von Balthasar in many other places and
instances, where the resurrection is given its due. It is just that he seems to lose

all sense of proportion when it comes to Holy Saturday. For a vigorous critique of Balthasar's Holy Saturday theology, see Alyssa H. Pitstick, *Light in Darkness: The Traditional Catholic Doctrine of Christ's Descent into Hell and the Theological Opinion of Hans Urs von Balthasar* (Grand Rapids: Eerdmans, 2005).

15. Further elaborated in Kelly, *The Resurrection Effect,* ix–xiii, 24–43.

16. J. H. Newman, "On the Introduction of Rationalistic Principles into Revealed Religion," in *Essays, Critical and Historical* (London: Longmans & Green, 1890), 1:34–35.

17. See William Desmond, "Is There Metaphysics after Critique?" *International Philosophical Quarterly* 41, no. 1 (2004): 221–41; see, too, the range of transpositions evident in William Norris Clarke, *The One and the Many: A Contemporary Thomist Metaphysics* (Notre Dame, IN: University of Notre Dame Press, 2001).

18. Thomas Aquinas *Summa theologiae* 1, q. 1, art. 13, obj. 1.

19. Ibid., q. 32, art. 1, ad 2.

20. Ibid., q. 43, art. 5, ad 2.

21. Thomas Aquinas *Summa theologiae* 2-2, q. 2, art. 2, ad 1.

22. Eric Voegelin, *Order and History,* vol. 4, *The Ecumenic Age* (Baton Rouge: Louisiana State University Press, 1974), 239–71.

23. Ibid., 242.

24. Ibid., 242–43.

25. Ibid., 246.

26. Ibid., 252–53.

27. Ibid., 253.

28. Ibid., 255.

29. Ibid., 260–66.

30. Ibid., 265–66.

31. It would be a productive exercise to contrast Voegelin's approach with that of Alain Badiou in his *Saint Paul: The Foundation of Univeralism,* trans. Ray Brassier (Stanford: Stanford University Press, 2003). Badiou, holding the chair of philosophy at the École Normale Supérieure in Paris, considers historical Jesus as largely a fable, and the resurrection a mythological objectification of something else, namely, the subject as a universal singularity. What interests Badiou is not Christian faith, let alone the Christian church, but the subjectivity of Paul's creative and provocative universalism calling into question all the dull sameness of the world based on distinctions between Jew and Greek, slave and free, male and female. Paul is to this extent our contemporary, witnessing to a new subjectivity, a new way of being human unencumbered by objectifying limitations of particular and oppressive modes of belonging based on social, cultural, or religious divisions.

32. For further perspective on Paul, see Kelly, *The Resurrection Effect,* 79–100.

33. In some ways, as Marion's critics point out, this emphasis on the sheer self-givingness of the phenomena is so extreme, so one-sided, that the conscious subject seems to have no role at all, in responding to and interpreting what is being given. But need subject and object be so adversarially opposed? I do not think so, as I shall later explain later in reference to the multiple dimensions of meaning the phenomenon provokes.

34. Jean-Luc Marion, *Being Given: Toward a Phenomenology of Givenness,* trans. Jeffrey L. Kosky (Stanford: Stanford University Press, 2002), 234–36.

35. Marion, *Being Given,* 5.

36. Dominique Janicaud et al., *Phenomenology and "The Theological Turn":* *The French Debate,* trans. Bernard G. Prusak (New York: Fordham University Press, 2000).

37. Marion, *"Le possible et la révélation,"* in *Eros and Eris: Contribution to a Hermeneutical Phenomenology; Liber Amicorum for Adriaan Peperzak* (Dordrecht: Kluwer Academic Publishers, 1992), 228.

38. Marion, *"Le possible et la révélation,"* 231; idem, *Being Given,* 242.

39. Marion, *Being Given,* 367.

40. Ibid., 235–36.

41. Marion, "The Saturated Phenomenon," *Philosophy Today* 40 (1996): 103.

42. Marion, *"Le possible et la révélation,"* 232.

43. Marion, *Being Given,* 236.

44. Ibid., 238.

45. Ibid., 239.

46. Ibid., 240.

47. Marion, "They Recognised Him; and He Became Invisible to Them," *Modern Theology* 18 (2002): 148.

48. Ibid., 149.

49. Ibid., 151–52.

50. For a theological phenomenology of voice, see Sergio Gaburro, *La Voce della Rivelazione: Fenomenologia della Voce per una Teologia della Rivelazione* (Milan: Edizioni San Paolo, 2005).

51. This account makes no pretense of giving a critical treatment of Marion's work in this area. I do, however, find in it a number of evocative starting points, taking us in the direction of the phenomenon of the resurrection.

52. Marion, *Being Given,* 140, 165, 172.

53. Ibid., 170–72.

54. Ibid., 201.

55. The phrase "eviential hermeneutics," while truer to the French text, does not travel so well in English.

56. Claude Romano, *L'événement et le monde* (Paris: Presses Universitaires de France, 1998), 60–69.

57. Ibid., 72–96.

58. Marion, *Being Given,* 203.

59. Marion, *God without Being: Hors-Texte,* trans. Thomas A. Carlson (Chicago: University of Chicago Press, 1991), 9–14; idem, *In Excess: Studies of Saturated Phenomena,* trans. Robyn Horner and Vincent Barraud (New York: Fordham University Press, 2002), 72.

60. Medard Kehl, "Hans Urs von Balthasar: A Portrait," in *The von Balthasar Reader,* ed. Medard Kehl and Werner Löser, trans. Robert J. Daly, S.J., and Fred Lawrence (Edinburgh: T&T Clark, 1985), 47–48.

61. Hans Urs von Balthasar, *The Glory of the Lord,* vol. 7, *Theology: The New Covenant,* trans. Brian McNeil, C. R. V. (Edinburgh: T&T Clark, 1989), 467.

62. David Bentley Hart, *The Beauty of the Infinite: The Aesthetics of Christian Truth* (Grand Rapids: Eerdmans, 2003).

63. Ibid., 15–28.

64. Ibid., 15–16.

65. Ibid., 334.

66. Ibid., 333.

67. Ibid., 334.

68. Marion, *Le phénomène érotique: Six meditations* (Paris: Grasset, 2003), 185.

69. Ibid., 170.

70. Marion, *In Excess,* 100; *Le phénomène érotique,* 170, 180–81.

71. Marion, *Being Given,* 239.

72. L. Wittgenstein, *Culture and Value,* trans. Peter Winch (Chicago: University of Chicago Press, 1980), 83. The paragraph reads:

> What inclines even me to believe in Christ's Resurrection? . . . If he did not rise from the dead, then he decomposed in the grave like another man . . . but if I am to be REALLY saved—what I need is certainty—not wisdom, dreams or speculation—and this certainty is faith. And faith is faith in what is needed by my *heart,* my *soul,* not my speculative intelligence. For it is my soul with its passions, as it were with its flesh and blood, that has to be saved, not my abstract mind. Perhaps we can say: only *love* can believe in the Resurrection.

73. Von Balthasar, *The Glory of the Lord,* 308–9.

74. See Michael Sheldon, *Orwell: The Authorised Biography* (London: Minerva, 1992), 343.

75. Ibid.

76. Emmanuel Lévinas, *Ethics and Infinity: Conversations with Philippe Nemo,* trans. Richard A. Cohen (Pittsburg: Duquesne University Press, 1985), 85.

77. Marion, *Being Given,* 216; idem, *God without Being,* 19.

78. Marion, *Being Given,* 232.

79. Marion, *In Excess,* 124.

80. Marion, *"Le possible et la révélation,"* 228.

81. See Joseph Sittler, *Evocations of Grace,* ed. Steven Bouma-Prediger and Peter Bakken (Grand Rapids: Eerdmans, 2000), 92–116.

82. Here I am using Lonergan's four dimensions of meaning, as found in Bernard J. F. Lonergan, SJ, *Method in Theology* (London: Darton, Longman and Todd, 1971), 76–81.

83. See Robert B. Stewart, ed., *The Resurrection of Jesus: John Dominic Crossan and N. T. Wright in Dialogue* (Minneapolis: Fortress Press, 2006).

84. For extensions of the "resurrection effect" into Trinitarian theology, ethics, and interfaith dialogue, see Kelly, *The Resurrection Effect,* 153–72.

8 | Habermas, Religion, and a Postsecular Society

JAMES SWINDAL

On June 25, 1962, the Supreme Court of the United States issued an 8–1 decision, *Engel v. Vitale,* in which the high court prohibited prayer in public schools. Effectively the decision banned a practice that was still, at the time, widespread. Justice Hugo Black, writing for the majority, wrote, "It is neither sacrilegious nor antireligious to say that each separate government in this country should stay out of the business of writing or sanctioning official prayers and leave that purely religious function to the people themselves and to those the people choose to look to for religious guidance."[1] This separate and, ostensibly, equal understanding of the functions of government and religion in a civil society stipulated that government does well to remain in its own sphere of competence and influence. Now over forty years later, the decision stands as, for the most part, an uncontroversial articulation of the separation of church and state as expressed in the first amendment of the United States Constitution. The separation is understood to be advantageous for both realms: each can function best within its proper domain of competence. But one wonders why there is no suggestion that the government might, in some cases, itself benefit from involvement with religious practices or that religious persons might find support from the government in carrying out their religious duties.

Such a decision was for the most part not heralded as a bolt out of the blue, but as a decision whose time had come. The separation-of-church-and-state clause in the First Amendment, initially crafted to prevent an established church, has slowly evolved to reflect the drift of cultural and economic development towards a greater separation of the respective functions of the state on the one hand and all religious institutions on the other. Such secularization was not intended to undermine religion as much as it was to purify government of the need to make decisions that "belong" in the religious realm—particularly given the increasing plurality of religious denominations, beliefs, and practices.

In his lone dissent in the *Engel* case, however, Justice Potter Stewart argued that such functional separation of church and state could come only at a price. He wrote, "I cannot see how an 'official religion' is established by letting those who want to say a prayer say it. On the contrary, I think that to deny the wish of these school children to join in reciting this prayer is to deny them the opportunity of sharing in the spiritual heritage of our Nation."[2] Stewart assumes that religion speaks to a part of us that has relevance to our citizenship. Moreover, schools impose many other activities, such as physical education, the study of poetry, or mathematics, that are not ostensibly related to citizenship but nonetheless contribute to civil society. Why should these be imposed while prayer is not even allowed?

It does not, however, take a great deal of reflection to realize that Justice Stewart's alternate understanding of the relation of church and state demands further specification. What exactly is the "spiritual heritage" of a nation, particularly of an ethnically, racially, and religiously pluralistic nation like the United States? Who decides what the precise understanding of this heritage is if no agreement exists as to what it means? Could such a spiritual heritage hamper impartial democratic will formation? Even more critically, does a secular state even need such a continuing heritage? Couldn't such a heritage, such as it was, possibly become obviated in the course of the state's evolution and progress?

It is to these general concerns of how a secular political order understands its relationship to religion—and vice versa—that this paper is addressed. Secularization can be analyzed historically, psychologically, sociologically, and, of course, theologically. But here I will examine some recent philosophical analysis that, I would submit, can contribute significantly to the understanding of the role of religion in a secular state. I shall proceed by analyzing the phenomenon of secularization, and then present some of Jürgen Habermas's highly theoretical analysis of it. Habermas has, however, somewhat modified his view on secularization recently, and even engaged in a somewhat uncharacteristic yet quite harmonious interchange on the matter with then Cardinal Joseph Ratzinger. Both think that we live now in a "postsecular" society that demands new ways of understanding the relation between politics and religion. I will close with some critical reflections of my own about future directions such a philosophical discussion could take.

THE DEVELOPMENT OF SECULARIZATION IN THE WEST

Secularization, of course, has a long history, particularly in the West. It can be read off of actual events, such as the decentralization and neutralization of much church authority that occurred during the Reformation, the subsequent rise of the separation of church and state in many nation states, and the development of cultures dedicated exclusively to individual success and fulfillment.[3] But an analysis of the development of secularization in the West and of the controversies it has engendered would be a vast undertaking.

Let's start instead with a conceptual approach. Etymologically, "secularization" derives from the Latin *saeculum,* which referred to a century of time, but more importantly to measurable chronological time as contrasted with eternity (e.g., *per saecula saeculorum*). Later it was used to describe property that had been alienated from church ownership. Etymology aside, secularization can be defined as the replacement of exclusively sacred and religious sources for the normative determination of individual actions and beliefs by some combination of argumentatively or contractually produced political, legal, and/or ethical sources. Notably, secularism does not *ipso facto* eliminate religion, but only undermines its *exclusive* role in determining the normativity of beliefs and actions. Moreover, a secular norm does not have to differ in appearance or function from a religious one: they can have content that is similar, if not, in many cases, identical. For example, it is arguable that our current secular norms regarding the value of human life, the civic values of education and tolerance, and the political virtues of justice and fair treatment coincide closely with most religious norms. Only the origin of, motivation for holding, and procedure for justifying the two types of norms differ.

What exactly are these differences? A religious norm is grounded in some event of revelation, even if it has long since past. Religious justification, in a broad sense, can be understood as transcendent: as underdetermined by a natural or scientific set of facts about the world. Secular beliefs, on the other hand, originate in some kind of contractual foundation backed by some form of originary narrative. Secular justification tends to be more empirical, benefiting from social scientific analyses of what promotes social coordination and cohesion. However, there is a close link between origins and justification in both cases. For example, the undercutting of a historical narrative can have a devastating effect on the justification set of either secular or religious beliefs. How many Americans still believe in the narrative of Manifest Destiny since it has been exposed to have been concocted to serve expansionist economic interests? Correlatively, what happens to devotion to a saint whose historical existence is questioned?

What causes secularization, then, to emerge? My thesis is that the emergence of the secular norms is best explained *relative to the prior religious norms they either modify or supplant*. Two broad models of this relationship between the sacred and secular suggest themselves:

1. Under one construal, secular norms are constructed by individuals and societies as direct alternatives to religious norms. They are formulated precisely in order to overcome religious dogmatism and narrowness. Voltaire's critique of religion—perhaps most recognizable in his ridicule of the reaction to the Lisbon earthquake—could fit under this category.[4] Secularization often requires at some point extrareligious (political, social, or even technological) stimuli in order to decrease dependence on religious authority. On this view, the Thirty Years' War, the French Revolution, and even perhaps the Internet revolution all have prompted increasing secularization.

2. On an alternative view, secular norms evolve inevitably from religious norms. For example, since Christianity promotes self-awareness

and unleashes a desire for individuation in its adherents, it can be concluded that secularization is the inevitable result of this uncoupling of the individual from religious authority.[5] The more a faith tradition affirms the unique goodness and freedom of each person, the more it furthers individualizing secular aims that in turn undermine its very spiritual power and authority.[6]

Habermas will develop a version of the first view; I shall conclude with a modified version of the second.

CRITICAL THEORY AND THE SECULAR

As a critical theorist, Habermas is supremely interested in human emancipation. Critical theorists are a loosely organized group of German intellectuals who have developed various models and strategies for human emancipation, minimally understood as the acquisition of "undamaged" subjectivity.[7] But their conceptions of emancipation, sensitive to the actual development of human societies throughout history, have been quite diverse. Much of their analysis has challenged prevailing religious beliefs and practices. Walter Benjamin relentlessly critiqued the evolutionary or teleological projections of future utopic states, and instead embraced a kind of negative transcendentalism that can hope to redeem only the past. Theodor Adorno developed a negative dialectics that decried what he called the immediacy inherent in most beliefs, religious or secular, in favor of an appeal to the social mediacy of all beliefs. Later, Max Horkheimer longed for a perfect justice emerging from abandonment to God's will by a critical realization that no other human practice suffices. Habermas, on the other hand, has embraced the emancipatory practice of a strict procedural methodology of *discourse* to establish norms in every major sphere of human life, for example, ethics, law, science, and even aesthetics.[8] Prima facie, Habermas is dismissive of religious practices since they cannot be rigorously discursive in the way he envisions.

For the bulk of critical theorists, secularism was not merely a theoretical notion but also the de facto condition of their lives. Benjamin, Horkheimer, and Adorno all came from reformed Jewish backgrounds. Despite their secular backgrounds, each of them respected an impetus towards some kind of messianism or redemption. For each it took a slightly different form. For Benjamin it was captured most clearly by an "awakening" that grasped, through an "anamnestic intoxication," flashes or dialectical pictures from various phantasmagoria.[9] These pictures were not inchoate templates for future instrumental action, but rather ways of forming a "salvaging critique" in the face of human suffering—particularly past suffering. For the neo-Marxist Adorno, messianism emerged as a hope that the transience of the finite, the conceptual, and even the beautiful could "negate the negation" of an alienated capitalist world.[10]

Habermas takes a significantly different tack. He argues that secularization emerges from the increasingly reflective grasp we moderns have developed regarding our own inherent power of intersubjective communication. This power of communication enjoins that no determination of meaning or truth ought ever in principle to be exempted from the tribunal of communicative reason each subject possesses. Religious authority, on the other hand, rests in principle on the communicatively resistant tribunal of only a few who possess the privileged authority. Habermas holds that, in fact, religions in the West have devolved into "privatized faiths," each with its own authority structure.[11] Religious thinking, in this paradigm, restricts rationality since it bestows on a dogmatic authority the right to limit the possibilities for rational determination of the meaning or truth of a belief. Habermas claims that only the successful intersubjective establishment of meaning, and ultimately of norms themselves, overcomes the inherent vulnerability and isolation of the human condition.[12]

Habermas does not, however, pronounce the religious attitude either as intrinsically faulty or as a rival to rationality; he sees it merely as obviated by a proper grasp of communicative reason. This grasp emerges from the general impetus of modernity to awaken people from their self-imposed immaturity, famously outlined in Kant's "What Is Enlightenment?"[13] The dynamics of intersubjectivity, embedded in language use, yield essentially all of the properties hitherto reserved to the divine. The power to communicate intersubjectively contains a virtual transcendence: a speaker can and must transcend his own subjectivity in order to take on the perspective of an other. Otherwise the speaker has, effectively, nothing to say. Habermas appeals here neither to a Sartrean gaze of the other, nor a Lévinasian face of the other, nor to the abyss of two absolute freedoms confronting each other, but rather to the reciprocal *self-transcending* idealizations that condition all successful communication. Habermas maintains that a speaker aims to communicate *something* to *someone:* the theory of communicative action is initially predicated on a binary set of interaction partners. The speaker must compose a comprehensible well-formed utterance, in either descriptive, imperative, or expressive form, to communicate to the other. The speaker's first aim is for the other to reach an understanding (*Verständnis*) of the utterance; once that is completed then the speaker desires the acceptance (*Einverständnis*) of the claim by the other as well. But the only way the hearer can accept the content of the utterance is by dint of validity claims that the speaker implicitly raises in the claim and that the hearer could redeem. The link between utterance and effect is completely noncausal.[14] These validity claims, if redeemed, give the extension of the original speech act universality and validity. *The transcendence of the conditions universalizes the scope of the redeemed claim.* Habermas even goes so far as to reconstruct a "postmetaphysical" view that embodies this quasitranscendental intersubjective viewpoint. Its argumentational economies are independent of all religious and metaphysical influence.[15]

What becomes of religious thought in this scheme? Habermas claims that religious practice circumvents the power of binary and social communicative power. The inherent elitism of religious authority undermines the transparency and inclusiveness needed for successful communication. In his famous idiom, the sacred realm has been increasingly "linguistified" in secular modernity.

> The socially integrative and expressive functions that were at first fulfilled by ritual practice pass over to communicative action; the authority of the holy is gradually replaced by the authority of an achieved consensus. This means a freeing of communicative action from religious controls. The disenchantment and disempowering of the domain of the sacred takes place by way of a linguistification of the ritually secured, basic normative agreement; going along with this is a release of the rationality potential in communicative action.[16]

Truth and morality are increasingly decoupled from religious control. The cultic values of secrecy and arcane ritual have given way increasingly to the publicity of inclusion and discussion.[17] Habermas does not, however, overlook the "burdens" of such a secular view. He is loath to celebrate, in a Promethean way, this diminishment of religion in the way a Nietzsche, a Sartre, or even, more recently, a Daniel Dennett might.

Habermas subscribes, then, to the view that secularism emerges, with some exogenous prompting, from religion itself. Following Klaus Heinrich, he thinks that the Jewish notion of a "confederation" or "covenant" between God and his faithful people provided an impetus for the "solidarity" now required for social cohesion in secular cultures.[18] The betrayal of another covenant partner, through any kind of crime against him or her, was understood as the betrayal of oneself.[19] Similarly, a secular society cannot ultimately tolerate deviance. Other religious discourses still provide unique resources for both the individual freedoms and social obligations integral to life in secular society.

Habermas insists that the guiding discourses of a secular society must function at multiple levels: at the level of self-reflection on one's own life projects and at the levels of practical imperatives, morality, aesthetics, politics, and law. Each is guided by the same exacting standards of intersubjectively redeemable validity claims. So although Habermas minimizes the role that religious belief plays in his theory of meaning and truth, he wants religious beliefs to be neither prohibited nor even merely tolerated. Moreover, he acknowledges that religious beliefs can offer consolation by giving new significance to unavoidable suffering, injustice, loneliness, sickness, and death. Moreover, they can give resources to motivate one to be moral in the face of extreme suffering and cruelty. Thus he can say that "the question of the salvation of those who have suffered unjustly is perhaps the most powerful moving force behind our continuing talk of God."[20]

Secularization is not, then, something that can be posited as ethically or politically superior to religious thinking. Nor is it a wholesale replacement for religion, inspired by certain radical critiques of religion. Moreover, under conditions of secularization, there is still a realm of transcendence immanent in communication itself. Habermas claims that all communication employs the idea of an open yet goal-directed process of interpretation that transcends the boundaries of social space from within from the perspective of actual situations.[21] Language use has this power of an inner transcendence by means of which we can reach mutual understanding with others and thereby lessen our intrinsic vulnerability. Only communicative reason can properly reconstruct the structures of meaning embedded in everyday speech and argumentation. This form of reason emerges neither from a primal ethos nor from a cultural homogeneity.[22] It bestows on human agents the procedural capacity to forge intersubjective agreements on the basis of which they can live responsible and free lives. He insists that discourse is "purely procedural" and, as such, is "disburdened of all religious and metaphysical mortgages."[23]

Though ostensibly not as messianic as his critical theory forbears, Habermas clearly thinks that we cannot understand our Western past without acknowledging the importance of Judeo-Christian contributions to notions of morality and ethics, persons and individuality, and freedom and emancipation. He also thinks that Kierkegaard in particular was quite right to defend the Christian notion of the supreme importance of the individual's existence against the universalizing assaults of the Hegelian Absolute. Habermas respects the historical influence of religious thinking that philosophy can neither subsume nor dislodge. Religion can help us to grasp the otherness of the concrete other. It renders us aware of the "fateful character of the events which confront us," the "fallibility of the human mind," and our "existential restlessness."[24] Yet his philosophical agnosticism remains firm. From the viewpoint of rationality as such, he still insists one must be a kind of "methodical atheist." We face our human vulnerability with neither hope in a consolation beyond this world nor a guarantee of its eradication in this world.

HABERMAS ON THE EPISTEMIC DUTIES OF RELIGIOUS AND SECULAR CITIZENS

Habermas has recently written extensively on the events of 9/11. He reads much of the ongoing conflict in religious terms: as a consequence of both the rise of fundamentalism in the world of Islam and the corresponding "Kulturkampf" in the United States. Europe, however, seems to be relatively isolated from these trends by its solid anchoring in secular human rights.[25] Yet, at the same time, Europe is less isolated politically from the post-9/11 conflict than the United States, since it is geographically closer to the maelstrom of the religious conflicts in the Middle East.

Initially, one might think that the religious extremism present in the events of 9/11 would lead a thinker like Habermas to promote an even stronger secularism. But just the opposite has occurred: it has prompted him to look afresh at the spiritual factors operative in the secular public sphere. He in fact finds two problematic features of the "spiritual situation of the age": a widening naturalistic view of the world, evident in many scientific practices such as the new genetic technologies, and a growing political influence of orthodox religions in many nation states.[26]

What is significant in Habermas's thought now is that the cognitive realm he outlines—understood both as that from which a meaningful claim draws content and that for which it provides verifiable inferences—now unambiguously includes religious beliefs. He makes this claim on the basis that any normative "ought" (in this case the need for religious believers to become full members of a secular state) requires the requisite "can" (in this case the cognitive attitudes by which the "ought" can be fulfilled).[27] Then he sets up a kind of cognitive division of labor: while theological reflection must use a form of cognitive reflection to confront the reality of religious pluralism in the secular order, nonreligious thought must use the reflexive resources of postmetaphysical thinking to deal with the pluralism of thought and ethics. Both of these effect *mental* changes of attitude. Without this epistemic— indeed "hermeneutic"—self-reflection, religious freedom could not be guaranteed by a state.

Before I explain this position, however, it will be instructive to examine some other remarks by Habermas. He takes up the question, raised initially by Ernst Böckenförde, of whether the secular state can live off of a normative order that it cannot itself guarantee.[28] John Rawls assumed that such a possibility is not inconsistent, since he maintains that the secular order is derived from the natural reason accessible to all persons.[29] This is the basis for his theory of justice. In his later work, Rawls allows into public discourse comprehensive doctrines, such as religious doctrines, as long as they are in fact reasonable.[30] Moreover, Habermas notes that even Catholicism does not oppose an autonomous grounding, independent of revelation, for morality and rights.[31] Nonetheless, Habermas finds that this assumption about the autonomy of these secular grounds needs to be critically examined.

Habermas finds this issue of grounds to concern what *motivates* persons to follow either religious or secular norms. On the basis of Böckenförde's question, he finds a prima facie motivational inconsistency in the secular order: a secular legal system requires a motivation structure for its citizens that it cannot itself guarantee. Habermas has, for several decades, given the name "constitutional patriotism" to the proper motivational structure for a democracy. But on the face of it, this remains notoriously underdetermined. When does this motivation arise? Who articulates it? How is it recovered if lost? Habermas concludes, like Rawls, that secular motivation arises from reason itself. Habermas holds that Rawls is right to see how each side now has to interpret the relation between faith and reason, but wrong to think that this very insight does not rely upon a self-reflexively determined intersubjectivity among all persons.[32] Rational motivation, Habermas thus concludes, is not a Rawlsian drive for a modus vivendi among comprehensive with noncomprehensive political notions, but rather the intersubjective communicative power that gives rise to the motives both to forge and to follow verified norms collectively.

Habermas then turns to theological motivation. He argues that theology in the modern era has examined this motivational question in the context of philosophical promptings emergent in the radical critique of reason—and talk of the "other of reason"—unleashed by Nietzsche, Heidegger, and others. On the one hand, philosophy realized that it could no longer arbitrate the truth of religious traditions (just as it could no longer do the same for the truth of the sciences). Theology is, in a sense, more autonomous than before. But on the other hand, at least in Habermas's view, theology's relation to its grounds becomes essentially *negative*. In contrast to its postmetaphysical thinking, which posits conditions of communicability among persons, such religious thinking can furnish much-needed intuitions of sin and suffering. These religious understandings contain something that, when lost, cannot be restored simply by expert knowledge. They recover a "sensibility for damaged life" and social pathologies, for the failures of individual life projects.[33] Their grounds are, then, primarily eschatological and soteriological.[34] In a claim stunning for him, he notes, "We still lack an adequate concept for the semantic difference between what is morally wrong and what is profoundly evil. There is no devil, but the fallen archangel still wreaks havoc—in the perverted good of the monstrous deed. . . . When sin was converted to culpability, and the breaking of divine commands to an offense against human laws, something was lost."[35] Religious beliefs can offer consolation by giving new significance to unavoidable suffering, unrecompensed injustice, loneliness, sickness, and death. In the post-9/11 world this translation involves the interpretive understanding of the values, and particularly religious values, embedded in other cultures.

Habermas claims that since it is no longer empowered to police theology, philosophy now needs to make explicit the "genuinely religious content" in many of its own notions, such as responsibility, autonomy, justification, history, memory, origins, repetition, emancipation, embodiment, and community. Philosophy needs to realize how it has *translated* religious beliefs into its own vocabulary.[36] For example, it translated the theological assertion that mankind is made in the image of God into the moral principle of the unconditioned value of each person.

Habermas's full answer to Böckenförde's question, then, is that philosophical and theological ways of knowing are "complementary." They both provide cognitive access to the shaping of cultural and ethical norms. Secular thinking remains critical of all religion's claims as it nonetheless "feeds on" its "normative substance."[37] Thus, postmetaphysical thought must be both agnostic *and* ready to learn from religion, though it is never authorized to carry out an apologetics for religion.[38] Moreover, both religion and reason provide ways of assuaging the damaging of life emerging from the capitalist markets and administrative power—dangers Habermas has trumpeted for decades. Yet religion maintains its autonomy throughout: only participants in a faith tradition can determine it to be "true." [39]

The acknowledgment of the complementarity of these religious and secular learning processes effects no less than a "postsecular society."[40] Such a society seizes on the normative insight that both religious and worldly mentalities are reflexively modified. Though such a hermeneutic-reflexive mentality is prepolitical and thus prenormative, it expresses a normative insight that has consequences for nonbelievers and believers alike.[41] In his recent essay "Faith and Knowledge," Habermas argues that postsecular societies not only must grant religious freedom, but also should foster the important resources for meaning that religious language provides for the public sphere. The secular character of the state is a necessary but not sufficient condition for a genuine religious freedom. He does continue to stipulate, however, that religions for their part must affirm the legitimacy of other denominations, adapt to the authority of the sciences, and agree to a constitutional state with a secular morality.

Religious consciousness structures a life form holistically, but it can do this only under the conditions of the secularization of knowledge, the neutralization of state power, and the universal recognition of religious freedom.[42] Naturalistic worldviews enjoy no prima facie priority over religious world-disclosive conceptions. A liberal political culture can even expect from the secularized citizens that they translate relevant contributions from religious into publicly accessible speech.[43] For example, a profane form of reason, "nonsecular secularization," can assist a postsecular society in dealing with the questions of theodicy.[44] Nevertheless, secular citizens do the translation themselves, since only secular grounds "count" in the secular realm.[45]

Now we can return to the prior argument that Habermas is making regarding the epistemic burdens of the secular and religious realms. He first considers Rawls's proviso that religious citizens must have a political justification for their comprehensive doctrines. He then raises the objection that such a demand would place an undue burden on the religious citizens. Along the lines of this objection, true faith is not merely doctrine, but a source of energy for a person's entire life. A believer fulfills his existence (*Existenz*) out of his faith. It can give a core or center of "existential certainty."[46] Because of this holistic view of the believer, Habermas does not suppose that a state can expect a believer to make his or her political attitudes independent of religious convictions. This would split the believer into a public and a private self. Religiously rooted existential convictions refer to the dogmatic authority of an inviolable center of an infallible truth of revelation. This is a "discursive extraterritoriality" that the secularist must respect. So religious belief cannot be subjected to an adaptation process—this would be Foucault's perspective.[47] Nevertheless, Habermas maintains, one must assume that the religious citizens accept the secular constitution on good grounds.[48] Even religious persons who speak only in religious terms are participants in a civic discourse in which persons are understood to be both the authors of and addressants of laws. So Habermas does continue to place some Rawlsian burdens on religious citizens: they must think self-reflexively, they must not see themselves in a contradictory relation with the secular world, and they must embed universalizable morals and rights in their comprehensive doctrines. Thus the secular counterpart to reflexive religious consciousness is a postmetaphysical thinking that employs judgments about religious truth, demands a strict distinction between faith and reason, and rejects any ontological statements that purport to conceive being as a whole (*im Ganzen*); yet it equally opposes a scientistically limited conception of reason or the exclusion of religious teaching from the genealogy of reason.[49]

Habermas thus demands that religious persons exercise an epistemic capacity to view their religious claims reflexively and then to tie them to secular conceptions. To fail to recognize this capacity undermines the integrity of the public sphere. The secular sphere never knows if it would be cutting off "important resources of meaning" if it were to cut off a religious community.[50] Often secular people can realize in dialogue with religious discourse something in their own "submerged intuitions."[51] Conversely, religious citizens must learn with effort the epistemic attitudes that come to their secular counterparts so easily. Only these attitudes can motivate the religious persons to carry out their secular obligations.

THE DIALOGUE WITH CARDINAL RATZINGER

Consistent with his growing interest in the contribution of religion to secular society, in 2004 Habermas engaged with then Cardinal Ratzinger in a dialogue about the roles of faith and reason in a political context. Though the topic of secularization initially guided the discussion, it devolved more towards the specific functions of politics and religion.[52] Both were worried about political responses to the religious radicalism growing in the post-9/11 world.

Ratzinger is searching for a legitimation of secular political powers. He argues, first, that scientific reason alone, expressed in some kind of evidentiary standards, cannot bring such legitimation about; some form of democratic positive law is needed. But law always brings with it the specter of disaffected minorities who contest a law's legitimacy. The problem of minorities led some to posit the existence of a universal theory of natural rights (*ius gentium*) that sets limits on majority power. Though a theory of natural right can provide a source for universally valid norms in highly pluralistic contexts, Ratzinger notes that its power has generally been upended by evolutionary thinking.[53] Correspondingly, Ratzinger provides no defense of natural law theory here, but instead endorses a rather idealized version of a universal political principle that he terms "interculturality" (*Interkulturalität*). Interculturality, itself a secular concept, analyses human existentiality by taking up the multiple perspectives that emerge in humanity.[54] It resists the positing of one culture as a primary or a world ethos. Thus Western secular rationality must realize that it cannot be made comprehensible to every culture and thus that it cannot be operative in all. Interculturality is, then, no longer a Eurocentric notion. Yet religion and reason constitute the world situation as no other cultural forces do. Reason and religion must intermingle and help each other to purify pathologies that interculturality lays bare.[55] Thus Ratzinger and Habermas agree strongly that we live in a postsecular, pluralistic, and global world which neither secular thinking nor religious thinking alone can manage yet both together must engage.

Though unmentioned by either, a close parallel emerges between Ratzinger's interculturality and Habermas's participant idealizations that guide discourse. Habermas's discourse emerges from idealizations embodied in a procedural regulation of the differences among others in actual argumentation, and Ratzinger's interculturality is similarly idealized inasmuch as it is a negative grasp of the lack of an existent universal culture that in turn prompts a positive solidarity among all diverse cultures.

Ratzinger has continued this rather novel line of reasoning in his recent writings as pope. In *Deus Caritas Est,* he maintains that the fundamental Christian demand for a just ordering of society is ultimately the responsibility not of the church but of the state. He sees as fundamental to Christianity the distinction between what belongs to Caesar and what belongs to God (cf. Matt. 22:21). The state may not impose religion, yet it must guarantee religious freedom and harmony between the followers of different religions. Yet the church, as the social expression of Christian faith, has a proper independence which the state must recognize. So the two roles overlap:

> Politics is more than a mere mechanism for defining the rules of public life: its origin and its goal are found in justice, which by its very nature has to do with ethics. . . . The problem is one of practical reason; but if reason is to be exercised properly, it must undergo constant purification, since it can never be completely free of the danger of a certain ethical blindness caused by the dazzling effect of power and special interests.[56]

Faith by its specific nature is an encounter with the living God, and as such it is a purifying force for reason. This is where Catholic social doctrine has its particular role: it empowers the state to fulfill this obligation. The church has an interest in forming political consciences and promoting justice. Thus, Ratzinger concludes, she must "play her part through rational argument and she has to reawaken the spiritual energy without which justice, which always demands sacrifice, cannot prevail and prosper."[57]

Thus Ratzinger prefers the religious term "purification" over Habermas's epistemic term "mutual learning processes." But both terms express the similar cognitive burdens required of both the religious and political spheres.

CONCLUDING REFLECTIONS

These recent discussions about secularism prove insufficient to prompt any definitive claims about, say, the relation between church and state. Nor could one assert that they foster any strong hope for the overcoming of religious extremism and secular scientism. The modest conclusion I wish to draw is simply that they provide evidence for—and encouragement to foster further—a shift in our epistemic understandings of how postsecular and religious beliefs interact. The reign of rigidly conceptualized notions of belief and action, guided only by scientific and legal norms, seems to be waning. This is not to say that such a moderating shift is without historical precedent. But new on the scene is the recognition of the failures of either rationality or religion alone to maintain the social order. Reason cannot by itself curb its constant temptation to be determinative rather than regulative; religion, bereft of reason's intervention, can easily slide into a benign otherworldliness. What is unfortunate is that each order has succumbed to its own demons at times, exacting significant damage on its age and peoples.

If I were to issue caveats regarding Habermas's and Ratzinger's solutions, though, I'd suggest two.

First, they both prioritize a cognitive solution to the problem of interaction between the secular and religious orders. But one can ask what role the *affective* dimension of human thought and action might play in this process. Elsewhere, of course, Habermas does speak of constitutional patriotism and Ratzinger does champion the spiritual aspects of the faith. But why were these brushed aside in their interchange? After all, it was precisely the affective—the "spiritual"—that motivated Justice Stewart's dissent in *Engel v. Vitale*. From a secular perspective, he realized that even a national culture requires the appeal to some kind of affective ground. This is the heritage, however fragmented, that a secular order does well not to relinquish. Doesn't, for example, much religious literature, ritual, and even sacramentality play a significant role in promoting effective citizenry? Doesn't, conversely, the secular order need its own highly developed cultural and public life to maintain a robust civic and legal order? Both Habermas's learning processes and Ratzinger's interculturality, each in its own way, can run the risk of becoming gnostic if not tempered by affective concerns.

Second, both Habermas and Ratzinger provide a rather functionalistic conception of both religion and reason. This poses no problem as long as their arguments are not presented in a reductionistic fashion. More worrisome is their tacit acceptance of a kind of "division of labor" between these functions—a division that the *Engel* majority opinion favored. Are these separate functions forever to remain so? If so, are we only to hope that there is a kind of preestablished harmony between them that will someday possibly be realized?

Let me close with the barest outline of some biblical conceptions that avoid an appeal to a division of labor between secular and religious realms altogether. They suggest that the secular not only is consistent with the religious, but might actually, under certain conditions, perfect it. Under such a construal, it is not inconsistent to say that the secular is emergent from or, more strongly, even sublates religious norms and thought.

One of the most astonishing eschatological episodes in the New Testament occurs, of course, in the last-judgment discourse of Matthew 25. In the dramatic scene that is presented, "all nations" are gathered for, and then receive, the final judgment of acceptance or rejection by the King—who represents Christ himself. Those accepted, who are told that they have been blessed and judged worthy of eternal life, express surprise. Presumably, they feel no surprise that they are receiving this invitation because they fed the hungry, welcomed strangers, clothed the naked, helped the sick, and visited prisoners. They are surprised precisely because *they did not realize* that when they did these acts, they did them to the King. They are being rewarded despite their failure to realize whom they were serving. In other words, they acted, presumably, not from religious but from secular motives. They become the secular peoples that the King admits to eternal life. Do secular motives, then, become *determinative* of salvation? Is the dismissal of religious particularism what is intended? More radically, would a religious motive for these selfless acts of charity in any way undermine their salvific power?

Other biblical passages endorsing the secular might suggest themselves here. One might easily argue that the most existential, particularizing, and nondiscursive—hence religious—relationships we experience in life are those between parent and child. Indeed, Jesus had such a relationship to the Father. Yet, astonishingly, Jesus at one point in the Gospels exhorts his disciples to *abandon* such relationships—if they are to follow him. Similarly, St. Paul in 1 Corinthians urges his disciples to eschew marriage and embrace celibacy. Marriage is allowed only as a compromise: something to be done only if one cannot overcome natural impulses. Yet isn't this abandonment of the exclusivity of family one of the necessary conditions for the foundation of the secular order of justice? Doesn't the secular demand that to be fully just we must treat everyone in principle the same—without any such particularizing familial commitments? Does the secular, then, actually instantiate a significant part of these New Testament imperatives?

I would not want, by any means, to draw from these brief biblical considerations the patently absurd claim that the secular order completely erases the religious. As even Habermas points out, religion is always entrusted with the existential crucible of one's own life. But these biblical accounts suggest not only that secular impulses cannot be understood as excluded from the kingdom of God but also that, under a certain radical construal, they contribute significantly to its perfection. If so, the secular order would certainly never compete with the religious. And conversely, how could something like prayer in public school ever be unwelcome?

Notes

1. *Engel et al. v. Vitale et al.,* 370 U.S. 42 (1962).

2. Ibid.

3. Nietzsche's *infamous* diatribes against Christianity are a case in point. He criticized its hatred of the "world." See "An Attempt at Self-Criticism," in *The Birth of Tragedy and the Case of Wagner,* trans. W. Kaufmann (New York: Vintage, 1967), 23.

4. Consider also Nicholas of Cusa's polemics against scholastic natural theology.

5. See Hans Blumenberg, *The Legitimacy of the Modern Age,* trans. R. Wallace (Cambridge, MA: MIT Press, 1983), 195. He sees the roots of such a drive for self-assertion in Ockham's nominalism.

6. Blumenberg famously argues that the roots of modern secularization can be understood as a second attempt, more successful than the first, at overcoming the gnosticism that emerges from a specific interpretation of certain biblical passages. See *Legitimacy of the Modern Age,* 126.

7. For an excellent analysis of critical theorists' understanding of revolution, see Raymond Guess, "Dialectics and the Revolutionary Impulse," in *The Cambridge Companion to Critical Theory,* ed. F. Rush (Cambridge: Cambridge University Press, 2004), 103–38.

8. Horkheimer argued that human longings for perfect justice could be satisfied only by the redemptive power of God's will. See his "Die Aktualität Schopenhauers," in *Gesammelte Schriften* (Frankfurt am Main: Suhrkamp, 1985–1991), 7:136–39.

9. For a good description of Benjamin's phantasmagoria, see Julian Roberts, *German Philosophy* (Atlantic Highlands, NJ: Humanities Press, 1988), 280.

10. See Theodor Adorno, *Aesthetic Theory,* trans. C. Lenhardt (London: Routledge & Kegan Paul, 1984), 5, 41–44; idem, *Negative Dialectics,* trans. E. B. Ashton (London: Routledge & Kegan Paul, 1973), 360.

11. Habermas, *Political-Philosophical Profiles,* trans. F. Lawrence (Cambridge, MA: MIT Press, 1983), 142.

12. Habermas, *Moral Consciousness and Communicative Action,* trans. C. Lenhard and S. Nicholsen (Cambridge, MA: MIT Press, 1990), 199.

13. Immanuel Kant, "What Is Enlightenment?," in *Practical Philosophy,* trans. M. Gregor (Cambridge: Cambridge University Press, 1996).

14. Habermas, "Religion in der Öffentlichkeit," in *Zwischen Naturalismus und Religion* (Frankfurt am Main: Suhrkamp, 2005), 147.

15. Ibid., 109.

16. Jürgen Habermas, *Theory of Communicative Action,* trans. T. McCarthy (Boston: Beacon Press, 1987), 2:77.

17. G. W. F. Hegel, for example, in the *Philosophy of Right* (trans. T. M. Knox [Oxford: Oxford University Press, 1952]), argued against the practice of private charity in favor of the public distribution of wealth.

18. Jürgen Habermas, *The Philosophical Discourse of Modernity,* trans. F. Lawrence (Cambridge, MA: MIT Press, 1987), 325.

19. See H. Düringer, *Universale Vernunft und Partikularer Glaube: Eine Theologische Auswertung des Werkes von Jürgen Habermas* (Leuven: Peeters, 1999), 69.

20. Jürgen Habermas, *Religion and Rationality,* ed. E. Mendieta (Cambridge, MA: MIT Press, 2002) 113.

21. Habermas, *Justification and Application,* trans. C. Cronin (Cambridge, MA: MIT Press, 1993), 145.

22. Habermas, "Vorpolitische Grundlagen des demokratischen Rechtsstaates," in *Zwischen Naturalismus und Religion,* 108.

23. Habermas, *The Philosophical Discourse of Modernity: Lecture XI,* quoted in D. Ingram, *Critical Theory: The Essential Readings* (New York: Paragon House, 1991), 277.

24. Habermas, *Religion and Rationality,* 133.

25. Habermas, "Einleitung," in *Zwischen Naturalismus und Religion,* 7. This was written, of course, before the summer 2005 Islamic unrest in France.

26. Ibid., 7.

27. Habermas, "Religion in der Öffentlichkeit," 132–33.

28. See Ernst Böckenförde, "Die Entstehung des Staates als Vorgang der Säkularisation," in *Recht, Staat, Freiheit,* ed. E. Böckenförde (Frankfurt am Main: Suhrkamp Verlag, 1991), 92 ff.

29. Habermas, "Religion in der Öffentlichkeit," 125.

30. Ibid., 128–30. As an example, Rawls cites the way that Martin Luther King Jr. used reasonable religious thinking in his political thought.

31. Habermas, "Vorpolitische Grundlagen," 107.

32. Ibid.

33. Habermas, "Vorpolitische Grundlagen," 115.

34. Habermas, "Religion in der Öffentlichkeit," 150.

35. Habermas, *The Future of Human Nature* (Cambridge: Polity, 2003), 110. This indicates, in fact, a trend in Habermas to make remarks that seem to contradict his systematic position that religion and communicative action are incompatible. See Edmund Arens, "Religion as Ritual, Communicative, and Critical Praxis," in *The Frankfurt School on Religion: Key Writings by the Major Thinkers,* ed. Eduardo Mendieta (New York: Routledge, 2004), 383.

36. Habermas, "Vorpolitische Grundlagen," 116.

37. Habermas, *Future of Human Nature,* 108.

38. Habermas, "Religion in der Öffentlichkeit," 149.

39. Ibid., 152.

40. Klaus Eder, "Europäische Säkularisierung—ein Sonderweg in die postsäkulare Gesellschaft," *Berliner Journal für Soziologie* 3 (2002): 331–43.

41. Habermas, "Religion in der Öffentlichkeit," 151–52; idem, "Vorpolitische Grundlagen," 116.

42. Habermas, "Vorpolitische Grundlagen," 117.

43. Ibid., 118.

44. Habermas, *Future of Human Nature,* 113–14. "A state neutrality with respect to world views—and a state power that guarantees the same ethical freedoms for each and every citizen—is incompatible with the political generalization of a secular point of view. Insofar as they appear qua citizens, secularized citizens may neither deny religious world views a role in truth determination nor contest the right of religiously motivated co-citizens to contribute to public discourse using religious language. A liberal political culture can even expect that secularized citizens will participate in the efforts required to translate relevant contributions from religious language into a publicly accessible one." See "Religion in der Öffentlichkeit," 118.

45. Habermas, "Religion in der Öffentlichkeit," 136.

46. Ibid., 136.

47. Ibid., 144.

48. Ibid., 135.

49. Ibid., 147.

50. Habermas criticizes Paul Weitman's solution—which relies on the religious persons' convictions, without arguments, concerning what their governments would favor—as too one-sided. See "Religion in der Öffentlichkeit," 139. He also criticizes Nicholas Wolterstorff's desire to allow lawmakers to use religious arguments, and even to serve in some cases as agents of a religious majority (140). Habermas maintains that the "existential value conflicts between faith convictions" are in some cases not suitable for compromise (141).

51. Ibid., 137.

52. Habermas even has recently said that he admires the "complexity, the level of differentiation, the gravity, and the rigor of the dialectical argument" of Aquinas, who stands as a "tower of strength among the shifting sands of religiosity." See Habermas, *Time of Transitions,* trans. C. Cronin and M. Pensky (Cambridge: Polity, 2006), 154.

53. Joseph Ratzinger, "Was die Welt Zusammenhält: Vorpolitische moralische Grundlagen eines freiheitlichen Staates," in *Dialektik der Säkularisierung* (Freiburg im Breisgau: Herder, 2005), 50–51.

54. Ibid., 53.

55. Ibid., 56.

56. *Deus Caritas Est,* sec. 28.

57. Ibid.

9 | "Transcendence from Within"

Benedict XVI, Habermas, and Lonergan
on Reason and Faith

FREDERICK G. LAWRENCE

[A] time of confusion . . . calls beliefs into question and, because they
are just beliefs, because they are not personally generated knowledge,
answers are hard to come by. So to confusion there are easily added
disorientation, disillusionment, crisis, surrender, unbelief. But . . . from
the present situation Catholics are suffering more keenly than others,
not indeed because their plight is worse, but because up to Vatican II
they were sheltered against the modern world and since Vatican II they
have been exposed more and more to the chill winds of modernity.
—Bernard Lonergan, "Belief: Today's Issue"

BENEDICT XVI'S REGENSBURG ACCOUNT OF THE NARROWING
OF REASON IN THE WEST

In his open letter to the *Neue Zürcher Zeitung* (February 10,
2007),[1] Jürgen Habermas comments on Benedict XVI's speech at Regensburg, saying that the pope's notion of rationality presupposes a "metaphysical" synthesis between reason and faith that held sway from Augustine to Thomas Aquinas. This is partially true. Benedict has consistently
emphasized the gravamen of one of the clearest patristic statements by

Tertullian, one that recalls the Platonic Socrates: "Christ called himself the Truth, not opinion."[2] Benedict has long stressed that the Septuagint's translation of the Tetragrammaton in Exodus 3:14 as "I Am" providentially initiated "a profound encounter between faith and reason," and that the Johannine phrase "In the beginning was the *logos*" is evidence that "the encounter between the Biblical message and Greek thought did not happen by chance." The Johannine passage, like Paul's Areopagus speech, was emblematic of an encounter between "genuine enlightenment and religion" and generated a "synthesis between the Greek spirit and the Christian spirit." Indeed, in 1983 then Cardinal Ratzinger stated, "Christianity is . . . the synthesis mediated in Jesus Christ between the faith of Israel and the Greek spirit."[3]

Yet Benedict has never been a devotee of scholastic metaphysics, however much he was sympathetic to its main goals.[4] This ambivalence was reflected in the Regensburg speech when Benedict described the synthesis between faith and reason in terms, not of the metaphysics, but of the "so-called intellectualism of Augustine and Thomas." Benedict uses the expression "so-called" because he does not wish to suggest any rationalist subordination of faith to reason; and the term "intellectualism" is drawn from medieval philosophical faculty psychology's convention of contrasting intellect (*intellectus*) and will (*voluntas*). Hence, the intellectualism of Augustine and Thomas Aquinas is opposed to the voluntarism of Duns Scotus. According to Benedict, Scotus initiated a tradition, radicalized by William of Ockham, in which "God's transcendence and otherness are so exalted that our reason, our sense of the true and the good, are no longer an authentic mirror of God, whose deepest possibilities remain eternally unattainable and hidden behind his decisions."

Bernard Lonergan's reading of Thomas Aquinas clarifies another nuance of the term *intellectualism,* although not in connection with the contrast between human intellect and human will. In Aquinas's gnoseology one may contrast *within* the exercise of intelligence itself the act of understanding (*intelligere*) and the inner word (*verbum intus prolatum*). The inner word may be either the concept proceeding from a direct insight into a phantasm or the judgment proceeding from the indirect or reflective act of understanding that grasps the sufficiency of the evidence for the truth of an affirmation.

In a January 1935 letter Lonergan noted "that Augustine talked a lot about *intelligere* and that Thomas didn't talk about universals—though knowledge of universals was supposed [by then dominant Thomistic interpreters] to be the be-all and end-all of science."[5] In *Verbum: Word and Idea in Aquinas* Lonergan later retrieved Aquinas's understanding of understanding and broke with both the closed and static conceptualism and the mistaken notion of judgment as a rubber-stamping synthesis upon which the pejorative and rationalist sense of the term "intellectualism" is based. The belief (1) that concepts, as impoverished replicas of what is presented by the senses and the imagination, precede acts of understanding and (2) that we know the existence or occurrence of things not by rational judgment but through sense perception, prevailed within Scholasticism from Henry of Ghent and Duns Scotus through Francisco Suárez to the post–*Aeterni Patris* Thomistic schools. Lonergan's close study of Thomas on the relationship between understanding and formulation/judgment in relation to the natural analogy for Trinitarian theology uncovered the factual psychological basis in experience for the metaphysical account of understanding and judgment in Thomas's writings: "Aquinas attributed the key role in cognitional theory not to inner words, concepts, but to acts of understanding."[6]

Benedict's expression "the rationality of faith" parses theology's task of *fides quaerens intellectum.* According to Lonergan, Aquinas's understanding of the phrase means not faith seeking certainty or proof according to the requirements of Aristotle's *Posterior Analytics,* as was the case in the thesis format of the post-Reformation manuals, but faith seeking understanding in the sense of working out analogies from nature, which Aquinas acknowledged as *rationes convenientiae* (i.e., what today we would call "possibly relevant hypotheses," rather than demonstrations or proofs).[7] Ironically, the notorious voluntarists Scotus and Ockham applied the Aristotelian *akribeia,* or unalloyed logical rigor and coherence, to theology in a way that Aristotle himself would have regarded as inappropriate. This bias toward an exclusively logical control of meaning was cultivated in Scholastic *Konklusionstheologie* (or *Denziger-theologie*) until the Second Vatican Council. It fit the needs of ahistorical orthodoxy, which did not acknowledge that "terms are . . . defined, but definitions are not unique: on the contrary, for each term there is a historical sequence of different definitions; there is a learned explanation for each change of definition."[8] This assumption was integral to the replacement of "the inquiry of the *quaestio* by the pedagogy of the thesis." Bishop and inquisitor Melchior Cano adapted the *loci* of Agricola's forensic rhetoric in the "thesis method" of pre–Vatican II seminary theology. The thesis stated church doctrines as propositions; after briefly listing the opinions of those who rejected them, it adduced proofs from Scripture, the Fathers, the councils and authoritative documents, the theologians, and finally from nature to establish how close they came to being *de fide definita.* This method presupposed "meanings fixed by definitions, with presuppositions and implications fixed by laws of logic," resulting in "what used to be called eternal verities but today are known as static abstractions."[9] It was a pedagogy that inculcated a preoccupation both with the certitudes of the faith and with the teaching authority and sanctions of the church.[10]

The most intelligent of those suspected of "modernism" thought in all probity that faith cannot be proven. Some turned to religious experience as the starting point for both theology and apologetics, and rejected dogmas and abstract propositional truths in favor of myths, symbols, metaphors, and rituals as expressions of religious experience. To be sure, the legitimate motivation for the old-style scholastic apologists, and for their opposition to starting with religious experience, was their Catholic conviction that Christian beliefs are to be believed because they are true, not because they happen to appeal to someone's subjective emotions or feelings. The so-called modernists opposed the post-Reformation and post-Enlightenment preoccupation with the *praeambula fidei* and with the old fundamental theology operating under the guise of science as *certa cognitio rerum per causas,* a preoccupation for which the core of science is understood to be logical demonstration: arguments for the existence of God, arguments for the ethical obligation to worship and adore God, arguments from prophecies and miracles to establish the divine origin of the Christian religion, and arguments for the church as the true religion. The rationale for this was always a dead-end undertaking. One in the position of "understanding seeking faith" tries to reach conclusions containing divinely revealed truths on the basis of premises that are simply rational or proportionate to "unaided reason." Such a procedure cannot justify a reasonable assent to divinely revealed truth. (The only consolation is that the reason of "the fool [who] says in his heart there is no God" [Ps. 14:1 NIV] cannot in this manner demonstrate the impossibility of such truths, either.)

While the ecclesiastical antimodernists worried about the certainty of the *praeambula* in terms of the logical control of meaning, Maurice Blondel in *L'Action* and John Henry Newman in the *Essay in Aid of a Grammar of Assent* debunked the stock-in-trade of old-style theology and apologetics—the putatively infallible intuitions, self-evident premises, and necessary conclusions—as the subjective constructions that they were. They opened the door to the widespread *ressourcement* that paved the way for Vatican II.

The stages of dehellenization to which Benedict ascribed the atrophy and shrinkage of reason in his Regensburg speech were virtually synthesized in what the church called modernism. First, the Reformation reacted to the putative subordination of faith and scriptural revelation to reason in late medieval scholasticism; and Kant radicalized the hermeneutic principles—*sola scriptura, sola fide*, and *sola gratia*—by his project of delimiting the scope of reason in order "to make room for faith." Reason as theoretical or speculative was confined to Kant's *simulacrum* of Newtonian science, which involved the mathematization of observable phenomena; reason as practical and aesthetic took over the traditional primacy from theoretical reason. Second, the historical-critical school of New Testament studies from Reimarus to Schweitzer went hand in hand with what Karl Barth called the *Kulturprotestantismus* he ascribed to liberal Protestants such as Friedrich Schleiermacher, Adolf von Harnack, Albrecht Ritschl, and Wilhelm Herrmann. As far as historical knowledge of Jesus is concerned, the *religionsgeschichtliche Schule*[11] and post-Bultmannian biblical studies oscillated between Wilhelm Wrede's "thoroughgoing skepticism" and Albert Schweitzer's "thoroughgoing eschatology."[12]

While liberal Protestantism (perhaps like liberal Catholicism after Vatican II) tended to replace worship with morality more or less in the Kantian mode, out-and-out scientism has come to dominate the third stage of dehellenization sketched by Benedict. Thus, current advocates of atheism such as Richard Dawkins dogmatically assert that genuine knowledge does not extend beyond the limits of algorithmic formulation and empiricist observation; even the human sciences must be trimmed to meet these limits. Any questions about the justification of scientific knowledge itself—not to mention questions regarding the overall meaning of human existence—are interdicted because they go beyond these limits, which are arbitrarily posited as exclusively valid.

THE AMBIGUITIES OF "HELLENIZATION"

The Nicene Case

Unfortunately, "dehellenization" is a misleading characterization of the processes at work in the truncation, immanentization, and alienation of reason that is destructive not only to faith itself but also to the human condition *tout court*. It was used by Protestants of the historical school to argue that Jesus's own first-century Palestinian mentality was distorted by Hellenism. Again, *Hellenization* does not refer simply to inculturation into Gentile culture. The councils at Nicea and after were not simply rephrasing beliefs in the language of a different culture. Indeed, Benedict's remarking the contrast between truth and opinion implies a movement among Christians from what-is-first-for-us to what-is-first-in-itself. This shift characterized the Trinitarian and Christological debates punctuated by the first six ecumenical councils, when church fathers reflected on the global and compact expressions in the ordinary or commonsense language of mythos and adopted the techniques of logical control to refine questions and to respond with definitions using technical terms.

The Council of Nicea's use of the term *homoousios* to define the relationship between the Father and the Son did not involve a rationalist subordination of Christian belief to Greek philosophy. Athanasius explained that the term defends the biblical meaning by logically ordering statements. "Therefore, because they are one, and because the divinity itself is also one, what is said (in the Scriptures) of the Father is also said of the Son, except the name, Father."[13] Arius, the rationalist, held that if the Son is *"ek tou patros,"* logically he must be a creature instead of Pantocrator. Neither Athanasius nor the assembled bishops at Nicea would have anything of such extreme Hellenization. Athanasius's balanced Hellenization only applied to a serious controversy the second-

order reflective resources made possible by the tradition of Greek philosophy; he did not borrow from any extant author or school. When
commenting on the Nicene decrees, Athanasius said that the Fathers
"were again compelled to gather up the mind (*dianoian*) of the Scriptures and to state and write again more clearly what they had said before, that the Son is consubstantial (*homoousion*) with the Father, in
order that they might make clear that the Son is not merely like, but is
from the Father as the same in likeness (*touton tē homoiōsei*)."[14] To say
the Son is "from the substance of the Father" (*ek tēs ousias tou Patros*)
differentiates the Son's generation from any creature's generation or production, while both synthesizing the biblical teaching about Son and
restating the mind of the Fathers at Nicea.[15] Alois Grillmeier has suc-
cinctly summarized the issue of Hellenization at Nicea:

> If we want to use a label like "the Hellenization of the Christian
> faith," we can see from this dispute where it really applies. It does
> not apply to the bishops of the council of Nicea (325) who rejected
> Arius' teaching. The fathers of the council used a term which fits
> very well into Greek philosophy, *homoousios,* identical in substance,
> consubstantial. But far from implying acceptance of Greek philoso-
> phy, their use of this term was a direct attack on it. They used it to
> stress the very point which no Greek philosopher would ever have
> conceived of, the true divinity of the Son and his begetting—not
> creation—by the Father. The council of Nicea chose the *difficilior
> lectio* of the Christian message. It resisted the temptation to adopt
> Arius' theory, although it was philosophically more plausible.[16]

The term "Hellenization" is appropriate to the extent that the
council fathers realized that they had to move from the first-for-us perspective of the Bible to the first-in-itself perspective of theory, which
Greek philosophy initiated. Lonergan clarified the theological task of
reason performed by Athanasius and the council fathers in the definition of the divinity of the Son: "(1) avoiding metaphors and anthropo-
morphisms, (2) selecting appropriate aspects of created things from
which, by analogy, one can ascend to some conception of God, and
(3) attending to and applying the words of sacred scripture, through
which alone the mystery of the Trinity is made known to us."[17] In this

process, the Christian faith does not change, but there occurs a growth in understanding that had not previously been attained.

Chalcedon

This positive sense of Hellenization becomes characteristic of the reasonableness of Christian dogma as a rule of belief. Athanasius gave a second-order interpretation of the *homoousios:* "Whatever is said about the Father . . . whatever is said about the Son . . ." After the Council of Nicea, Severus of Antioch and the Monophysite tradition, wishing in all goodwill to adhere to the teachings of the council and of Athanasius, did not want to admit more than one nature in Christ, and so resisted the further questions, raised by Apollinaris on the one hand and by Nestorius on the other. On the way to the teaching of the Council of Chalcedon (451) about two natures united in "one and the same" Jesus Christ, Diodore of Tarsus, Theodore of Mopsuestia, Pope Leo the Great, and Cyril of Alexandria articulated the questions and attempted to respond to them. Here the challenge was actually methodological: to answer new and further questions by moving beyond the first-for-us perspective of the faithful (*both* in terms of the Scriptures *and* in terms of the preceding Fathers and councils) to the first-in-itself perspective of theology and systematic thinking.[18] Once again, according to Grillmeier, the technique of reflection on scriptural propositions was used to reach the orthodox response:

> The council of Chalcedon canonized no metaphysical "theory of Christ." Still less did it leave any room for mythological ideas. The whole "formalistic" style of the fathers' definitions, far from making the mystery manageable, emphasizes its difficulty. The council doesn't give us an answer to the question, "Who is Jesus Christ?" It gives us instructions about how to think and talk. Whether we go into further metaphysical questions or not, we are required to resist oversimplifications and always to describe the man Jesus in such a way that God is clearly visible in his humanity, and always to describe the eternal Son of God in such a way that he has the features of the man Jesus of Nazareth.[19]

A Medieval Case

In 1277, the bishop of Paris, Étienne Tempier, under pressure from Peter of Spain and Pope John XXI, condemned 219 propositions associated with Latin Averroism, some of which were ostensibly those of Thomas Aquinas as one who made use of the philosophy of Aristotle.[20] The Stagirite's comprehensive philosophy of nature, not influenced by *theologoumena,* did not completely accord with Christian biblical doctrine. According to Ernest Fortin, the condemnations were in all likelihood aimed not at the then recently deceased "Angelic Doctor" but at exponents of what became pejoratively known in later scholarship as Latin Averroism — Siger of Brabant and Boethius of Dacia. Fortin points out that Siger, who was so exalted by Dante in *The Divine Comedy,*[21] tethered his mind neither to the authoritative teachings of the Bible nor to church tradition. Should any doctrines not pass muster before the tribunal of reason (in Aristotelian terms), he insisted on saying what he thought was true, even if doing so would be costly. In Fortin's view, Siger's determination to follow Aristotle wherever his thought might lead was a conscious commitment to be open to the breadth and depth of Aristotle's thought as opposed to its putatively "constricted"[22] version in orthodox theology. This was a rationalist Hellenization against which the Dominican Richard Kilwardby and many Franciscans such as John Peckham reacted. J.-P. Torrell calls Peckham "the type . . . of the conservative Augustinian tendency that opposed the new Aristotelian ideas." Thomas Aquinas was not a rationalist.[23]

Perhaps the underlying motive for this reaction was a failure to acknowledge the need in the medieval context for a "*Wendung zur Idee*" or an articulation of theology as a science in order to answer questions raised by the gradual entry of Aristotle's works into the Latin West. As Yves Congar put the matter:

> For Albert the Great and St. Thomas the sciences represent a genuine knowledge of the world and of the nature of things. For things have their own consistence and intelligibility and this knowledge is valid even in the Christian economy. Therefore, the sciences in their order have a verifiable autonomy of object and method, just

as in their order they convey their own truth. In this perspective the expression "handmaid of theology," which St. Thomas also uses, has a very different meaning from the primitive Augustinian sense, for "the better to assure the services of its slave, theology begins by freeing her."

Now we understand better why Albert and St. Thomas followed the thought of Aristotle. They were looking not only for a master of reasoning but a master in the knowledge of the nature of things, of the world, and of man himself. Certainly St. Thomas was not ignorant any more than St. Bonaventure that all things must be referred to God. But alongside that reference to God in the order of use or exercise, he recognized an unconditioned bounty to the speculative intellect in the nature or specification of things, which was a work of God's wisdom. There was question of speculatively reconstructing the order of forms, of *rationes,* put into things and into the very mysteries of salvation by the wisdom of God. Such a program could be realized only by a knowledge of forms and natures in themselves. This is why St. Thomas' Aristotelianism is not external to his theological wisdom or to the very conception he has fashioned of it.[24]

In Lonergan's analysis, the medieval context required more than the logical coherence of the doctrines that were problematized by Peter Abelard's *Sic et Non* in 158 propositions "pro" and "con." What was needed was a sapiential ordering of *quaestiones* that was capable of dealing with the fundamental issues from which other connected issues followed. Such an ordering was not available in the order of discovery (*via analytica/ inventionis*) as evident in Peter Lombard's *Sentences.* Such a wisdom needed what Aquinas called the *disputatio magistralis,* which instructed listeners to lead them to an understanding of the truth already believed by them, involving an investigation going to the root of the truth by presenting its reasons or grounds and by making students know why what is said is true.[25] The theologian has to pass from what is first in Scripture and what is first in the patristic authorities to what is first-in-itself, thus making the transition from the *ordo inventionis* to the *ordo doctrinae.* We can note how Thomas goes back and forth between the two orders in the fourth book of his *Summa Contra Gentiles,* where chapters alternate between arguments ascertaining facts of Christian belief by appeals to authorities on the one hand and, on the other, magisterial disputations in which reason is used to acquire further understanding of the truths believed.[26] This is an achievement of theology as a science, or of theology as systematic in a more contemporary sense.

Modern Dehellenization

For Lonergan, modern dehellenization has two principal causes, the rise of modern science and the emergence of historical consciousness. Lonergan did not stress the *Wirkungsgeschichte* of the Reformation as Benedict did in Regensburg, because he agreed with Herbert Butterfield's position that the origin of modern science "outshines everything since the rise of Christianity and reduces the Renaissance and the Reformation to the rank of mere episodes, mere internal displacements, within the system of medieval Christendom."[27]

Modern science has in common with the Aristotelian notion of science only one feature: the movement from the "first-for-us" of the commonsense cognitional perspective expressed in ordinary language to the "first-in-themselves" of a theoretical cognitional perspective expressed in technical terms and relations. As Lonergan explains, commonsense understanding is descriptive in the sense that it understands things-in-relation-to-our-senses. Thus, operating in terms of common sense, we speak of the sun rising and setting, and of the sun as revolving around the earth. In contrast, the perspective of the theoretical understanding characteristic of science is explanatory in the sense that it understands things-in-relation-to-each-other. So the scientist puts the sun at the center of the solar system and knows that the earth spins on its axis every twenty-four hours at the same time as it revolves around the sun. In general, ancient science passed from common sense to theory by using logic and dialectic to replace opinions with *epistēmē,* with definitions *omni et soli.* But modern science moves from the raw experience of sense perception to its version of classical science (which grasps possibly relevant correlations) by measurement, and then maps the results on a number field; this evokes hypothesis formation (1), the drawing of implications from the hypothesis (2), and empirical testing of the implications (3), for the sake of a more or less probable, indirect verification of the hypothesis (4). This procedure is commonly simplified by saying that the modern sciences are based on *observation* (in contrast to the verbalisms of premodern science) and the *mathematization* of nature (so that valid knowledge admits only what is susceptible of algorithmic formulation). When either the more complicated or simplified conceptions of scientific procedure enter into modern rationalist ideologies, then anything that goes beyond the limits of world-immanent existence comes to be regarded as the realm of unreality expressible in metaphor, symbol, and myth (taken in the pejorative sense of the term). This is connected inextricably with the so-called end of metaphysics.

The second factor in modern dehellenization is the rise of historical consciousness and of the procedures of critical history in the nineteenth century. Lonergan cited the Anglican theologian Alan Richardson:

> One should never forget that it was one and the same movement of critical enquiry which first culminated in the seventeenth-century scientific achievement and later in the emergence of the fully developed historical critical method of the nineteenth. The critical faculty, once awakened, could not rest satisfied with the successful exploration of the realm of nature; it was bound to go from there to the critical investigation of the more intractable realm of human nature, and when the idea of development was fully understood, to seek to understand scientifically how, in fact, man and his institutions have come to be what they are. Since the nineteenth century it has been an axiom of Western thinking that men and their institutions cannot be understood apart from their history. . . . The historical revolution in human thinking, which was accomplished in the nineteenth century, is just as important as the scientific revolution of two centuries earlier. But they are not two different revolutions; they are aspects of the one great transitional movement from the mediaeval to the modern way of looking at things.[28]

Augustine's *De doctrina Christiana,* which presided over the theological reading of the Bible until early modern times, set forth a hermeneutics of belief or of love. Briefly, it was considered a matter of course to read the Bible in light of the Christian creeds that emerged from the formulations of the early baptismal formulae. Although he did not champion the *sensus literalis* of Scripture above all, there was something hermeneutically correct about his account of the way Christian belief and worship and the practice of love influence a faithful reading of the biblical texts. In general, Hans-Georg Gadamer's account of the shortcomings of the "prejudice against prejudice" allows us to recover the real strengths in Augustine's teachings again.[29] But to do so fully requires one to overcome the specific cognitional theoretic and rationalist biases that since Baruch Spinoza's *Theologico-Political Treatise* have been regularly taken for granted by those practicing the critical historical reading of the Scriptures.

During Benedict's professorial career the prime instance of this unbalanced type of historical scholarship was Rudolf Bultmann.[30] This brilliant sometime collaborator of Karl Barth and colleague of the Martin Heidegger of the *Sein und Zeit* period at Marburg united the Kantianism he received from his teacher Wilhelm Herrmann with a historicist basis for the modern split between the Christ of faith and the Jesus of history; these presuppositions have not been completely abandoned by everyone in New Testament studies. I believe Ben F. Meyer has well formulated the underlying issue:

> The key issue was the claims of reason. To practically all participants in the quest, much of what Luther and Melanchthon considered essential to Christianity ran counter to reason; i.e., it violated the conception of reality as an impermeable system of finite causes. Bultmann is the spokesman of a two-hundred-year tradition when he says that "for modern man" the conceptions of spirits and miracles, redeemer and redemption, are "over and done with." To hold the contrary would involve a *sacrificium intellectus* "in order to accept what we cannot sincerely consider true." Spoken in the tradition of Goethe and Schiller, of Kant, Schelling, and Hegel, of the post-Enlightenment mainstream. Here Christian and agnostic, rationalist and idealist, liberal and existentialist find common ground.[31]

This "conception of reality as an impermeable system of finite causes" lies at the heart of Spinoza's "hermeneutics of suspicion," as we see in the *Theologico-Political Treatise*'s chapter "Of Miracles," upon which all the great Germans listed in Meyer's statement ultimately depended. But as Meyer notes, Christians themselves shared the blame for this rationalist conception of nature, because they espoused it in their apologetics. Meyer quotes Butterfield on this: "If earlier in the [seventeenth] century religious men had hankered after a mathematically interlocking universe to justify the rationality and self-consistency of God, before the end of the century their successors were beginning to be nervous because they saw the mechanism becoming possibly too self-complete."[32] Quoting Butterfield further, Meyer then says, "Unwittingly, they had opened the way for 'a colossal secularization of thought in every possible realm of ideas at the same time.' This is what Paul Hazard called 'the crisis of the European mind,' and Peter Gay, 'the rise of modern paganism.'"[33] As Meyer reports, "Avant-garde Protestant theology allied itself with the spirit of the time. In eighteenth-century Germany, orthodoxy in the Wolffian mode gave way to rationalism or its opposite, Pietism." Meanwhile Catholic theology "retired to its dogmatic corner"[34] (continuing to do so in its antimodernist stance), because, as Lonergan phrased the matter, the church "acknowledged the transformation of our knowledge of nature and of our knowledge of man, not as a single momentous development in philosophy, but as a series of regrettable aberrations that unfortunately were widely accepted."[35]

LONERGAN'S ALTERNATIVE APPROACH TO THE PROBLEM OF DEHELLENIZATION

Besides addressing the kinds of problems Roman Catholic theology encountered in connection with dehellenization,[36] Bernard Lonergan spent his life trying to respond to the modernist crisis. As is evident from what has already been said, he gave careful consideration to these issues in his theological work. But the overall crisis in Catholic philosophy and theology brought about by the rise of modern science and of modern historical studies compelled him to push beyond theology proper into what he conceived of as philosophy's contemporary role, namely, foundational methodology. Lonergan's analysis of the crisis highlights the great transition in Western culture from the classicist perspective that had permeated ecclesiastical and theological consciousness:

Always in the past it had been the Catholic tradition to penetrate and Christianize the social fabric and the culture of the age. So it entered into the Hellenistic world of the patristic period. So it was one of the principal architects of medieval society and medieval thought. So too it was almost scandalously involved in the Renaissance. But only belatedly has it come to acknowledge that the world of the classicist no longer exists and that the only world in which it can function is the modern world.

To a great extent this failure is to be explained by the fact that modern developments were covered over with a larger amount of wickedness. Since the beginning of the eighteenth century Christianity has been under attack. Agnostic and atheistic philosophies have been developed and propagated. The development of the natural and of the human sciences was such that they appeared and often were said to support such movements. The emergence of the modern languages with their new literary forms was not easily acclaimed when they contributed so little to devotion and so much, it seemed, to worldliness and irreligion. The new industry spawned slums, the new politics revolutions, the new discoveries unbelief. One may lament it but one can hardly be surprised that at the beginning of this century, when churchmen were greeted with a heresy that logically entailed all possible heresies, they named the new monster modernism.

If their opposition to wickedness made churchmen unsympathetic to modern ways, their classicism blocked their vision. They were unaware that modern science involved a quite different notion of science from that entertained by Aristotle. When they praised science and affirmed the Church's support for science, what they meant to support was true and certain knowledge of things through their causes.

But modern science is not true and certain; it is just probable. It is not fully knowledge; it is hypothesis, theory, system, the best available opinion. It regards not things but data, phenomena. While it still speaks of causes, what it means is not end, agent, matter, form, but correlation.[37]

The problems raised by the shift from the Aristotelian to the modern conception of science were exacerbated by the added problems due to historical consciousness. As Lonergan remarks, classicist churchmen worried that "the historical sciences were the locus of continuous attacks on traditional views of the Church in its origins and throughout its development." And so, as classicists they "believed that [they] could escape history, that [they] could encapsulate culture in the universal, the normative, the ideal, the immutable, that, while times would change, still the changes necessarily would be minor, accidental, of no serious significance."[38]

Hence, Lonergan was convinced that, "in brief, the contemporary issue is, not a new religion, not a new faith, but a belated social and cultural transition," namely, "the transition from classicist to modern culture." The task was that of "disengagement from classicist thought-forms and viewpoints, and simultaneously, of a new involvement in modern culture." It is important to insist here that Lonergan "did not think things wrong because they were classicist; on the contrary, [he] found a number of things [he] thought wrong, and, on putting them together, [he] found what he named classicism. Again, [he did] not think things are right because they are modern, but [he] did find a number of things [he] thought right and they are modern at least in the sense that they were overlooked in the nineteenth century Catholic theological tradition." And so, as he went on to point out, "If we are not just to throw out what is good in classicism and replace it with contemporary trash, then we have to take the trouble, and it is enormous, to grasp the strength and the weakness, the power and the limitations, the good points and the shortcomings of both classicism and modernity."[39]

This is an enormous challenge for Catholic philosophers and theologians, one for which knowledge is not enough.

One has to be creative. Modernity lacks roots. Its values lack balance and depth. Much of its science is destructive of man. Catholics in the twentieth century are faced with a problem similar to that met by Aquinas in the thirteenth century. Then Greek and Arabic culture were pouring into Western Europe and, if it was not to destroy Christendom, it had to be known, assimilated, transformed. Today modern culture, in many ways more stupendous than any that ever existed, is surging round us. It too has to be known, assimilated, transformed. That is the contemporary issue.[40]

HABERMAS, BENEDICT, AND LONERGAN AND POSTMETAPHYSICAL THINKING

In his open letter to the *Neue Zürcher Zeitung*, Jürgen Habermas notes concerning Benedict XVI's Regensburg speech that the pope's brief account of the gradual decline of reason includes a brief historical genealogy of postmetaphysical thinking:

The progress from Duns Scotus to nominalism leads nonetheless not only to the voluntarist God of the Protestants, but also levels the path to modern science. Kant's critical turn leads not only to a critique of the proofs for the existence of God, but also to the notion of autonomy, which has first made our modern understanding of law and democracy possible. And historicism leads forcibly not only to a relativistic self-denial of reason. As a child of the Enlightenment, [historicism] makes us sensitive to cultural differences and protects us from the overgeneralization of context-dependent judgments.[41]

Habermas holds that modern natural sciences and history challenge philosophy not only to become self-critical but to bid farewell "to metaphysical constructions of the whole of nature and history," because "nature and history pertain to the empirical sciences, while little more is left to philosophy than the competences of knowing, speaking, and acting subjects."[42] Habermas, Ratzinger, and Lonergan agree in the main about the historical stages in the development of philosophical and theological knowledge, starting with the "axial period" defined earlier by Karl Jaspers.[43] All three reject the Enlightenment rationalist accounts of d'Alembert or Comte, which deny cognitive status to anything but modern empirical science.

Benedict has always affirmed that human beings can know both reality as factual and good and evil objectively even when the subject matter is not reducible to what can be observed by the senses. Habermas believes Benedict's assertion is grounded in premodern metaphysics whereas postmetaphysical thinking signals the decline of an "emphatic concept of theory, which was supposed to render not only the human world but nature, too, intelligible in their internal structures."[44] Moreover, having undertaken the linguistic turn, postmetaphysical thinking replaces consciousness as a starting point for philosophy. It rejects transcendental approaches and reflects on the fact that "the rules (according to which signs are linked, sentences are formed, and utterances are brought forth) can be read off from linguistic formations *as if from something lying before one.*"[45] Again, postmetaphysical thinking eschews thought as abstract, disembodied, and detached to consider thought only within social space and historical, cultural time, and it affirms the primacy of practice over theory.

What can be made of Habermas's proposal to adopt a postmetaphysical standpoint in the cultural conversation between secular reason and religious reason? Vittorio Possenti has rejected Habermas's proposal out of hand, arguing that unless one has a metaphysical basis, it is impossible to discriminate between either truth and falsehood or good and evil.[46] I propose instead Lonergan's foundational methodology as an account of postmetaphysical thinking to which Benedict (whose position may well be close to that propounded by Possenti) and Habermas may each be able to subscribe. In its philosophical dimension, foundational methodology displaces metaphysics from its traditional primacy within scholasticism. As Lonergan stated in a review of E. Coreth's *Metaphysik*:

> I should not equate metaphysics with the total and basic horizon, the *Grund- und Gesamtwissenschaft.* Metaphysics as about being, equates with the objective pole of that horizon; but metaphysics, as science, does not equate with the subjective pole. In my opinion, [the metaphysical] subjective pole is under a measure of abstrac-

tion that is quite legitimate when one is mediating the immediacy of latent metaphysics, but is to be removed when one is concerned with the total and basic horizon. In the concrete, the subjective pole is indeed the inquirer, but incarnate, liable to mythic consciousness, in need of a critique that reveals where the counterpositions come from. The incarnate inquirer develops in a development that is social and historical, that stamps the stages of scientific and philosophic progress with dates, that is open to a theology that Karl Rahner has described as an *Aufhebung der Philosophie.*[47]

Lonergan agrees with Habermas that the methods of modern science ought to make a difference for philosophy. Just as modern science seeks to understand all the phenomena provided by the data of the senses, now philosophy must expressly adopt an empirical method. Philosophy today, Lonergan argues, must start from a *generalized* empirical method that encompasses the data of consciousness as well as the data of the senses. The phenomenologies of Heidegger, Merleau-Ponty, Gadamer, and Ricoeur have moved in this direction insofar as they radicalized the pioneering work of Edmund Husserl. A perhaps even more relevant precedent for Lonergan's approach is Jean Piaget's completely independent genetic epistemology, an organized account of empirical studies of developing human operations, including not merely biological, but also psychic and intellectual operations.[48] By starting with generalized empirical method, foundational method develops an empirically based cognitional theory to answer the question, what are we doing when we think we know? The key here is asking a factual question about what we are doing when we are learning what something is and whether it is so, instead of first asking whether we know. By scrutinizing experiences of understanding in mathematics, in the classical and statistical investigations of the natural sciences, and in the self-correcting learning processes of common sense, one attends not so much to the contents of knowing as to its compound of cognitional operations precisely as verifiable in experience. This provides a factual entrée to a methodically controlled justification for the validity of knowledge (epistemology), on the one hand, and on the other, to an explanatory heuristic structure of what we can know when we deploy this basic group of operations in theoretical or scientific experiencing, understanding, and judging (metaphysics).[49]

Lonergan's *Insight* is understood to be a transposition of Thomas Aquinas's gnoseology, which Lonergan recovered in *Verbum: Word and Idea in Aquinas,* already mentioned above. He claims that "from the structural and dynamic features of scientific knowing" he can

> cast into a single perspective such apparently diverse elements as (1) Plato's point in asking how the inquirer recognizes truth when he reaches what, as an inquirer, he did not know, (2) the intellectualist (though not conceptualist) meaning of the abstraction of form from material conditions, (3) the psychological manifestation of Aquinas's natural desire to know God by his essence, (4) what Descartes was struggling to convey in his incomplete *Regulae ad directionem ingenii,* (5) what Kant conceived as a priori synthesis, and (6) what is named the finality of intellect in J. Maréchal's vast labor on *Le point de depart de la métaphysique.*[50]

The point of the study is all-important, because it establishes an empirically verifiable meaning for the term *reason* as a common ground upon which all people of intelligence—secular or religious—may meet. As Lonergan wrote:

> Unless one breaks the duality in one's knowing one doubts that understanding correctly is knowing. Under the pressure of that doubt, either one will sink into the bog of a knowing that is without understanding, or else one will cling to understanding but sacrifice knowing on the altar of an immanentism, an idealism, a relativism. From the horns of that dilemma one escapes only through the discovery—and one has not made it yet if one has no memory of its startling strangeness—that there are two quite different realisms, that there is an incoherent realism, half animal and half human, that poses as a halfway house between materialism and idealism, and on the other hand that there is an intelligent and reasonable realism between which and materialism the halfway house is idealism.[51]

Four things should be noted here. First, while it is true that for Lonergan the starting point for such self-appropriation of oneself as a knower is consciousness, it is consciousness as accessible to reflection upon our experiences of experiencing, understanding, and judging, which we perform again and again all the time.

Second, Lonergan conceives of understanding as grasping intelligibility in the concreteness of images and of formulation as the constructive activity of expressing descriptively in symbol or metaphor or narrative, or explanatorily in technical terms and relations (concepts, definitions, functional correlations, algorithms), the intelligibility one has grasped. Further, he accepts Piaget's conception of "the real world as something that is constructed," because construction implies idealism or subjectivism only for one who thinks that "knowing is taking a good look at what is already out there now," an assumption that Lonergan identifies with the "incoherent realism" noted above, which is naïve.[52]

Third, for Lonergan, establishing the correctness of one's knowing is not achieved through an essentialism, which is the legitimate target of post-Kantian critiques of metaphysics, but through the grasp of a virtually unconditioned, that is, a conditioned, intelligibility whose conditions have in fact been fulfilled: "Thus the question, Does it exist? presents the prospective judgment as a conditioned [one]. Reflective understanding grasps the conditions and their fulfillment. From that grasp there proceeds rationally the judgment, It does exist."[53] In confining judgment to matters of fact and excluding everything that putatively "could not be otherwise," Lonergan eliminates all the exorbitant claims about the knowledge of the truth against which so-called fallibilists rightly object.

And fourth, Lonergan's starting point does not prejudice but acknowledges the linguistic turn, because the horizon of conscious intentionality is concretely conditioned by the horizon of language. Thus, we use language when, in order to respond to a question about data, we dispose the images in relation to which insights arise; we use language to express the contents of our acts of understanding in symbols and metaphors or technical terms; we normally verify (i.e., check the warrants for and judge the truth or falsity of) guesses or hypotheses formulated in language. Prior to all these operations, moreover, we have difficulty even perceiving what we cannot name in language. Hence, the horizons of language and of consciousness are mutually entwined with each other, and it is a mistake to isolate either horizon. One can prescind from either horizon, where "prescind" means to treat one at a time while realizing that the two can and should be brought back into relation to each other.

Because generalized empirical method basically takes seriously the empirical character, the constructive character, the contingency, and the linguistic character so emphasized by postmetaphysical communicative, genealogical, and deconstructive "antifoundationalism," it can ground an entirely nonreductionistic account of the methods of science, scholarship, philosophy, and theology.

Insight transposes Aquinas's gnoseology into a cognitional theory "sufficiently refined to do justice to the problems caused by symbolic logic, by mathematics, by the probable principles employed in the natural sciences, and by the ontological argument for God's existence."[54] As Lonergan turned his attention to other dimensions of foundational methodology, he made explicit the isomorphism between Aquinas on understanding and judging on the one hand and the basic procedures of modern empirical science on the other.[55] Then he was able to use Piaget's conception of the stages of human cognitive development (in terms of differentiating operations and grouping operations) through an analogy with group theory[56] in order to replace the notion of *habitus* (for example, Aristotle's conception of moral and dianoetic habits [*hexeis*]), which was not directly accessible to internal experience, but only metaphysically deduced. In its place he used the empirically verifiable notion of differentiations of consciousness. Thus, the general characterization of development as moving from global and compact expressions of worldviews or commonsense knowing to more differentiated and specialized accounts can be specified more exactly. The key differentiations of conscious intentionality that Lonergan works out regard commonsense, theory or system (as in the exact sciences of nature), scholarship (as in history or the humanities), interiority (as in intentionality analysis or generalized empirical method), and religion or transcendence. Lonergan did this in order to resolve apparently irreconcilable "chasms" among different universes of discourse (e.g., between symbolic and mythic realms and theoretical, explanatory lan-

guage) that have troubled theology in different ways throughout its development.[57] Lonergan used the notion of differentiated consciousness
to analyze the control of meaning,[58] and also the stages of meaning,[59]
which are relevant for understanding cultural or doctrinal pluralism.[60]
He also found a methodological resolution for many of theology's contemporary problems caused by varieties of undifferentiated, or combinations of multiply differentiated, consciousness by recourse to his notion of the unity of differentiated consciousness.

From the perspective of Lonergan's own development between
the completion of the writing of *Insight* in 1952 and the publication
of *Method in Theology* in 1972, we see how much more difficult was the
transposition of Aquinas's thought on grace and freedom[61] than had
been the task of transposing Aquinas's obnubilated gnoseology in *Verbum*. Emblematic of the further complicatedness involved in this transposition is the completely new appropriation in himself of what he
calls the transcendental notion of value, of the massive role of feelings
as intentional responses to values, of the reversal of the scholastic dictum *nil amatum nisi prius cognitum,* and of the expansion of his understanding of the good:

> In *Insight* the good was the intelligent and the reasonable. In *Method*
> the good is a distinct notion. It is intended in questions for delib-
> eration: Is this worthwhile? Is it truly or only apparently good? It
> is aspired to in the intentional response of feeling to values. It is
> known in judgments of value made by a virtuous or authentic per-
> son with a good conscience. It is brought about by deciding and liv-
> ing up to one's decisions. Just as intelligence sublates sense, just as
> reasonableness sublates intelligence, so deliberation sublates and
> thereby unifies knowing and feeling.[62]

The full impact of these changes from *Insight* can be seen in *Method*'s
chapter on the human good,[63] in which the structure of the human good
discussed in the former work is transformed by later breakthroughs connected with the fourth level of conscious intentionality.

On the way to *Method,* Lonergan also combined the notion of mediation adapted from Henri Niel's discussion of Hegelian dialectic[64] together with insights from Piaget to distinguish the world of immediacy,

in which objects are immediately present to our operations, from the world mediated by meaning, in which we operate "in a compound manner; immediately with respect to image, word, symbol; mediately with respect to what is represented or signified in this fashion."[65] Once we learn our mother tongue, we operate for the most part in the world mediated by meaning and guided by value, which is constructed by our operations of understanding, judging, and evaluating. As Lonergan put it in an early formulation of his breakthrough to a notion of meaning far more comprehensive than the simple relationship between a sign and that which it signifies:

> I have been meeting the objection that meaning is a merely secondary affair, that what counts is the reality that is meant and not the mere meaning that refers to it. My answer has been that the functions of meaning are larger than the objection envisages. I would not dispute that, for the child learning to talk, his little world of immediacy comes first, and that the words he uses are only an added grace. But as the child develops into a man, the world of immediacy shrinks into an inconspicuous and not too important corner of the real world, which is a world we know only through the mediation of meaning. Further, there is man's transformation of his environment, a transformation that is effected through the intentional acts that envisage ends, select means, secure collaborators, direct operations. Finally, besides the transformations of nature, there is man's transformation of man himself; and in this transformation the role of meaning is not merely directive but also constitutive.[66]

This notion of the constitutive function of meaning becomes absolutely central for Lonergan:

> For it is in the field where meaning is constitutive that man's freedom reaches its highest point. There too his responsibility is greatest. There there occurs the emergence of the existential subject, finding out for himself that he has to decide for himself what he is to make of himself. It is there that individuals become alienated from

community, that communities split into factions, that cultures flower and decline, that historical causality exerts its sway.[67]

LONERGAN, BENEDICT, AND HABERMAS ON THE SECULAR/RELIGIOUS DIALOGUE

For Benedict, faith without reason leads to fundamentalism, fanaticism, and terrorist violence, but faith that insists on reason is only strengthened thereby; Christian faith historically has also been a great supporter of reasonableness. Hence, his claim regarding Europe's apostasy is not just a plea for a return to Christian beliefs and praxis, but a warning about Europe's loss of traditional identity: "This is, in fact, an historical, cultural, and moral identity before being geographical, economic, or political; an identity constituted by a collection of universal values that Christianity has contributed to forging, thereby acquiring a role that is not only historical, but also foundational in relation to Europe."[68] Thus, Benedict, in accord with his universal values, had reflected on salutary and humane social, economic, and political perspectives for Europe and the West in his dialogue with Habermas on January 19, 2003.[69]

Habermas, in moving beyond his earlier Weberian stance on the role of religion in society,[70] demands in the secular/religious dialogue a hermeneutical self-reflection from the side of religious faith. He insists on the following stipulation: "Under the conditions of postmetaphysical thinking, whoever puts forth a truth claim must, nevertheless, translate experiences that have their home in religious discourse into the language of a scientific expert culture—and from this language, translate them back into praxis."[71]

Now if existentialists helped Lonergan to understand the world not only mediated but also constituted by human acts of meaning, phenomenologists helped him to discover the fundamental notion of horizon, which enabled him to transpose the traditional theological idea of conversion into the terms of intentionality analysis. Conversion is not a change within a given horizon, but a change from one horizon to another horizon. Great obstacles to genuine dialogue are caused by differences in horizon. One of the great Catholic conversation-partners with secular reason of the pre–Vatican II era was the learned American Jesuit John Courtney Murray, an early architect of *Dignitatis Humanae,* Vatican II's Decree on Religious Freedom.[72] He once explained rather humorously to one of his putative secular interlocutors, "Not only are our minds not meeting, they are not even clashing." More often than not, this is the situation of the dialogue between secular and religious reason today. In Lonergan's analysis the postmetaphysical terms of horizon and conversion are at the center of questions of dialectic and dialogue. These terms are clearly also indispensable for an adequate hermeneutical philosophy of dialectic and dialogue, and they raise issues less clearly expressed in terms of Habermas's stipulation that persons of faith must translate truth claims. Here, perhaps, Lonergan offers a bridge between the approach of Benedict and that of Habermas.

Lonergan highlights these issues surrounding horizon and conversion in *Method*'s treatment of the theological functional specialty of dialectic, which handles the concrete, the dynamic, and the contradictory within human movements. His definition of dialectic in theology is relevant to the secular/religious dialogue: "a generalized apologetic, conducted in an ecumenical spirit, aiming ultimately at a comprehensive viewpoint, and proceeding toward that goal by acknowledging differences, seeking their grounds real and apparent, and eliminating superfluous oppositions."[73] Conflicts and oppositions are rooted in horizonal differences that may be complementary and genetic, or dialectical if the oppositions are contradictory.[74] Finally, dialectical contradictions ultimately depend on the presence or absence of three distinct kinds of conversion: intellectual, moral, and religious.

For Lonergan conversion is a "transformation of the subject and his world"; it is "existential, intensely personal, utterly intimate." As lived, conversion "affects all of a man's conscious and intentional operations. It directs his gaze, pervades his imagination, releases the symbols that penetrate to the depths of his psyche. It enriches his understanding, guides his judgments, reinforces his decisions."[75] Intellectual conversion adds to the personal appropriation of rational self-consciousness the decision to live in accord with all the implications of discovering that knowing is irreducible to "taking a look," of rejecting "objectivity" conceived as the perceptual overcoming of the putative subject-object split, and of denying that reality is identical with the "already-out-there-now." Intellectual conversion brings the realization that knowing is an enactment of the compound composed of experience, understanding, and judgment, that objectivity is the achievement of authentically self-transcendent subjectivity, and that reality (or being) is the objective correlative of human acts of understanding and true judgment. Moral conversion shifts the criterion of one's decisions from satisfactions as interpreted via a reductive psychology of motivations to the criterion of true values implicitly interpreted though a philosophy of orientation. Religious conversion, finally, brings about a shift from oneself as the center of the universe to the real center, which Christians understand and affirm as the transcendent mystery of love and awe. True, religious and perhaps moral conversions may be correlated with people's changing the stories in the light of which they live, and yet there is a dimension to both human horizon and all the kinds of conversion that is irreducible to its linguisticality. In any case, for Lonergan, religious conversion is not confined to Christians.[76]

Habermas has spoken of the limit situation that the praxis of autonomy must inevitably encounter:

> Of course, effective socializing or pedagogical praxis, which under the aegis of an anticipated autonomy [*Mündigkeit*] seeks to provoke freedom in the other, must take into account the appearance of circumstances and spontaneous forces that it cannot at the same time control. And, with an orientation toward unconditional moral expectations, the subject increases the degree of his or her vulnerability. This then makes the subject especially dependent upon a considerate moral treatment from other persons. Yet, the risk of failure, indeed, of the annihilation of freedom precisely in the processes that should promote and realize freedom, only attests to the constitution of our finite existence. I refer to the necessity, which [Charles Sanders] Peirce emphasized again and again, of a self-relinquishing, transcending anticipation of an unlimited community of communication. This anticipation is simultaneously conceded to us and demanded of us.[77]

Isn't Habermas here translating into his own postmetaphysical terms what in Christian religious terms is, at least partially, a question of salvation? However, to maintain his postmetaphysical standpoint, Habermas observes the ground rules set by Kant's *Kritik der reinen Vernunft*:

> But, in the passage through the discursive universes of science and philosophy, not even the Peircean hope in a fallible theory of the development of being as a whole, including that of the *summum bonum*, will be able to be realized. Kant already had answered the question, "What may we hope for?" with a *postulate* of practical reason, not with a premodern certainty that could inspire us with *confidence*.[78]

And so he must offer this conviction: "I believe myself to have shown that in communicative action we have no choice but to presuppose the idea of an undistorted intersubjectivity . . . as the formal characterization of the necessary anticipation for the forms, not able to be anticipated, of a worthwhile life."[79] This Piercean reformulation of Kantian practical reason vouchsafes a kind of heuristic hope.

> In communicative action, we orient ourselves toward validity claims that, practically, we can raise only in the context of *our* languages and of our forms of life, even if the convertibility [*Einlösbarkeit*] that we implicitly co-posit *points beyond* the provinciality of our respective historical standpoints. We are exposed to the movement of a transcendence from within, which is just as little at our disposal as the actuality of the spoken word turns us into masters of the structure of our language (or of the *Logos*).[80]

Kant's definition of the Enlightenment as the human race's attainment of *Mündigkeit* as a praxis "under the aegis of an anticipated autonomy" requires that human beings become responsible for themselves instead of obeying external authorities. Yet we can reinterpret *Mündigkeit* in terms of Lonergan's explication of the difference between, on the one hand, human psychological operations that are merely conscious and spontaneous (including any actuation of a spiritual capacity, such as raising a question, or getting insights, or performing habitual acts) and, on the other, those that are conscious and autonomous.[81] Then autonomy—etymologically, giving oneself the law—is grounded in the specifically spiritual causality of what Aquinas called intelligible emanation,[82] a causality that explains the movement (1) from insight to formulation of possibly relevant intelligibility whenever that formulation is due to one's understanding (e.g., the contrast between a memorized answer and one uttered on the basis of understanding), (2) from the mind's grasp of the sufficiency of evidence to judgment (affirmation or denial that some possibly relevant intelligibility is actually relevant) because of one's understanding of the virtually unconditioned (i.e., what is absent in a rash or precipitous or silly judgment), and (3) from authentic apprehension of values to value judgments occurring with an easy conscience (which, when the procession or emanation does not occur, gives rise to the uneasy or guilty conscience). Intelligible emanations also ground the movement from judgments of true values to authentic decisions in the desire to make our actions consistent with our knowledge of values. This reinterpretation of *Mündigkeit* not only specifies the meaning of autonomy more precisely than did Kant's interpretation of it; it also brings Lonergan's account of reason and of the role of reason in deciding and acting into accord with Benedict's as worked out in his essay "Conscience and Truth."[83] Lonergan's account of autonomy is advanced in his account of genuineness in *Insight*.[84] From a philosophical viewpoint, Lonergan (unlike Benedict) carefully distinguishes what can be affirmed in terms of proportionate being as intrinsically or extrinsically conditioned by space and time from issues that can be coherently raised and solved only once one takes care of the question of the general transcendence proper to an infinite act of understanding or to God. Still, the thrust of *Insight*'s project is the unfolding of the pure, unrestricted, and disinterested desire to know as an immanent source of transcendence, which we experience and do not simply posit or presuppose, as in fact both Kant and Habermas do. Furthermore, it seems that they confine themselves to the realm of immanence at the cost of obscurantism. Benedict, relying on the authority of St. Basil of Cappadocia, reaches roughly the same conclusion as Lonergan in his theological discussion of the anamnetic and judicial aspects of conscience's ability to know good and evil, an ability due to an in-built light rather than a law imposed from without.

This agreement between Lonergan and Benedict is, of course, based on a shared Christian horizon and on their shared Christian religious conversion. Perhaps this is why they are less sanguine than Habermas that human beings can overcome by human means alone the disabling of freedom by sin and evil. It is important to note that because of his inter-pretation of the universalist Catholic doctrine that "God wills that all hu-mankind be saved," so that the gift of God's love is offered to everyone on account of Jesus Christ, Lonergan does not restrict religious conversion to Christians. We can wonder then whether the presence of such an in-cognito gift might explain Hans Jonas's insight that, once one takes into account Kant's teaching on basic evil in *Die Religion innerhalb der Gren-zen der blossen Vernunft,* together with his notion of the will's autonomy, one realizes that human freedom is dialectically equiprimordial with moral renunciation and insufficiency.[85] As far as I know, Habermas does not seem to have meditated on this aspect of Kant very clearly. Even so, I think that something akin to this sensitivity has motivated Habermas's *Philosophical Discourse of Modernity,* where he argues vigorously against radical transformations of Kant's ideas of morality and dignity in the wake of Nietzsche, who first deconstructed the Enlightenment project of emancipation in order to come to terms with his disappointment with the historical failure of modernity evident in *Zarathustra*'s "last man."[86]

If we can describe the goal of political good of order as institutions that enable "peaceful activity in accord with the dignity of man,"[87] in-stead of organized collective selfishness or the institutional protection of the manipulation, suppression, and exploitation of each by all, it seems that one would have to go beyond Habermas's admission of "the weak-ness of the motivational power of good reasons" along with the attesta-tion "that rational motivation by reason is more than nothing [*auch nicht nichts ist*]" or that "moral convictions do not allow themselves to be overridden without resistance."[88] For both Benedict and Lonergan, this political order can be realized only if the individual choosers are habitu-ally willing to align particular goods and concrete goods of order with the good of the universe; and they are more likely to do this if they be-lieve that the goods of the order within which they live participate in a transcendent order, a transcendent good. As Lonergan loved to say, quoting Aquinas, "The purpose of the universe is a good existing in it, namely, the order of the universe itself";[89] and, "The universe as a whole is a more perfect participation in and reflection of the divine goodness than any individual creature."[90]

Notes

The phrase with which my title begins is taken from Jürgen Habermas, "Transcendence from Within, Transcendence in This World," in *Habermas, Modernity, and Public Theology,* ed. Don S. Browning and Francis Schüssler Fiorenza (New York: Crossroad, 1992), 226–50; repr. in Jürgen Habermas, *Religion and Rationality: Essays on Reason, God, and Modernity,* ed. Eduardo Mendieta (Cambridge, MA: MIT Press, 2002), 67–94.

1. Jürgen Habermas, "Ein Bewusstsein von dem, was fehlt," letter to the editor, *Neue Zürcher Zeitung,* February 10, 2007.
2. Tertullian *De virginibus velandis* 1.1, quoted in Joseph Ratzinger, *Einführung in das Christentum: Vorlesungen über das Apostolische Glaubensbekenntnis* (Munich: Deutscher Taschenbuch Verlag, 1971 [1st ed. 1968]), 93.
3. See Joseph Ratzinger, "Europa—verpflichetendes Erbe für Christen," in *Europa: Horizonte der Hoffnung,* ed. Franz König and Karl Rahner (Graz: Styria, 1983), 68.
4. See Joseph Ratzinger, *Milestones 1927–1977* (San Francisco: Ignatius Press, 1998), on his trials and tribulations with Thomistic theologians, especially when writing his *Habilitationsschrift.*
5. Lonergan to Henry Keane, January 1953, quoted in Frederick E. Crowe, *Lonergan* (Collegeville, MN: Liturgical Press, 1992), 22.
6. See Bernard Lonergan, "*Insight* Revisited," in *A Second Collection,* ed. W. J. Ryan and B. J. Tyrrell (London: Darton, Longman & Todd, 1974), 267.
7. See Bernard Lonergan, "Theology and Understanding," in *Collection: Papers by Bernard Lonergan,* Collected Works of Bernard Lonergan (hereafter CWL) 4, ed. Frederick E. Crowe and Robert M. Doran (Toronto: University of Toronto Press, 1988), 114–32.
8. See Bernard Lonergan, "Dimensions of Meaning," in *Collection,* 243.
9. See Bernard Lonergan, "The Future of Thomism," in *A Second Collection,* 47.
10. See Bernard Lonergan, "Theology in Its New Context," in *A Second Collection,* 55–67.

11. The school was born in Göttingen in the 1890s and included A. Eich-horn, H. Gunkel, W. Bousset, J. Weiss, and W. Wrede.

12. See N. T. Wright, "The 'Quests' and Their Usefulness," in *The Contemporary Quest for Jesus* (Minneapolis, MN: Fortress Press, 2002), 1–22; see, too, Stephen Neill and Tom Wright, *The Interpretation of the New Testament 1861–1986,* 2nd ed. (Oxford: Oxford University Press, 1988), especially the updating chapter added to this edition by Tom Wright, "History and Theology," 360–449.

13. Athanasius *Orat. 3 contra Arianos* 4, quoted in Bernard Lonergan, *The Way to Nicea: The Dialectical Development of Trinitarian Theology,* trans. Conn O'Donovan (Philadelphia: Westminster Press, 1976), 101.

14. Ibid.

15. See Alois Grillmeier, "Hellenisierung—Judaisierung des Christentums als Deutungsprinzien der Geschichte des kirchlichen Dogmas," in *Mit ihm und in ihm: Christologische Forschungen und Perspektiven* (Freiburg im Breisgau: Herder, 1975), 423–88; see also Bernard Lonergan, "The Structure of the Ante-Nicene Movement," in *Way to Nicea,* 105–37; Brian E. Daley, SJ, "'One Thing and Another': The Persons in God and the Person of Christ in Patristic Theology," *Pro Ecclesia* 16, no. 1 (2007): 17–46.

16. See Alois Grillmeier, "God's Divinity and Humanity," in *The Common Catechism* (New York: Seabury Press, 1975), 241.

17. Lonergan, *Way to Nicea,* 103.

18. See Bernard Lonergan, *De Deo Trino, 2: Pars systematica* (Rome: Gregorian University Press, 1964), 47–53; English translation: *The Triune God: Systematics,* trans. from *De Deo Trino: Pars systematica* (1964) by Michael G. Shields; ed. Robert M. Doran and H. Daniel Monsour (Toronto: University of Toronto Press, 2007), 93–100.

19. Grillmeier, "God's Divinity and Humanity," 258.

20. See Fernand van Steenberghen, *Thomas Aquinas and Radical Aristotelianism* (Washington, DC: Catholic University of America Press, 1980); idem, *Aristotle in the West: The Origins of Latin Aristotelianism* (Brussels: E. Nauwelaerts, 1955).

21. Ernest L. Fortin, *Dissent and Philosophy in the Middle Ages: Dante and His Precursors,* trans. Marc A. LePain (Lanham, MD: Lexington Books, 2002); *Dissidence et philosophie au moyen âge* (Montréal: Fides, 1984), 50.

22. Fortin, *Dissent and Philosophy,* 44.

23. See Jean-Pierre Torrell, OP, *Saint Thomas Aquinas,* vol. 1, *The Person and His Work,* trans. Robert Royal (Washington, DC: Catholic University of America Press, 1996), 183–87 on Peckham, and 303–16 on Peckham, Kilwardby, and the controversy over the condemnation of Thomas.

24. See Yves Congar, OP, *A History of Theology,* ed. and trans. Hunter Guthrie, SJ (Garden City, NY: Doubleday, 1968; based on Congar's article

"Théologie," which first appeared in *Dictionnaire de Théologie* [Paris: Editions Letouzy & Ané]), 15:107–8.

25. See Thomas Aquinas *Quodlibetum* 4, a. 18.

26. See Lonergan, *De Deo Trino,* 2, 8–9, 47, 49, 53; *The Triune God,* 9–11, 93–100.

27. Herbert Butterfield, *The Origins of Modern Science, 1300–1800,* 2nd ed. (New York: Collier Books, 1966), 7, cited in Lonergan, "Theology in Its New Context," 55–67.

28. See Alan Richardson, *History, Sacred and Profane* (London: SCM Press, 1964), 32–33, quoted in Bernard Lonergan, "Questionnaire on Philosophy: Response," in *Philosophical and Theological Papers 1965–1980,* in CWL 17 (Toronto: University of Toronto Press, 2004), 354.

29. See the second part of Hans-Georg Gadamer, *Wahrheit und Methode: Grundzüge einer philosophischen Hermeneutik* (Tübingen: J. C. B. Mohr, 1963).

30. See Joseph Ratzinger, "II. Jesus der Christus: Die Grundform des christologischen Bekenntnisses. *1. Das Dilemma der neuzeitlichen Theologie: Jesus oder Christus?*" in *Einführung in das Christentum,* 138–42.

31. See Ben F. Meyer, "A Review of the Quest," in *The Aims of Jesus* (London: SCM Press, 1979), 57.

32. Butterfield, *Origins of Modern Science,* 85, quoted in Meyer, *Aims of Jesus,* 57.

33. Butterfield, *Origins of Modern Science,* 137, quoted in Meyer, ibid.; the references are to Paul Hazard's *La crise de la conscience européene* (Paris: Boivin, 1935), and Peter Gay's *The Enlightenment: An Interpretation,* vol. 1, *The Rise of Modern Paganism* (New York: Knopf, 1966).

34. Lonergan, "Theology in Its New Context," 58.

35. Lonergan, "Questionnaire on Philosophy," 353–54.

36. See, for instance, Bernard Lonergan, "The Dehellenization of Dogma," in *A Second Collection,* 11–32, which was originally a review of Leslie Dewart, *The Future of Belief: Theism in a World Come of Age,* that appeared in *Theological Studies* 28 (1967): 336, 351. It is a very significant piece for understanding Lonergan, because many of Dewart's opinions incorporate specifically modern counterpositions.

37. See Bernard Lonergan, "Belief: Today's Issue," in *A Second Collection,* 93–94.

38. See Bernard Lonergan, "The Absence of God in Modern Culture," in *A Second Collection,* 112.

39. Lonergan, "Belief: Today's Issue," 93–94, for quotations in this paragraph.

40. Ibid., 99.

41. Habermas, "Ein Bewusstsein von dem, was fehlt."

42. Ibid.

43. See Karl Jaspers, *Vom Ursprung und Ziel der Geschichte* (Frankfurt am Main: Fischer Bücherei, 1955).

44. See Jürgen Habermas, *Postmetaphysical Thinking: Philosophical Essays,* trans. William Mark Hohengarten (Cambridge, MA: MIT Press, 1992), 6.

45. Ibid., 7. Italics added.

46. See Vittorio Possenti, "Metafisica o postmetafisica? A proposito del dialogo tra ragione secolare e ragione religiosa: Note a commento dello scritto di Jürgen Habermas sulla 'Neue Zürcher Zeitung' del 10 febbraio 2007," reported by Sandro Magister at www.chiesa.espressonline.it (March 10, 2007).

47. See Bernard Lonergan, "Metaphysics as Horizon," review of Austrian philosopher Emerich Coreth's *Metaphysik: Eine methodisch-systematische Grundlegung,* in *Collection,* 204.

48. See, for example, Jean Piaget, *Introduction à l'épistémologique,* 3 vols. (Paris: Presses Universitaires de France, 1950).

49. See Bernard Lonergan, *Insight: A Study in Human Understanding,* CWL 3, ed. Frederick E. Crowe and Robert M. Doran (Toronto: University of Toronto Press, 1992).

50. Ibid., 16.

51. Ibid., 22.

52. See Bernard Lonergan, "Piaget and the Idea of a General Education," in *Topics in Education: The Cincinnati Lectures of 1959 on the Philosophy of Education,* CWL 10, ed. Robert M. Doran and Frederick E. Crowe (Toronto: University of Toronto Press, 1993), 204.

53. See Bernard Lonergan, "*Insight:* Preface to a Discussion," in *Collection,* 150.

54. Ibid., 149–50. On the reference to logic and mathematics in the quotation, see Bernard Lonergan, *Phenomenology and Logic: The Boston College Lectures in Mathematical Logic and Existentialism,* CWL 18, ed. Philip McShane (Toronto: University of Toronto Press, 2001), esp. 3–166 on the foundations of mathematics.

55. See Bernard Lonergan, "Isomorphism of Thomist and Scientific Thought," in *Collection,* 133–41.

56. "The principal characteristic of the group of operations is that every operation in the group is matched by an opposite operation and every combination of operations is matched by an opposite combination. Hence, inasmuch as operations are grouped, the operator can always return to his starting-point and, when he can do so unhesitatingly, he has reached mastery at some level of development" (Bernard Lonergan, *Method in Theology* [New York: Herder & Herder, 1972], 27–28).

57. These issues were traced and explicitly named in Lonergan's seminar courses at Rome's Gregorian University before the publication of *Method in Theology* in 1972: *De intellectu et methodo,* 1958–1959, documented in typed

notes of Francesco Rossi de Gasperis and P. Joseph Cahill and in some of Lonergan's own notes; *De systemate et historia,* 1959–1960, documented in the handwritten notes of Francesco Rossi de Gasperis and in some of Lonergan's own notes; and *De methodo theologiae,* 1961–1962, in which Piaget's ideas are applied for the first time.

58. "For if social and cultural changes are, at root, changes in the meanings that are grasped and accepted, changes in the control of meaning make up the great epochs in human history" (Lonergan, "Dimensions of Meaning," 235).

59. See Lonergan, *Method in Theology,* 85–99.

60. See, for example, Bernard Lonergan, *Doctrinal Pluralism* (Milwaukee: Marquette University Press, 1971), and the chapters entitled "Doctrines" and "Systematics," in *Method in Theology,* 295–333, 335–53.

61. Bernard Lonergan, *Grace and Freedom: Operative Grace in the Thought of St. Thomas Aquinas,* CWL 1, ed. Frederick E. Crowe and Robert M. Doran (Toronto: University of Toronto Press, 2000).

62. Bernard Lonergan, "*Insight* Revisited," in *A Second Collection,* 277.

63. Lonergan, *Method in Theology,* 27–55.

64. See Henri Niel, *De la Médiation dans la philosophie de Hegel* (Paris: Aubier, 1945); see, too, Lonergan's exposition of the notion of mediation in "The Mediation of Christ in Prayer," in *Philosophical and Theological Papers 1958–1964,* CWL 6, ed. Robert C. Croken, Frederick E. Crowe, and Robert M. Doran (Toronto: University of Toronto Press, 1996), 160–82, esp. 160–76.

65. Lonergan, *Method in Theology,* 28.

66. Bernard Lonergan, "Dimensions of Meaning," 234–35; but for the expanded view see the chapter on meaning in *Method in Theology,* 57–99.

67. Lonergan, "Dimensions of Meaning," 235.

68. According to Sandro Magister at his website, www.chiesa.espresson line.it, "The pope formulated this diagnosis while receiving in the Vatican's Sala Clementina on March 24 [2007] the cardinals, bishops, and politicians who were taking part in a conference organized in Rome by the Commission of the Bishops' Conferences of the European Community, COMECE, dedicated to the theme of 'Values and perspectives for the Europe of tomorrow.'" The citation comes from Benedict XVI's address, "That the Church May Again Be 'Leaven for the World,'" quoted in English translation by Sandro Magister at his website on March 28, 2007.

69. Jürgen Habermas and Joseph Ratzinger, *Dialektik der Säkularisierung: Über Vernunft und Religion* (Freiburg im Breisgau: Herder, 2005).

70. See Jürgen Habermas, "Transcendence from Within, Transcendence in This World," in *Habermas, Modernity, and Public Theology,* ed. Don S. Browning and Francis Schussler Fiorenza (New York: Crossroad, 1992), 237, or in his *Religion and Rationality: Essays on Reason, God, and Modernity,* ed. Eduardo Mendieta (Cambridge, MA: MIT Press, 2002), 79 (in subsequent citations to

this essay, I will separate page references to the two works with a slash): "I would also submit that I subsumed rather too hastily the development of religion in modernity with Max Weber under the 'privatization of the powers of faith' and suggested too quickly an affirmative answer to the question as to 'whether then from religious truths, after the religious world views have collapsed, nothing more and nothing other than the secular principles of a universalist ethics of responsibility can be salvaged, and this means: can be accepted for good reasons on the basis of insight.'"

71. Habermas, "Transcendence from Within, Transcendence in This World," 234/76.

72. See John Courtney Murray, *We Hold These Truths: Reflections on the American Proposition* (New York: Sheed & Ward, 1960); idem, *Religious Liberty: Catholic Struggles with Pluralism*, ed. J. Leon Hooper, SJ (Louisville: Westminster John Knox, 1993); idem, *Bridging the Sacred and the Secular: Selected Writings by John Courtney Murray, SJ*, ed. J. Leon Hooper, SJ (Washington, DC: Georgetown University Press, 1994).

73. Lonergan, *Method in Theology*, 130.

74. Ibid., 236–37.

75. Ibid., 131.

76. Ibid., 241–43.

77. Habermas, "Transcendence from Within, Transcendence in This World," 237/79–80.

78. Ibid., 239–40/82.

79. Ibid., 240/82.

80. Ibid., 237–38/80.

81. See Lonergan, *The Triune God*, 179–81.

82. See Bernard Lonergan, *Verbum: Word and Idea in Aquinas,* CWL 2, ed. Frederick E. Crowe and Robert M. Doran (Toronto: University of Toronto Press, 2997), 46–47: "All causation is intelligible, but there are three differences between natural process and the processions of an inner word. The intelligibility of natural process is passive and potential: it is what can be understood; it is not an understanding; it is a potential object of intellect, but it is not the very stuff of intellect. Again, the intelligibility of natural process is the intelligibility of some specific natural law, say, the law of inverse squares, but never the intelligibility of the very idea of intelligible law. Thirdly, the intelligibility of natural process is imposed from without: natures act intelligibly, not because they are intelligent, for they are not, but because they are concretions of divine ideas and a divine plan. On the other hand, the intelligibility of an inner word is not passive and potential; it is active and actual; it is intelligibility because it is the activity of intelligence in act; it is intelligible, not as the possible object of understanding is intelligible, but as understanding itself and the activity of understanding is intelligible. Again, its intelligibility defies formulation in any specific law; inner

words proceed according to the principles of identity, noncontradiction, excluded middle, and sufficient reason; but these principles are not specific laws but the essential conditions of there being objects to be related by laws and relations to relate them. Thus the procession of an inner word is the pure case of intelligible law: one may say that such procession is a case of 'omne agens agit sibi simile'; but one has only to recall that this agent may be similar to anything, that it is 'potens omnia fieri,' to see that really one has here not a particular case but the resume of all particular cases. Thirdly, it is native and natural for the procession of inner word to be intelligible, actively intelligible, and the genus of all intelligible process; . . . intelligible procession [is native and natural] to intelligence in act; for intelligence in act does not follow laws imposed from without, but rather it is the ground of the intelligibility in act of law, it is constitutive and, as it were, creative of law; and the laws of intelligible procession of an inner word are not any particular laws but the general constituents of any law, precisely because of this naturalness of intelligibility to intelligence, precisely because intelligence is to any conceived law as cause to effect."

83. See Joseph Ratzinger, "Conscience and Truth," lecture presented at the Tenth Workshop for Bishops, February 1991, in Dallas, TX; sponsored by the Pope John XXIII Medical-Moral Research and Education Center and through the generosity of the Knights of Columbus.

84. Lonergan, *Insight,* 499–503, 646, 647.

85. See Hans Jonas, "The Abyss of the Will: Philosophical Meditation on the Seventh Chapter of Paul's Epistle to the Romans," in *Philosophical Essays: From Ancient Creed to Modern Technological Man* (Chicago: University of Chicago Press, Midway Reprint, 1974), commenting on Immanuel Kant, *Religion within the Limits of Reason Alone,* trans. and ed. Allen Wood with George di Giovanni (Cambridge: Cambridge University Press, 1998), where "radical evil" is characterized as being rooted in the freedom of moral choice. See 54: "A propensity to evil can only attach itself to the moral faculty of choice [*Willkür*]"; 53–54: "The propensity for evil affects the use of freedom, the capacity for acting out duty—in short, the capacity for actually being autonomous."

86. Jürgen Habermas, *The Philosophical Discourse of Modernity,* trans. Frederick G. Lawrence (Cambridge, MA: MIT Press, 1987).

87. This phrase is Leo Strauss's from *Natural Right and History* (Chicago: University of Chicago Press, 1952), 147.

88. Habermas, "Transcendence from Within, Transcendence in This World," 239/81.

89. Thomas Aquinas *Summa theologiae* 1, q. 47, art. 3, corpus.

90. Thomas Aquinas *Summa theologiae* 1, q. 103, art. 2, ad 3.

Contributors

JEFFREY BLOECHL is associate professor of philosophy at Boston College and honorary professor of philosophy at the Australian Catholic University. He has published widely in contemporary European philosophy, philosophy of religion, and philosophical anthropology. He is founding series editor of *Levinas Studies: An Annual Review* (Duquesne University Press) and, with Kevin Hart, the series Thresholds in Philosophy and Theology (University of Notre Dame Press).

PETER J. CASARELLA is professor of Catholic Studies at DePaul University, where he is also the director of the Center for World Catholicism and Intercultural Theology (CWCIT). Major publications include *Cusanus: The Legacy of Learned Ignorance* (2006) and numerous articles exploring medieval thought, theology, and culture and the work of figures such as von Balthasar, Przywara, and Gadamer.

KEVIN CORRIGAN is Samuel Candler Dobbs Professor of Interdisciplinary Humanities and the director of the Institute of Liberal Arts at Emory University. He has published fifteen books and scholarly editions in the areas of Platonic and Neoplatonic philosophy and patristic theology. These include *The Life of Saint Macrina by Gregory, Bishop of*

Nyssa (translation with introduction and notes, 1987), *Plotinus' Theory of Matter-Evil and the Question of Substance: Plato, Aristotle, and Alexander of Aphrodisias* (1996), *Reading Ancient Texts,* vol. 2, *Aristotle and Neoplatonism,* co-edited with Suzanne Stern-Gillet (2007), and *Evagrius and Gregory: Mind, Soul and Body in the Fourth Century* (2009).

KEVIN HART is Edwin B. Kyle Professor of Christian Studies and chair of the Department of Religious Studies at the University of Virginia. His major publications in the areas of theology, philosophy, and literature include *The Trespass of the Sign: Deconstruction, Theology, and Philosophy* (1989), *The Dark Gaze: Maurice Blanchot and the Sacred* (2004), *The Exorbitant: Emmanuel Levinas between Jews and Christians,* co-edited with Michael A. Signer (2010), and *Jean-Luc Marion: The Essential Works* (forthcoming).

ANTHONY J. KELLY is professor of theology at the Australian Catholic University. His many books include *The Trinity of Love: A Christian Theology of God* (1989), *Touching on the Infinite: Explorations in Christian Hope* (1991), *The Creed by Heart: Re-learning the Nicene Creed* (1996), *Eschatology and Hope* (2006), and *The Resurrection Effect: Transforming Christian Life and Thought* (2008).

JEAN-YVES LACOSTE is lifetime member of Clare Hall, Cambridge University. He has taught philosophy and theology in Chicago, Paris, Jerusalem, and Washington, DC. He has edited the *Dictionnaire critique de théologie* (2002; English translation 2005), and authored, among others, *Note sur le temps* (1990), *Expérience et Absolu* (1994; English translation 2004), *La Phénoménalité de Dieu* (2008), and *Être en danger* (2011).

FREDERICK G. LAWRENCE is professor of theology at Boston College and a leading authority on the thought of Bernard Lonergan. Recent publications include "Expanding Challenge to Authenticity in Insight: Lonergan's Hermeneutics of Facticity" (2004), "Grace and Friendship" (2004), "The Dialectic Tradition/Innovation and the Possibility of a Theological Method" (2006), and "The Ethics of Authenticity and the Human Good" (2007).

CYRIL O'REGAN is Catherine Huisking Professor of Theology at the University of Notre Dame. He has published *Gnostic Return in Modernity* (2001), *Gnostic Apocalypse: Jacob Boehme's Haunted Narrative* (2002), *Theology and the Spaces of Apocalyptic* (2009), and *The Anatomy of Misremembering: Balthasar and the Spectre of Hegel* (forthcoming, 2012).

ADRIAAN T. PEPERZAK is Arthur J. Schmitt Chair of Philosophy at the Loyola University of Chicago. He has published over three hundred articles and over thirty books in several languages. Recent books include *Reason in Faith: On the Relevance of Christian Spirituality for Philosophy* (1999), *Modern Freedom: Hegel's Legal, Moral, and Political Philosophy* (2001), *The Quest for Meaning: Friends of Wisdom from Plato to Levinas* (2003), *Philosophy between Faith and Theology: Addresses to Catholic Intellectuals* (2005), and a forthcoming study of the act and phenomenon of trust.

JAMES SWINDAL is associate professor of philosophy and acting dean of Liberal Arts at Duquesne University. He has written extensively on the philosophy of Jürgen Habermas, action theory, and Catholic philosophy. His publications include *Reflection Revisited: Jürgen Habermas's Discursive Theory of Truth* (1999), *The Sheed and Ward Anthology of Catholic Philosophy,* co-edited with Harry Gensler (2004), and *Action and Existence: A Case for Agent Causation* (2011).

Index